THE CHARTERED INSTITUTE OF MARKETING

Professional Certificate in Marketing

STUDY TEXT

Marketing Essentials

Valid for assessments up to September 2013

First edition July 2012

ISBN 9781 4453 9141 0

e-ISBN 9781 4453 7614 1

British Library Cataloguing-in-Publication Data
A catalogue record for this book
is available from the British Library

Published by

BPP Learning Media Ltd
Aldine House, Aldine Place
142-144 Uxbridge Road
London W12 8AA

www.bpp.com/learningmedia

Printed in the United Kingdom by Polestar Wheatons

Hennock Road
Marsh Barton Industrial Estate
Exeter, Devon
EX2 8RP

Your learning materials, published by BPP Learning Media Ltd, are printed on paper obtained from traceable sustainable sources.

The contents of this book are intended as a guide and not professional advice. Although every effort has been made to ensure that the contents of this book are correct at the time of going to press, BPP Learning Media, the Editor and the Author make no warranty that the information in this book is accurate or complete and accept no liability for any loss or damage suffered by any person acting or refraining from acting as a result of the material in this book.

Every effort has been made to contact the copyright holders of any material reproduced within this publication. If any have been inadvertently overlooked, BPP Learning Media will be pleased to make the appropriate credits in any subsequent reprints or editions.

We are grateful to The Chartered Institute of Marketing for permission to reproduce in this text the unit syllabus.

Lead Author: Mark Davis

A note about copyright

Dear Customer

What does the little © mean and why does it matter?

Your market-leading BPP books, course materials and e-learning materials do not write and update themselves. People write them: on their own behalf or as employees of an organisation that invests in this activity. Copyright law protects their livelihoods. It does so by creating rights over the use of the content.

Breach of copyright is a form of theft – as well as being a criminal offence in some jurisdictions, it is potentially a serious breach of professional ethics.

With current technology, things might seem a bit hazy but, basically, without the express permission of BPP Learning Media:

- Photocopying our materials is a breach of copyright
- Scanning, ripcasting or conversion of our digital materials into different file formats, uploading them to facebook or e-mailing them to your friends is a breach of copyright

You can, of course, sell your books, in the form in which you have bought them – once you have finished with them. (Is this fair to your fellow students? We update for a reason.) Please note the e-products are sold on a single user licence basis: we do not supply 'unlock' codes to people who have bought them second-hand.

And what about outside the UK? BPP Learning Media strives to make our materials available at prices students can afford by local printing arrangements, pricing policies and partnerships which are clearly listed on our website. A tiny minority ignore this and indulge in criminal activity by illegally photocopying our material or supporting organisations that do. If they act illegally and unethically in one area, can you really trust them?

Contents

Page

1 Studying for The Chartered Institute of Marketing (CIM) qualifications

There are a few key points to remember as you study for your CIM qualification:

(a) You are studying for a **professional** qualification. This means that you are required to use professional language and adopt a business approach in your work.

(b) You are expected to show that you have 'read widely'. Make sure that you read the quality press (and don't skip the business pages), read *Marketing*, *The Marketer*, *Research* and *Marketing Week* avidly.

(c) Become aware of the marketing initiatives you come across on a daily basis; for example, when you go shopping look around and think about why the store layout is as it is; consider the messages, channel choice and timings of ads when you are watching TV. It is surprising how much you will learn just by taking an interest in the marketing world around you.

(d) Get to know the way CIM writes its exam papers and assignments. They use a specific approach (the Magic Formula) which is to ensure a consistent approach when designing assessment materials. Make sure you are fully aware of this as it will help you interpret what the examiner is looking for (a full description of the Magic Formula appears later).

(e) Learn how to use Harvard referencing. This is explained in detail in our CIM Professional Certificate Assessment Workbook.

(f) Ensure that you read, very carefully, all assessment details sent to you from CIM. There are strict deadlines to meet, as well as paperwork to complete for any assignment or project you do. You also need to make sure to have your CIM membership card with you at the exam. Failing to meet any assessment entry deadlines or complete written work on time will mean that you will have to wait for the next round of assessment dates and will need to pay the relevant assessment fees again.

2 The Professional Certificate Syllabus

The Professional Certificate in Marketing is aimed at anyone who is employed in a supporting marketing role such as Marketing Co-ordinator or Executive. You may also be a manager with a senior role within a small or medium-sized company where marketing only forms part of a wider work remit. Or you may be looking to move into your first marketing role or to specialise.

The aim of the qualification is to provide a strong foundation of marketing knowledge. You will develop the breadth of knowledge of marketing theory but also appreciate issues faced within the organisation as CIM qualifications concentrate on applied marketing within real work places.

The complete Professional Certificate qualification contains four units:

- Unit 1 Marketing Essentials
- Unit 2 Assessing the Marketing Environment
- Unit 3 Marketing Information and Research
- Unit 4 Stakeholder Marketing

CIM stipulates that each module should take 40 guided learning hours to complete. Guided learning hours refer to time in class, using distance learning materials and completing any work set by your tutor. Guided learning hours do not include the time it will take you to complete the necessary reading for your studies.

The syllabus as provided by CIM can be found below, with reference to the coverage within this Study Text.

Unit characteristics – Marketing Essentials

The aim of this unit is to provide a detailed explanation of the key theories and practice behind marketing as an exchange process and a business function, but also as a means of creating customer value in the short to medium term. This unit introduces individuals to the importance of the marketing planning process and the role of marketing across the organisation.

The unit also aims to provide knowledge of the key marketing tools to support an innovative range of marketing activities. Students will be taught the nature and implications of the use of marketing tools as both independent tools and tools that are often integrated to maximise the impact of the marketing proposition.

On completion, students should be able to explain how to utilise all elements of the marketing mix and how they can be co-ordinated to create a value proposition that reflects the organisation's objectives.

Overarching learning outcomes

By the end of this unit students should be able to:

- Explain how marketing has evolved and the importance of market orientation in creating customer value
- Assess the importance of marketing, its cross-functional role and the contribution it makes to the organisation and society
- Identify and explain the stages in the marketing planning process
- Assess the key elements of the internal and external marketing environment that impact upon the organisation, its objectives and its activities
- Identify and describe the characteristics and applications of each element of the marketing mix (7Ps)

SECTION 3 – The marketing mix (weighting 50%)

		Covered in chapter(s)
3.1	Explain and illustrate the principles of product and planning: ▪ Branding ▪ Product lines/ranges (depth and breadth) ▪ Packaging, eg sustainability, design, eg recycling ▪ Service support	5
3.2	Explain the concept of the product life cycle (PLC) and its limitations as a tool for assessing the life of the product/services: ▪ Development ▪ Introduction ▪ Growth ▪ Maturity ▪ Decline ▪ Obsolescence ▪ Limitations including failure of the product to succeed/no measurable outcome	5
3.3	Explain the importance of new products and services into the market: ▪ Changing customer needs ▪ Digital revolution ▪ Long-term business strategies	5
3.4	Explain the different stages of the process of new product development: ▪ Idea generation ▪ Screening new ideas ▪ Concept testing ▪ Business analysis ▪ Product development ▪ Test marketing ▪ Commercialisation and launch	5
3.5	Explain the importance of price as an element of the marketing mix: ▪ Brings together the marketing mix elements to fulfil customer needs ▪ Income, revenue and profit generation ▪ Contributing to the organisation's business and financial objectives ▪ Limitations of price as a competitive tool	6
3.6	Identify and illustrate a range of different pricing approaches that are adopted by organisations as effective means of competition: ▪ Absorption costing ▪ Cost base and marginal costing ▪ Cost plus ▪ Price skimming ▪ Penetration pricing ▪ Loss-leader ▪ Promotional pricing	6

		Covered in chapter(s)
3.7	Define the different channels of distribution, and the roles they play in a co-ordinated marketing mix: ■ Wholesaling ■ Retailing ■ Direct marketing ■ Internet marketing ■ Vending ■ Telephone selling ■ Franchising ■ Digital/e-channels	7
3.8	Explain the factors that influence channel decisions and the selection of alternative distribution channels: ■ Multiple channels ■ Location of customers ■ Compatibility ■ Nature of the goods/services ■ Geographic/environmental/terrain ■ Storage and distribution costs ■ Import/export costs	7
3.9	Evaluate a range of marketing communications tools that comprise the marketing communications mix and consider their impact in different contexts: ■ Direct Response Advertising ■ Personal selling ■ Sponsorship ■ Public relations ■ Direct marketing ■ Sales promotions ■ Digital technologies ■ Website	8
3.10	Evaluate the range of marketing communications media and consider their impact in different contexts: ■ TV ■ Cinema ■ Bill boards ■ Press ■ Magazine ■ Web-advertising ■ Sales promotions	8
3.11	Explain the importance of a co-ordinated services marketing mix, its characteristics and implications for the marketing of service products: ■ Co-ordinated approach to people, physical evidence and process ■ Characteristics/implications: inseparability, intangibility, variability, perishability and non-ownership	9

		Covered in chapter(s)
3.12	Explain the different methods used for measuring the success of marketing activities: ▪ Budget measurement ▪ Objectives attained ▪ Sales/revenue, profit/loss ▪ Efficiency/effectiveness ▪ Zero defects/returns ▪ Customer service complaints ▪ Increased awareness and changing attitudes ▪ Repeat purchase and loyalty	10
3.13	Explain the process of product and service adoption, explaining the characteristics of customers at each stage of adoption: ▪ Innovators ▪ Early adopters ▪ Early majority ▪ Late majority ▪ Laggards	5
3.14	Explain the concept of developing a co-ordinated approach to the marketing mix, as a means to satisfying customers' requirements and competing effectively: ▪ Designing a mix which is compatible and co-ordinated effectively ▪ Being mindful of the target market, their needs and expectations ▪ Being mindful of tactical competitive activities ▪ Being mindful of the impact of other elements of the marketing mix	4

3 Assessment

The unit covered by this Study Text (Unit 1 Marketing Essentials) is assessed in a three-hour formal examination. In order to help you revise and prepare for the exam we have also written a Professional Certificate in Marketing Assessment Workbook which is available either through your usual book retailer or our website, http://www.bpp.com/learningmedia.

4 The Magic Formula

The Magic Formula is a tool used by CIM to help both examiners write exam and assignment questions, and you, to more easily interpret what you are being asked to write about. It is useful for helping you to check that you are using an appropriate balance between theory and practice for your particular level of qualification.

Contrary to the title, there is nothing mystical about the Magic Formula and simply by knowing it (or even mentioning it in an assessment) will not automatically secure a pass. What it does do, however, is help you to check that you are presenting your answers in an appropriate format, including enough marketing theory and applying it to a real marketing context or issue.

The Magic Formula for the Professional Certificate in Marketing is shown below:

Figure A The Magic Formula for the Professional Certificate in Marketing

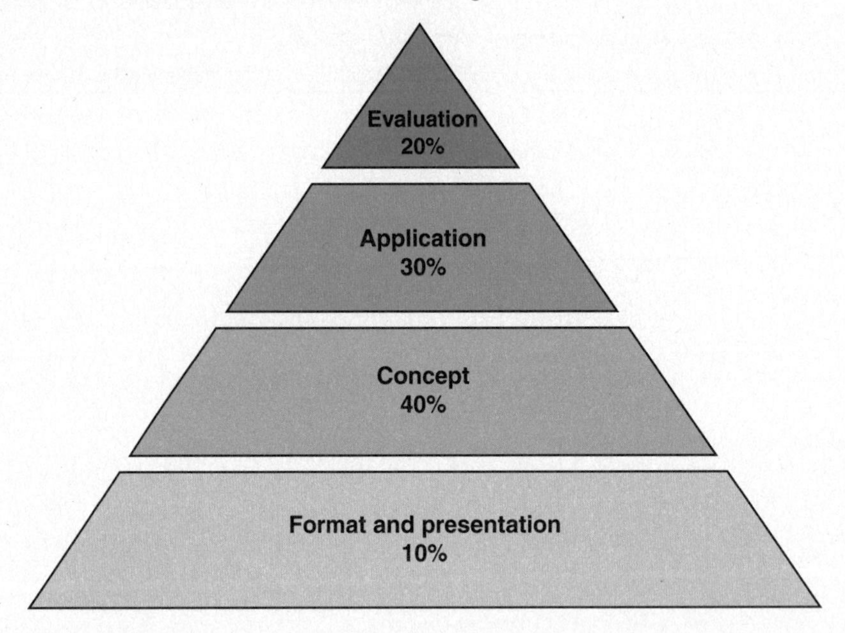

You can see from the pyramid that, for the Professional Certificate, marks are awarded in the following proportions:

- **Presentation and format – 10%**

  You are expected to present your work professionally, which means that assignments and projects should **always** be typed. Even in an exam situation attention should be paid to making your work look as visually appealing as possible. CIM will also stipulate the format that you should present your work in. The assessment formats you will be given will be varied and can include things like reports to write, slides to prepare, emails, memos, formal letters, press releases, discussion documents, briefing papers, agendas and newsletters.

- **Concept – 40%**

  Concept refers to your ability to state, recall and describe marketing theory. The definition of marketing is a core CIM syllabus topic. If we take this as an example, you would be expected to recognise, recall and write this definition to a word perfect standard to gain the full marks for concept. Understanding marketing concepts is the main area where marks will be given within your assessment at the Professional Certificate level.

- **Application – 30%**

  Application-based marks are given for your ability to apply marketing theories to real-life marketing situations. For example, a question may ask you to discuss the definition of marketing and how it is applied within your own organisation. Here, you are not only using the definition but are applying it in order to consider the market orientation of the company.

- **Evaluation – 20%**

  Evaluation is the ability to asses the value or worth of something, sometimes through careful consideration of related advantages and disadvantages, or weighing up of alternatives. Results from your evaluation should enable you to discuss the importance of an issue using evidence to support your opinions.

  For example, if you were asked to evaluate whether or not your organisation adopts a marketing approach, you should provide reasons and specific examples of why you think they might take this approach, as well as considering why they may not take this approach, before coming to a final conclusion.

5 A guide to the features of the Study Text

Each of the chapter features (see below) will help you to break down the content into manageable chunks and ensure that you are developing the skills required for a professional qualification.

Chapter feature	Relevance and how you should use it
Introduction	Shows why topics need to be studied and is a route guide through the chapter
Syllabus reference	Outlines the syllabus learning outcomes covered in the chapter
Chapter topic list	Study the list; each numbered topic denotes a numbered section in the chapter
Key Term	Highlights the core vocabulary you need to learn
Activity	An application-based activity for you to complete
The Real World	A short case study to illustrate marketing practice
Exam tip/Assessment tip	Key advice based on the assessment
Chapter roundups	Use this to review what you have learnt
Quick quiz	Use this to check your learning
Further reading	Further reading will give you a wider perspective on the subjects you're covering

6 Additional resources

To help you pass the entire Professional Certificate in Marketing we have created a complete study package. The **Professional Certificate Assessment Workbook** covers all four units for the Professional Certificate level. Practice questions and answers, tips on tackling assignments and work-based projects are included to help you succeed in your assessments.

Our A6 set of spiral-bound **Passcards** are handy revision cards which are ideal to reinforce key topics for the Marketing Essentials and Assessing the Marketing Environment exams.

7 Your personal study plan

Preparing a Study Plan (and sticking to it) is one of the key elements of learning success.

CIM has stipulated that there should be a minimum of 40 guided learning hours spent on each unit. Guided learning hours will include time spent in lesson, working on fully prepared distance learning materials, formal workshops and work set by your tutor. We also know that to be successful, students should spend **at least** an additional 60 hours conducting self study. This means that for the entire qualification with four units you should spend 160 hours working in a tutor-guided manner and at least an additional 240 hours completing recommended reading, working on assignments, and revising for exams. This Study Text will help you to organise this 60-hour portion of self study time.

Now think about the exact amount of time you have (don't forget you will still need some leisure time!) and complete the following tables to help you keep to a schedule.

	Date	Duration in weeks
Course start		
Course finish		Total weeks of course:
Examination date:	Revision to commence:	Total weeks to complete revision:

Content chapter coverage plan

Chapter	To be completed by	Revised?
1 What is marketing?		
2 The nature and scope of marketing		
3 Planning within the marketing context		
4 The marketing mix		
5 The marketing mix – product		
6 The marketing mix – price		
7 The marketing mix – place		
8 The marketing mix – promotion		
9 The marketing mix – people, process and physical evidence		
10 The marketing mix – evaluation		

Section 1:

The nature and scope of marketing (weighting 25%)

This section accounts for 25% of the whole course, so it should take around 10 hours of study time for the average student. Some of this will consist of reading through this study text and working the examples and case studies, and some may be class time with a tutor or with a correspondence course. Clearly, though, if you have studied for less than 10 hours, you either are exceptionally bright or have missed something – experience shows that it is often the latter case. At this level, the examiner will be expecting you to be able to apply your learning, not just quote it: when you are reading case studies or examples, try to develop the habit of asking yourself 'What would I have done in those circumstances?' Do not assume that the marketers involved came up with the perfect answer simply because they are working for a large company.

It is a good idea to give yourself plenty of time away from studying, so that your subconscious can absorb the materials better. Cramming at the last minute might get you through the exam, but remember you are doing this course because the knowledge and thought patterns you gain from it will help you in your career – the piece of paper is of no use if your boss finds out you actually do not know anything!

The Chartered
Institute of Marketing

CHAPTER 1

What is marketing?

Introduction

In this chapter we will introduce the concept of marketing and define marketing as an exchange process.

Marketing is all about markets. Originally this would have been the physical arena where buyers and sellers would meet and this is still the case in some places around the world. However today marketing is much different. Although buyers and sellers still exist, they no longer have to be in the same place, or meet face to face. Often marketing today is about developing a set of tools to make that exchange process more effective for both sides.

At its core marketing is about the satisfaction of need and that requires an exchange to take place between one individual or organisation and another individual or organisation. So we will concentrate on the organisations, individuals, firms, businesses or whatever they are called in that exchange process.

This chapter will look at how this exchange will affect the philosophy, development and management of those organisations. We will also look at how an organisation should function in its community and the ethical standards it should apply to everything it does.

After working through this chapter and reading around the subject, you should be able to:

- Define marketing and what is a marketer
- Explain the evolution of marketing orientation
- Describe the contribution of marketing as a means of creating customer value and competitive advantage
- Describe the factors which contribute to a marketing-oriented approach to run the organisation
- Be aware of the difficulties which might be encountered in developing a marketing orientation within the firm
- Be aware of the role of relationship marketing

Topic list

Syllabus references

1.1	Explain the evolution of market orientation: ■ Product orientation ■ Production orientation ■ Sales orientation ■ Market versus marketing orientation
1.2	Assess the contribution of marketing as a means of: ■ Creating customer value ■ Creating and responding to competition
1.3	Appreciate the different characteristics of a market-oriented approach to business: ■ An exchange process ■ A philosophy of business ■ A managerial function ■ A dynamic operation, requiring analysis, planning and action ■ A catalyst for change

1 What is marketing?

> **Key term**
>
> **Marketing** is the management process responsible for the identifying, anticipating and satisfying of customer requirements profitably (CIM, 2012)

There are many differing definitions of marketing however The Chartered Institute of Marketing (CIM) states that it is the

'Management process responsible for the identifying, anticipating and satisfying of customer requirements profitably' (CIM, 2012)

This definition has its limitations in terms of the large number of differing types of organisation that exist in the business world today. If we take a short visit to our local high street, for example, we will expect to see retailers who are profit-making businesses, as well as charity shops which will be there to make a surplus for the benefit of others; and then we may well find libraries or doctors who are funded by the government to offer a service to the customer, which is free at the point of delivery. So we can see that the word 'profit' is difficult to deal with if we consider that all organisations should aspire to be marketing-based organisations. So perhaps a better definition is:

'Marketing consists of individual and organisational activities that facilitate and expedite satisfying exchange relationships in a dynamic environment through the creation, distribution, promotion and pricing of goods, services and ideas' (Dibb *et al*, 2005)

Once again, however, this definition seems to put great store on the price of the product or service we are selling and, in the examples above, we can see that money may not be involved at the point at which the product or service is provided.

Would it be better, therefore, to consider that to achieve the organisation's objectives or goals you will need to ensure the customers are satisfied with what has been delivered to them; and if this is undertaken in the correct way and in the right environment, they will not complain and will return in the future if that service or product is required. Therefore it is common sense that we, as organisations, try to achieve satisfied customers, so it could be argued that the simplest definition of marketing is: 'Common sense applied'.

Peter Liney, who was Marketing Manager of the Concorde project, first quoted this simple but effective definition of marketing. The *Collins English dictionary* states that common sense is 'plain ordinary good judgment' and the Microsoft *Encarta* dictionary describes it as 'sound practical judgment derived from

experience rather than study'. In other words we know what satisfies customers because we have experienced it ourselves as customers.

This definition therefore allows us to cover any organisation, whose outcomes are different, but to achieve those outcomes in a marketing way, from doctors to tank manufacturers, they all need to satisfy their customers' desires and needs for continued employment and organisational survival.

THE REAL WORLD

The UK's National Health Service (NHS)

This case study looks at the basic facts around what individuals think marketing is and what it should achieve. The NHS is a government-run, free at the point of delivery service offered to everyone in the UK. However it still needs to offer a customer focused approach where everyone in the organisation is working to achieve the same goal – satisfied customers.

Firstly you need to explore what would appear to be the central problem for marketers within the NHS context, the extent to which 'marketing' is accepted and how it is perceived amongst the employees. Many of the staff within the NHS will have a fundamental misunderstanding of the role of marketing and the benefits it can deliver. They would talk of 'glib, meaningless statements' and paint a picture of an organisation that would be forced to waste its resources to compete with itself. The Trade Unions are not slow to join in: 'The very idea that hospitals should spend taxpayers' money on advertising for patients instead of treating patients is ridiculous' to quote one of their members. However, with the development of a communication plan and a change process over a period of time, there has been a gradual acceptance of what marketing could deliver and demonstrate to all stakeholder groups within the NHS and, therefore, why marketing is needed.

Marketing in the National Health Service should focus on two key factors: Firstly, internal marketing is needed to show doctors and managers the benefits of the customer-led approach, and to create a more joined-up organisation where doctors and managers work towards a common end, a common sense approach in satisfying the customer. Changing the service processes in this way could have a huge positive impact on the success of the NHS. Secondly, marketing strategies can be used to improve quality – from the perspective of both the customers and the doctor. By implementing marketing techniques, hospitals and doctors can tailor their products and services to offer the **right** solution in the **right** place at the **right** time. Once again, achieving a common sense approach to the service offered to the customers by hospitals, doctors and the NHS as a whole.

(CIM, 2012)

2 What is a marketer?

Marketers tend to think differently from other people in the organisation. This is because they are much more concerned with people, and especially people outside the organisation, than are (say) the finance manager or the production manager. Marketers tend to be risk-takers: they are more prepared to try something new, because this is usually the only way to establish a competitive advantage over other firms – following a standard, tried-and-tested approach means simply copying what other people have done, which will not generate any advantage. For this reason, marketers tend to be creative and innovative.

Marketers often think of themselves as **having common sense**: after all, if the company does not look after its customers, the customers will soon find someone who will and will spend their money elsewhere. To a marketer, this seems obvious, yet to many managers from other disciplines, it does not – they see the marketers as someone who is paid to go out and find customers for products which the company already supplies.

If the finance managers of two companies in the same industry were exchanged, they would almost certainly be able to carry on with their jobs without pause: the same would be true of company lawyers or administrators. If the marketers were exchanged, though, they would be completely lost in each other's firms because each marketer should be following a completely different programme of new product development, promotion, pricing and so forth. This is because each marketer seeks to differentiate his or her company from all the others in the market, as a way of reducing (or at least circumventing) the competition.

3 The evolution of marketing orientation

Marketing is a relatively young discipline and is thought to have evolved from previous business paradigms as follows.

3.1 Production orientation

> **Key term**
>
> **Production orientation**: the organisation's emphasis is on making products as efficiently and cost-effectively as possible, making them more affordable.

In this paradigm, the key to success in business is to produce as cheaply as possible and keep prices low. This paradigm was typical in the 19th century, when mechanised production could out-compete hand production in cost terms. The basis of production orientation is that people will buy anything as long as it is cheap enough. The drawback, of course, is that consumers are expected to accept a standardised product which is unlikely to meet their needs exactly: only a very few products are acceptable on a one-size-fits-all basis. Many firms still operate this way, but people have come to expect (and can afford) more customised products, and global production runs mean that economies of scale can still be generated. The drawback from a manufacturing viewpoint is that the company is competing on price, which invariably cuts profit margins: there is always someone somewhere in the world who is able to produce more cheaply or is desperate enough (or naïve enough) to sell below the costs of production.

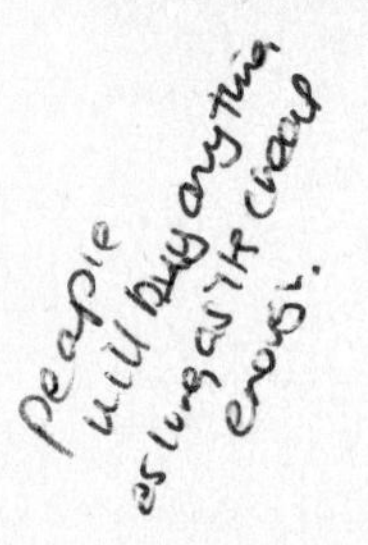

3.2 Product orientation

> **Key term**
>
> **Product orientation**: organisations concentrate on the product itself and not on customers' needs.

In order to compete effectively, the product needs to have features which appeal to individual consumers. In a product-oriented firm, the products are designed to incorporate a large number of features in order to meet the needs of a large number of consumers. Such products can become extremely complex, since people's needs vary considerably, even for basic, everyday products such as biscuits and cleaning materials. Unfortunately, the cost of a 'state of the art, all the bells and whistles' product becomes too high for most people, and of course consumers do not want to pay for features which they are unlikely ever to use.

3.3 Sales orientation

> **Key term**
>
> **Sales orientation**: selling function is most important in these organisations. They sell what they have, rather than what the customer needs.

As mass production developed to the point where there was an over-supply of goods, firms supposedly switched to a sales orientation. Sales-oriented firms believe that people will only buy if they are subjected to a high-pressure sales pitch: the assumption is that people do not want to buy things and will only do so if persuaded. Furthermore, sales orientation assumes that people will not mind being persuaded and will be happy for the salesperson to call again: from the producer's viewpoint, success is thought to come through using aggressive promotional techniques. In effect, sales orientation aims to change customers in order to meet the needs of the organisation. The major problem from a producer's viewpoint is that salespeople are an expensive item, so much so that it is almost always cheaper simply to produce things that people want to buy.

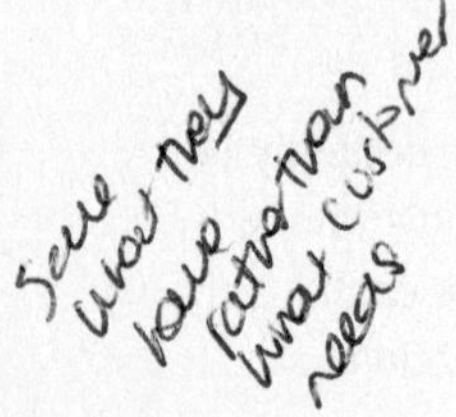

Sales orientation has little or nothing to do with the practice of selling, of course: high-pressure techniques simply result in cancelled orders once the sales rep has left.

3.4 Market orientation

> **Key term**
>
> **Market orientation**: here the organisation is driven by the market and what the groups of customer within that market want and need.

Here the firm looks at what the market (ie consumers) actually needs and acts accordingly. For the market-oriented firm, the customer's needs and wants are at the centre of everything the firm seeks to achieve, and the aim of the firm is to fit the firm to the customers rather than try to fit the customers to the firm. One key element in market orientation is that consumers can be grouped according to their needs, so that quite large subsections (or segments) of the market can be identified and targeted accordingly. Different products can be offered to each group, which enables the firm to compete by differentiation rather than competing on price: provided the cost of making changes is less than the additional premium people are prepared to pay for a more 'customised' product, the firm will make a greater profit and will also shut out competition, at least for a while.

3.5 Marketing orientation

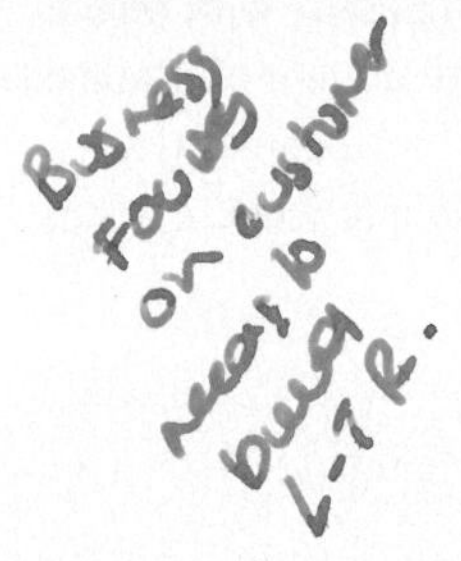

> **Key term**
>
> **Marketing orientation**: where a business focuses on customer needs and wants to build long term relationships.

However, **marketing orientation** means that customer needs become the driving force throughout the supplying organisation: a truly marketing-oriented firm will use customer need as the 'touchstone' for setting policy, for resolving differences between different departments within the firm and for considering competitive responses. **Customer orientation** is the degree to which the company understands its customers: the better understanding the firm has of their needs, the better it will be able to make more attractive offers, for which the firm can charge a premium price. **Competitor orientation** is the degree to which the firm understands the other offers in the marketplace: other firms may offer radically different solutions to the customer's needs, but each firm needs to consider whether the alternatives represent better value from the customer's viewpoint. Identifying who the competition is can be a major problem in itself – bus companies compete not only with each other, but also with trains, cars, bicycles, aeroplanes and even, in some cases, with the internet. Some people have managed to cut out commuting by working from home, but most bus companies would not recognise this as competition.

> **Exam tip**
>
> These business paradigms need to be learned by heart, unfortunately! There is a strong possibility that you might have to list them and explain them in an exam question, as well as identify which one a particular company is using. Although they are often presented as stages of an evolutionary process, examples of each of them are easy to find in any country and you are likely to see examples in examinations.

3.6 Societal marketing

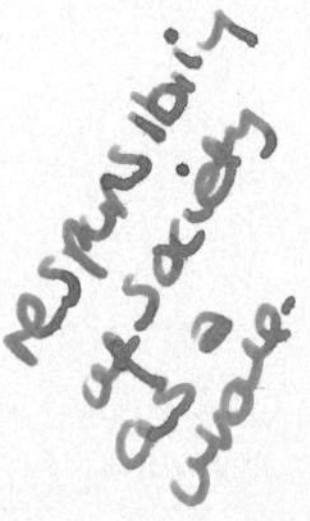

A more recent addition to the evolution of marketing debate is the concept of **societal marketing**. This is the view that marketers should take some responsibility for the welfare of society as a whole and for the long-term sustainability of their activities. This need not necessarily conflict with meeting the everyday needs of consumers, but it does add another dimension of decision making.

For example, Kotler *et al* (2010) have developed a classification of products according to their immediate satisfaction potential and their long-term benefits or disadvantages.

- Products which are highly satisfying and also have high long-term benefits are classified as **desirable products**: a natural fruit juice which is high in vitamins and also tastes good would fit this category.
- Products which are not immediately satisfying but which have high long-term benefits (such as a household smoke alarm) are categorised as **salutary products**.
- Products which are bad for people in the long run, but are satisfying in the short term (such as alcohol or confectionery) are called **pleasing products**.
- Finally, products which are neither good for people nor satisfying are called **deficient products**: for example, slimming products which do not work or toys which have no educational value and are boring to play with. In theory, firms should aim to produce desirable products, but consumers often choose pleasing products instead, for example, eating unhealthy foods when they feel unhappy (Garg *et al*, 2007).

3.7 Debate

There is considerable academic debate about whether the marketing concept actually evolved in a linear manner. In other words, there may not have been the kind of orderly move from production orientation to market orientation that is implied by the model: however, there is little doubt that the different orientations do exist and companies do operate under the various paradigms to this day. In fact, the company you work for may well not be market oriented – you may want to consider the implications of this.

The orientations themselves can still be seen in daily life: some companies are **sales-orientated**, employing high-pressure salespeople to persuade people to buy. This might be typical of a home improvements company, because there is unlikely to be much repeat business: selling someone a new kitchen or a fitted bedroom is usually a one-off process, as is selling timeshare properties or even cars. **Production orientation** exists in many Far Eastern countries, where, for example, T-shirts or baseball caps are produced in their millions, with only a few sizes being available. Product orientation is staging something of a renaissance with the advent of iPhones: people are moving towards the idea of one piece of equipment that functions as a GPS set, as a camera, as internet access, as a word processor, as a music system and so forth. Many teenagers no longer wear watches, because their telephones will tell them the time.

THE REAL WORLD

This example shows how a company with a product orientation (and, to some extent, a sales orientation) can still be successful. However, we might ask ourselves whether the company would do better if it were customer oriented.

Jim Kirby produced his first cleaning system in 1906, using water to separate the dirt from carpets and soft furnishings. This product was not a great success, since it left everything wet and also required the owner to clean out dirty water from the machine. In 1907, Kirby produced the first of his vacuum cleaners, using air to force the dirt into a cloth bag, but it was in 1925 that he launched the first multi-attachment vacuum cleaner.

Right from the start Kirby used door-to-door salespeople to sell the vacuum cleaners. As time went on, the product became steadily more sophisticated, with special attachments for cleaning bedding, curtains, linoleum, sofas and chairs and indeed almost anything else in the house which needed a clean now and then. The Kirby Cleaner could even be configured either as a cylinder model or as an upright model, as these competing designs came into the market in the 1930s and 1940s. The latest version has a multi-speed motor allowing it to be used to buff floors, and it has a carpet shampooing function, a special pet-hair removing attachment, and even a headlight for cleaning under furniture.

In fact, the Kirby Cleaner solves all the cleaning problems any normal householder will ever encounter, and does it extraordinarily well. So how come it is not the biggest-selling vacuum cleaner in the world?

First is the price. With all the attachments, it costs over £1,200 – which is quite a lot of money for a vacuum cleaner. Second, it is complex to use, and most people soon get tired of fitting each different attachment – once the novelty has worn off, most people only use it for basic carpet cleaning. Third, some people do not like the sales pitch. The salesperson comes to the customer's house and vacuums various items (the bed being one – people are amazed at how much dirt comes out of their mattresses).

Almost everybody finds this embarrassing, and many find it intrusive – but equally, many find it hard then not to buy the cleaner, when this otherwise appears to be an admission that they do not mind living in a dirty house and sleeping in a dirty bed.

The Kirby Cleaner provides us with a prime example of a product-oriented company and, to a large extent, a sales-oriented company. The product has all the features anyone could want, but of course most people will only want two or three of the features and will not want to pay £1,200-plus for a lot of features they do not need and will never use.

Since the product would be unlikely to sell in a normal electrical retail outlet, the company has resorted to home demonstrations and powerful sales pitches –to be fair, the cleaner's amazing cleaning power would not be evident without a demonstration, but the cost of sending sales people out to people's homes is obviously extremely high.

The Kirby Company continues to dedicate itself to perfecting just one product – a home care system based on Jim Kirby's first vacuum. In 2012 they are still successfully selling the state-of-the-art model, the 'Sentria', launched in 2008, which follows their transition of quality, reliability and performance to the next century.

The company has been selling vacuum cleaners for over 90 years now and operates in 70 countries with millions of satisfied customers. They must be doing something right! The question remains: Does Kirby's approach to the competitive world of vacuum cleaner marketing remain effective in the 21st century?

(Kirby, 2012)

Equally, many companies are not truly marketing oriented. Some only say that they are **customer-centred**, without actually having a very clear idea of their customers' needs: it is very common for managers to guess what their customers might need rather than find out through market research or by careful analysis of the market.

Exam tip

It is not unusual for a case study to concern a company which is not market oriented, and in fact of the last five case studies used in CIM exams, only two were about customer-oriented companies. If you think the company is operating under one of the other business paradigms, say so – you will gain marks. You might also be able to make suggestions for bringing the company closer to a market orientation.

Remember, too, that marketing orientation and customer centrality do not mean that we simply give the customer everything he or she wants – what we aim to do, as marketers, is **sell** the customer everything he or she wants, for the best price we can get.

4 The contribution of marketing

Marketing operates on the basis of **adding value** for customers. Marketers always begin by considering **customer needs**, whatever the business problem: customers are at the centre of everything they do, whether developing a new product which will make life easier and more convenient for consumers or designing an advertising campaign that will entertain, inform and catch the attention of the target audience. Creating customer value means that people are more likely to be prepared to give them their money, and they are more likely to return to them when they need something new: it has been said that marketing is about selling products that do not come back to customers that do.

Exam tip

In any question of marketing, always begin with the customer. If you are asked to develop a marketing communications campaign, always relate it to the target audience: What media do they use? What type of communication will appeal to them most? What do they want from the product, and from the advertisement? Likewise, if you are discussing new product development, you need to consider: What needs the product is intended to address? What price range will consumers be prepared to pay? Which type of person will the product appeal to?

Many candidates lose sight of this basic consideration and only think about problems from the company's viewpoint: in addition, there is a tendency to talk about 'the consumer' as if referring to one person. People differ in their needs and wants, as companies differ in their capabilities to meet those needs and wants.

This is basic to marketing thinking: if you take nothing else away from the course, take this!

Customer value is a key concept in marketing because it gives importance to the idea that we should always be looking for ways to improve the customers' experience of dealing with us and with our products. Customer value can be increased by adding something that our competitors do not have – although care should be taken not to slide into product orientation by providing everything that any customer could possibly want. The value should only be added if either it costs us nothing to do it or the cost will add less to the price we sell for than the value gained by the customer. If this were not the case, the customer would not see the product as continuing to offer value for money and would simply shop elsewhere. Customer value should not be confused with customer lifetime value, which is the value of the customer to the firm and is a key concept in relationship marketing.

Of course, marketers are not looking after the customer out of altruism. Meeting customer need effectively is the easiest way of creating an exchange (usually financial) and therefore is the most effective way for the firm to meet its own objectives. Marketing is not, therefore, about persuasion or fooling people: it is about providing useful, desirable products and services at a price that people regard as reasonable (or good) value for money.

If we are better at recruiting and retaining customers than our competitors, it seems likely that we will be able to compete more effectively in general. Customer retention has become even more important in recent years, and this has led to the development of relationship marketing, in which long-term relationships are established with customers so that an income stream is generated rather than a one-off transaction. There is a great deal more about relationship marketing throughout the course, since it is seen as the logical next stage in customer centrality.

THE REAL WORLD

Tesco

This case study shows how customer orientation works in practice. Tesco supermarkets are to be seen in nearly every town throughout the United Kingdom and have become hugely successful through putting the needs of customers first. In less than 100 years, the company has gone from a market stall to a giant retailer, meeting the needs of widely differing groups of customers, despite strong competition from other supermarket chains.

In 1919, a young Londoner called Jack Cohen used his First World War Army gratuity to start a business selling groceries from a market stall in the East End of London. His fledgling business went well enough for him to start his own tea company, in partnership with a man by the name of TE Stockwell. Stockwell's initials plus the first part of Cohen's name provided Tesco with its brand name.

In 1929, Cohen opened his first grocery shop in Burnt Oak, Edgware. His motto was always 'Pile it high, sell it cheap' and during the depression-hit 1930s this proved to be a winning formula. During the 1930s, Cohen opened many more stores, but it was not until after the Second World War that supermarket methods came to Britain. Tesco's first self-service store was opened in 1948, and their first true supermarket was opened in 1956, in a converted cinema in Maldon. Because staff costs are much lower in supermarkets, and because Cohen was able to buy in bulk, prices should have been much lower at Tesco stores than in other stores, but until 1964 manufacturers were allowed by law to fix the retail prices of their goods. In other words, all retailers had to sell at the same price, so price competition was impossible. Tesco attacked this problem in two ways – first, the company gave out trading stamps which loyal customers could collect and redeem against gifts of household goods, and second, Jack Cohen was active in lobbying Parliament for a change in the law. In 1964, the Resale Price Maintenance law was repealed and Cohen was able to pursue a vigorous price-cutting approach to business (although trading stamps continued until 1977).

During the 1960s the United Kingdom experienced a rapid rise in prosperity. More people owned cars, more people owned freezers (and so were able to bulk-buy their food) and credit cards were just beginning to be used. In 1967, Tesco introduced the concept of the edge-of-town superstore when the company opened a 90,000-square-foot store at Westbury in Wiltshire. This store was intended to be used by car drivers – ample parking, large trolleys for bulk-buying and a much greater range of goods in

the store meant that car owners could shop much more easily. The edge-of-town location meant lower costs for the store, which could be passed on to customers. This policy proved hugely successful, so through the 1970s Tesco gradually closed down its town-centre stores (with their high overheads) and concentrated on out-of-town superstores. In 1974, the company began selling petrol at discounted prices, again encouraging motorists to come to the store. By 1991 Tesco was Britain's biggest independent petrol retailer.

In the 1990s Tesco returned to the city centre by opening Tesco Metro stores, smaller supermarkets with a smaller range of goods and smaller pack sizes, designed to meet the needs of the local community and inner city dwellers. In 1997, the first Tesco's Extra superstore was opened, offering a range of non-food goods, household appliances and clothing, as well as the traditional groceries available in all Tesco's stores. Altogether, Tesco operates six different store formats: Tesco Extra, Tesco Superstore (standard-sized supermarkets), Tesco Metro, Tesco Express (neighbourhood convenience stores, mainly stocking high-value convenience products) and One Stop, which is a hangover from the company's purchase of T&S Stores in 2002. This is the only format without Tesco in the title and will probably be incorporated into the Tesco Express format eventually.

In 1995, Tesco was the first retailer to offer a loyalty card. Customers present the card at the checkout, and the Tesco central computer records their purchases. Every three months the customer receives a mailing containing vouchers which are redeemable at Tesco stores for groceries or other products; customers also receive special discount vouchers for specific products. Other retailers followed suit, offering their own loyalty cards, but by then Tesco had already seized a substantial market share. A spin-off from the loyalty scheme was that Tesco now had very detailed information about each customer's purchasing behaviour – how often they shop, where they live and what products they buy. This has proved invaluable for future planning and for fine-tuning the service to meet customer needs more effectively and was reported as having been used to thwart Wal-Mart's entry into the UK supermarket business through its Asda subsidiary.

Tesco's customer focus has moved ahead of Jack Cohen's 'Pile it high, sell it cheap' price competition focus. Being cheap is no longer enough – because every other supermarket chain operates on the same basis. Tesco found that most people object to queuing in supermarkets – so they introduced the 'one in front' system. If the queue is such that there is more than one person in front of the customer, the store opens more tills until either all the tills are open or the queue has subsided. The system is monitored centrally – every 15 minutes the tills freeze and can only be released by the cashier entering the number of people in the queue. The figure is fed through to Tesco's main computer, and if there are more than two people in the queues for more than 5% of the times the number is entered, the store manager is asked for an explanation.

Tesco has three own-brand ranges: the 'Value' range, which consists of cheap basic products; the 'Tesco' range, which aims to compete head-on with mainstream brands; and the 'Tesco's Finest' range of upmarket, luxurious products. Each brand meets the needs of a different group of Tesco customers. These now represent about half of all Tesco sales. The company also offers a range of organic products and is now Britain's biggest retailer of organic products. In 2000 the company launched Tesco.com, its online retailing system, which is the biggest online grocery outlet in the world. The online system owes its success to the fact that it is based in the stores themselves, not in a central warehouse, so that staff have local knowledge and the delivery routes are shorter.

Tesco's advertising uses the strapline 'Every little helps' and usually consists of products photographed against a white background, with a voice-over explaining the latest offers. The voice-overs use various well-known British actors such as Jane Horrocks, Martin Clunes, Terry Wogan and Dawn French: in 2007, the company's Christmas campaign featured The Spice Girls. Tesco also takes the lead in new product development: in 2009, they announced that they had developed a new type of tomato which is less juicy, so that it does not make sandwiches soggy. The company has also extended the brand hugely, offering mobile phones (using the O2 network), financial services such as insurance and savings accounts and even loans and credit cards. On the PR front, Tesco sponsors The Tesco Cup, a football competition for young players throughout the United Kingdom, and continues to offer its Computers for Schools programme, in which shoppers can collect vouchers to give to local schools which can redeem them against computer equipment. This scheme has been hugely successful: it encourages a sense that Tesco cares about the local community, while giving customers the chance to be generous towards local schools. It encourages people to shop in the stores rather than elsewhere, of course, but it also has a less obvious spin-off: Tesco has created a generation of computer literate people who feel positive towards the company and would make good employees.

Tesco's customer orientation has certainly paid off. It is now the United Kingdom's leading supermarket chain with 29% of the market. It operates in 14 countries overseas and is the market leader in 6 of those: 65% of the company's retail space is outside the United Kingdom. The company now offers personal finance products (insurance, credit cards, loans) at the checkout and has many other innovations on the way – customer champions, innovative buying policies and so forth.

All of which is a very far cry from a market stall in the East End.

(Tesco, 2011)

ACTIVITY 1.1

Consider the Tesco example above.

1 Having low costs coupled with high prices must have made Tesco very profitable in the 1950s and the early 1960s. Why would Jack Cohen have lobbied for the abolition of Resale Price Maintenance?

2 Presumably Tesco's various customer-focused innovations cost money. Why not simply cut prices even further?

3 Why have three separate own-brand labels?

4 What is the difference between the trading-stamp system and the loyalty-card system? What advantages do loyalty cards have for customers and for Tesco?

5 Why stock a range of organic products as well as ordinary products?

5 Aspects of the market-oriented approach

Exam tip

Consider the organisation you work for (or one you are familiar with in some other way) and decide which of these aspects of the market-oriented approach come into play. Consider how you might be able to change things, if you were put in charge.

The purpose of doing this is to help you practise relating theory to real-world situations. Examiners will often ask you to comment on your own firm, and even if they do not, you will be expected to carry out this type of thinking on a case study.

Marketing can be viewed in several different ways, according to its role and status within the organisation.

5.1 A process of managing exchange

Key term

Exchange process: organisations that are marketing orientated will see this process as both parties being better off and makes the process as easy as possible.

Many academics define marketing as the process of managing exchange, and from a practitioner viewpoint this is not at all a bad definition. Managing the exchange process means that each party will be better off than they were before: if this were not the case, trade would be impossible. One of the problems with the definition is that many exchanges would not, by most observers, be regarded as marketing: an offer to help a friend with his car maintenance in exchange for help with the garden is certainly an exchange, but most people would not regard it as marketing. The key issues with this definition are that it is the marketers who manage the exchange process, and the exchange itself makes both parties better off – therefore, marketers seek to make it as easy as possible for the exchanges to happen (eg by ensuring that the products are readily available or that financing packages are available). The more exchanges that happen, the better off will the company be.

5.2 A driving philosophy of the business

This means that the firm devotes all its efforts to meet customer needs, and every decision at every level of the firm is taken with the customer in mind. Note that customers and consumers might not be the same people – the purchase may be a gift or it may be a family purchase where one person makes the buying decision, with the needs of the other family members in mind. In such cases, the customer (the person doing the buying) has needs even if the product is for someone else, for example, a need for a convenient location from where to buy the product, or perhaps for sales assistance in choosing the most appropriate product. Customers may be professional buyers buying on behalf of a company, in which case they will have very specific needs in terms of career aspirations and so forth. Astute marketers consider the needs of everyone involved in buying and consuming their products. If marketing is the driving philosophy, it acts as a co-ordinating force within the firm: everyone in the company will be aiming for the same end goal, customer satisfaction, and the marketers will have the role of ensuring that everyone is aware of customer needs and their own role in meeting those needs.

5.3 A managerial function

If marketing is viewed as a managerial function only, the company will take marketing decisions on the basis that they will move the company nearer to its objectives, which may be shareholder value, growth, survival, profit or any one of many possible objectives. This moves marketing to a somewhat lower position than it would otherwise occupy if it were regarded as the driving philosophy of the business, but marketers will still occupy a position of importance with regard to the other business functions of production, finance and personnel management. This role is probably typical of many successful companies – it is certainly possible to be successful without being entirely customer-centred.

5.4 A dynamic operation, requiring analysis, planning and action

This view of marketing implies that marketers need to think on their feet and be prepared to change course very rapidly as circumstances dictate. Because customer needs change, and of course new customers are recruited and old ones defect to the competition, marketers will need to be dynamic in their approaches to markets. Equally, competitive responses can force changes on marketers: whatever one firm does, others will either follow or retaliate, so the dynamics of the game are constantly shifting.

5.5 A catalyst for change

Because marketers operate at the interface between the company and its customers, they frequently act as advocates of the customer's viewpoint, thus making changes within the firm based on customer needs. This means that marketers are expected to be working on behalf of customers to improve the firm's offer and will often find themselves in the position of advising (or seeking to influence) changes within the organisation. Much depends on the position of marketing within the organisation: if marketing is seen as a managerial function rather than the driving force within the organisation, marketers will be one voice among several, supporting the needs of one group of stakeholders (customers) in negotiations with representatives of other groups of stakeholders (employees, shareholders, management and so forth). Internal marketing (the use of marketing techniques to change attitudes and behaviour within the organisation) is linked to this view of marketers as advocates for the customers.

These ways of looking at marketing are not necessarily mutually exclusive. It is possible to view marketing as both an exchange management process and a catalyst for change, for example. Change is managed (for marketers) through a process of advocating an improvement in what is being offered for exchange with customers. Having said that, the idea of marketing as the driving philosophy of the organisation does not sit well with the idea of it being only a managerial function – the 'driving philosophy' view moves marketing to a strategic level, rather than simply a tactical level.

ACTIVITY 1.2

Obtain a copy of your company's mission statement or corporate strategy statement. Where do you think marketing fits into the overall picture? How well does this coincide with your view of where marketing sits within the firm?

If possible, ask some non-marketing colleagues about their views on this – Are we all marketers now or is marketing still a separate function?

Exam tip

CIM exams (and indeed many other exams) are usually based on case studies. Questions are likely to emphasise one or other of the above aspects, even if the examiner does not specifically say so: it is worthwhile considering which aspect is likely to be uppermost in the examiner's mind and ensure that your answer relates to it. Many candidates seem to expect that the case studies are always about companies which are customer-centred, or where marketing occupies a central position, but this is not always the case.

The way to do this is to read the case study carefully first, then decide whether you are being asked to comment on the day-to-day aspects of handling marketing problems (in which case you should think in terms of exchange management, managerial function or dynamic processes) or whether the question is geared more towards strategic issues such as where the company is going in the long term or what objectives are being set (in which case you will be considering the question from the marketing philosophy or catalyst for change aspects).

As you progress through the CIM programmes, you will be expected to take a more strategic approach. You should be aware of this, and be ready to 'change gear', since a very similar question might require a completely different answer at a higher level.

Another view of the development of marketing has been offered by Kotler (2003). This is shown in Figure 1.1.

In Figure 1.1, marketing starts out as being only one of the main four business functions, having equal status. It then moves up to being a more important business function than the others, later evolving to being the most important function and having control over the other functions.

This is not, however, the whole story. In a truly customer-oriented business, the customer will be the driving force for all the business functions: in the final stage of Kotler's view of marketing, the customer becomes central, with marketing acting as the co-ordinating and integrative function, operating between the customer and the firm.

There is no evidence that this model represents an evolutionary process, but (rather like the evolution of marketing model) it is certainly possible to identify firms which put marketing into those roles.

Figure 1.1 Evolution of the role of marketing

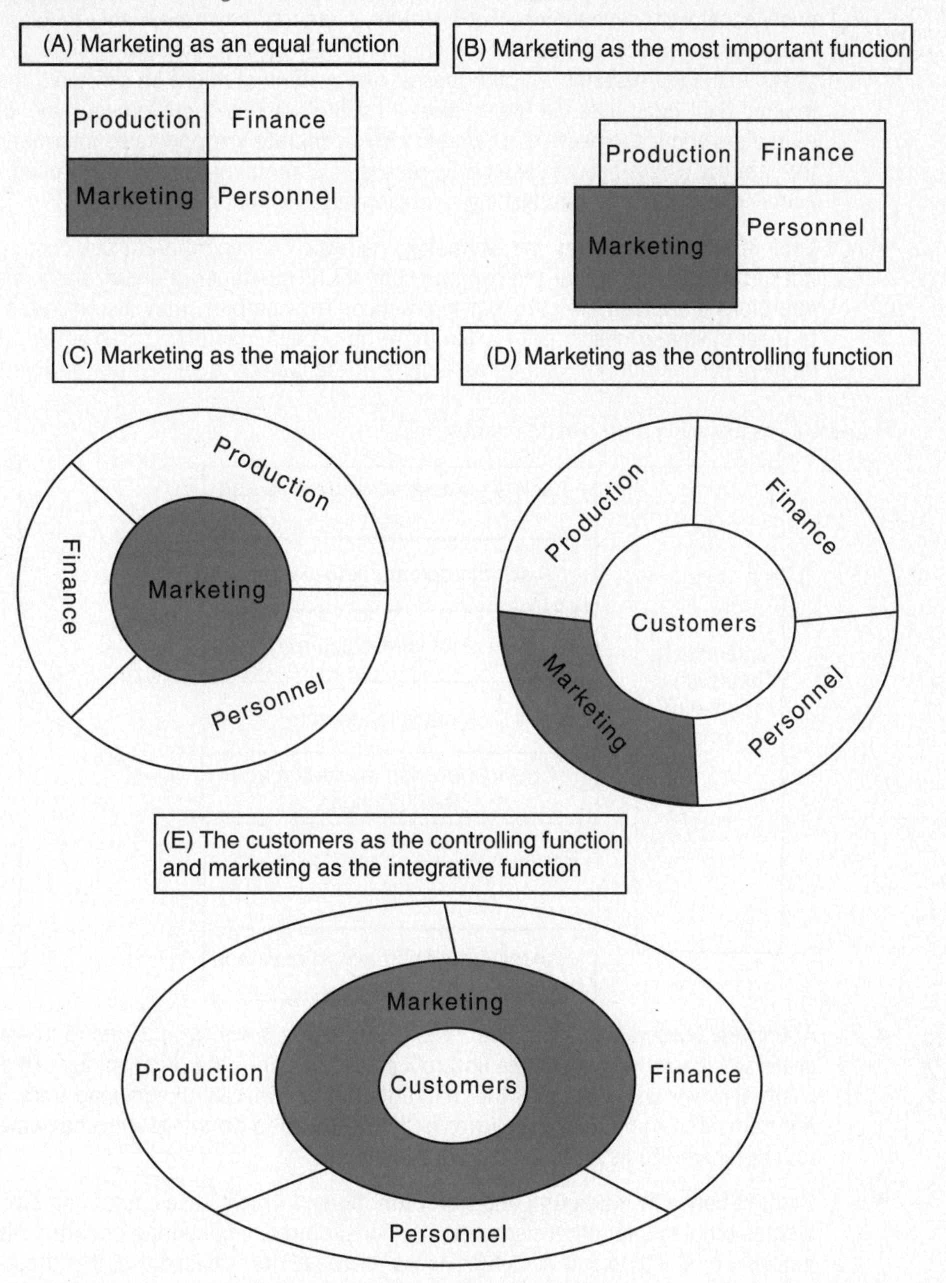

6 Difficulties in developing a marketing orientation

Even though marketers might feel that a market orientation is the obvious way for the firm to go, in practice there are likely to be barriers to developing such an orientation. Some of these come from senior management, some come from colleagues and some are simply the result of organisational inertia. Possible barriers are as follows (see Figure 1.2).

- **Lack of committed leadership and vision**. If the senior management are not on board, it is unlikely that the company can become market-oriented. In some cases, boards of directors can be obstructive: partly this is because they have a legal obligation to put shareholders' interests first and may not see the connection between customer orientation and shareholder value, and partly it may arise from ignorance of what marketing is actually about.

- **Lack of customer knowledge**. Clearly it is difficult for firms to become customer-oriented if they lack knowledge of their customers. For example, a retailer may not be able to keep good, detailed records of every customer who comes into the shop and may lack the necessary skills or finance to carry out effective market research. In other cases, the customers might be scattered throughout the world, making their purchases via the internet. In still other cases, customers may not be prepared to tell the marketers about themselves or (worse) may deliberately supply false information – this is not unusual on the internet where people become worried that information might be misused. Good customer knowledge is basic to establishing a relationship marketing approach.
- **Lack of infrastructure** (eg the technology necessary to record and track customer behaviour). This does not necessarily mean that the company cannot be customer-oriented, but it may mean that the good intentions are difficult to carry out in practice. The company may also lack the infrastructure to be able to meet customer needs, even when these have been identified: for example, if customers need a rapid delivery service but the road infrastructure of the country does not permit this, the need cannot be met.

Figure 1.2 Barriers to establishing a marketing orientation

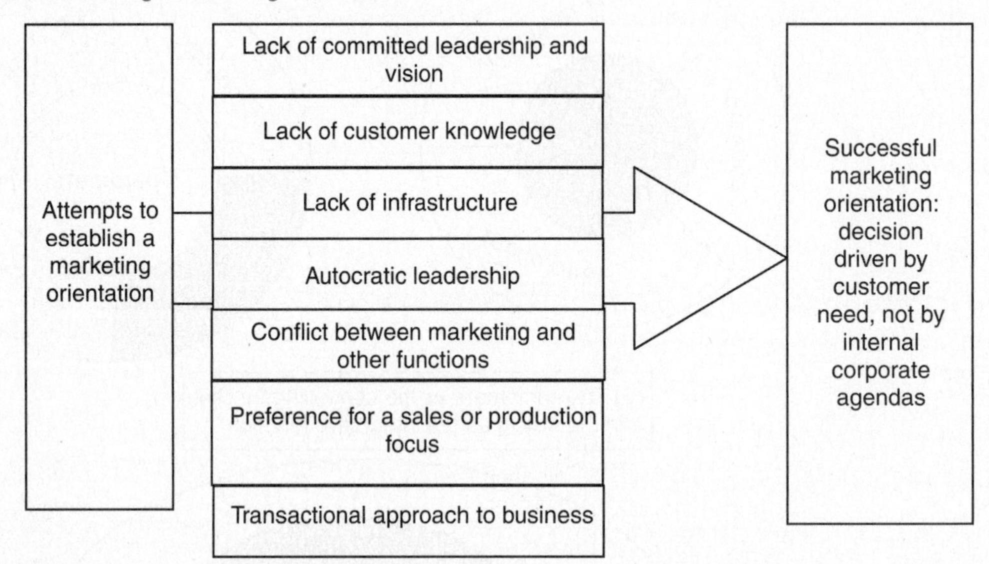

- **Autocratic leadership**. A manager who is autocratic is one who wants to make all the decisions himself or herself, based on experience and (of course) power in the organisation. This often acts as a barrier to customer orientation because the market-oriented firm will take its lead from what the customers need, not from what the manager believes is the best way to do things. In other words, the manager is unlikely to be prepared to listen to customers sufficiently.
- **Conflict between marketing and other functions**. In most cases, adopting a market-oriented approach creates problems for other departments. For example, engineering departments are often unwilling to redesign products to suit customer needs, because they believe that it is the job of the marketers to find customers who want to buy the product ('sell what we can make' rather than 'make what we can sell' philosophy). Equally, company finance managers will tend to see customer-based initiatives such as innovative communication campaigns as a cost rather than an investment.
- **Preference for a production or sales focus**. Both these approaches are likely to create quick results: customer orientation takes time to develop and show results, whereas a good salesperson gets results within a few days, and production orientation makes cost savings almost immediately. These approaches are much more easily measured than market orientation, so are often seen as preferable.
- **Transactional approach to business**. If the firm takes the attitude that the sale is the end of the process, a true customer orientation will not happen. For example, very few car dealers ever follow up on a sale once the customer leaves the forecourt, yet a truly customer-oriented dealer

> **Key term**
>
> **Transaction**: supplier organisations give customers goods and services, often in exchange for money and little else.

would call the customer a couple of months after the car has been sold to check everything is still working properly and would probably also call two years or so later to see if the customer is ready to trade the car in. There is more later on about relationship marketing.

Although most firms try to look after their customers, many firms conduct business as if the customers were of no importance except as sources of money: the next 'The Real World' provides some examples.

THE REAL WORLD

The Beiersdorf development – Nivea for men

The example shows how a company with a product orientation can still be successful. However we might ask ourselves whether the company would do better if it were customer orientated.

In 1882 Paul C Beiersdorf, a pharmacist based in Hamburg, took out a patent for a new method of manufacturing medical adhesive dressings. This marks the development of Beiersdorf as a company whose reputation around the world would be built on innovative products and high quality standards. It was another 22 years before the development of Nivea Crème, which has become a global iconic brand in skin care.

In the mid 20th century, of course, it was important that German organisations did not lose their opportunities to grow and, in a bid to retain the UK market, the company changed its name to Herts Pharmaceuticals Ltd. Herts Pharmaceuticals was then bought by Smith & Nephew Ltd; however in the early 1990s Beiersdorf bought back the Nivea and Atrixo trademarks from Smith & Nephew in the UK and in some ex-commonwealth countries and Nivea Visage was immediately launched together with a new skincare cream, called Nivea Soft. As Nivea and Beiersdorf move into the 21st century, new products are launched at different markets: Nivea Hand, Nivea for Men and Nivea Lip Care, into the global population of over 6 billion where everyone is unique when it comes to skin care. Beiersdorf and Nivea are very aware of this fact and have responded successfully to these multifaceted requirements with an individual and constantly expanding portfolio of products for the last 125 years.

As a product-oriented company, Nivea has mainly focused on Europe, Asia, and the Americas and in particular on the growth markets within these regions with a continuously enhanced range of innovative skin care products. In 2011 Nivea celebrated 100 years of the product and launched its first product range made from natural origin ingredients – Pure & Natural.

Growing a business can involve many differing aspects, but in Nivea's case this has been a consistent review of the product to ensure increased turnover, profits and enlarged geographic coverage. A company like Nivea grows by expanding into regions that offer new opportunities. Nivea has engaged in organic and external growth over the last 100 years. However it has concentrated on organic growth, not surprising as Nivea's brand is so well known globally. Nivea's most recent developments illustrate, once again, its organic growth strategy: the launching of Nivea for men and Pure & Natural developing new markets in new countries and expanding the sales of the existing products in well-established markets. Nivea's plan for growth concentrates heavily on product research and development as a basis for innovation. The company benefits from the synergy that comes from developing brand families around the famous Nivea products. This can be represented by a turnover of €6,194 million in 2010, an increase of 7% on 2009 turnover, and pre-tax profits of €553 million.

Nivea continues to look for a global presence, whilst at the same time assessing the local differences and strengths in the products it provides to those markets.

Nivea is Europe's leading skincare company. It continually seeks to grow through developing its products. The company continues to build a successful business by developing new and existing products and markets as well as diversifying into new markets with products. The company has been selling skin care products for 100 years and operates in all the major markets of the globe with millions of satisfied customers. So they must be doing something right! However the question remains: does the product-led organic growth strategy remain effective as we move into the 21st century?

(Beiersdorf, 2012)

ACTIVITY 1.3

In your own firm, make a list of the people who would be most likely to create barriers to the acceptance of a marketing orientation in the firm. What reasons might they have for blocking marketing? Are those reasons justified? How could you overcome their resistance?

Seeing the problem from the other person's viewpoint is something all marketers need to become good at.

THE REAL WORLD

Intervention by regulators

This example shows how some firms exploit customers. Even without the government regulators, these companies are unlikely to succeed in the long run – customers soon pass the word that they are bad firms to do business with.

In August 2007, the Office of Fair Trading (OFT) announced that it had reached an agreement with an airline regarding price fixing in the long-haul flights market. The airline was to pay a total of £121.5 million as a penalty: the other party to the price fixing was not penalised, because it had come forward to report the price fixing to the OFT. This procedure ensures that it is strongly in the interests of colluding firms to blow the whistle – the other party will be fined, whereas the reporting firm will not and will also have benefitted from the price-fixing arrangement. In September 2009, the OFT imposed fines on six recruitment agencies for price fixing in the construction industry; in 2008, the OFT fined several supermarkets and tobacco manufacturers for price fixing.

Meanwhile, in the voluntary sector, the Advertising Standards Authority (ASA) was also busy. Advanced Hair Studios were told to withdraw an advertisement which implied that their products would grow new hair on balding men, when in fact the effects were merely cosmetic. Agora Lifestyles Ltd was told to remove an advertisement which implied that their herbal remedies for serious problems such as heart failure and cataracts were being withheld by the medical profession. The ASA ruled that the advertisements could lead people to withdraw from conventional medical treatments – even though Agora pointed out that they were not in fact offering the products for sale, but instead were seeking to sell subscriptions to their health newsletter.

In the same week, the ASA found that an escort agency had breached the regulations by failing to mention that there would be an up-front fee for becoming an escort. The agency concerned mentioned some fees, but not the crucial £350 initial fee: one of the recruits complained after he was not offered any work, despite having paid the fee.

Not all the adjudications went against the advertiser, though. DIY giant Homebase was cleared of misleading advertising when it claimed that prices for garden furniture had been reduced: the complaint had been made by arch-rival B&Q, but was not upheld. A complaint about National Express trains regarding the availability of fares between London and York 'from £13' was also rejected by the ASA, who accepted that the word 'from' would be unlikely to make passengers think that all the tickets would be available at £13.

The ASA, unlike the OFT, has no statutory powers. It cannot force advertisers to comply, and in some cases advertisers have been known to ignore the ASA adjudications. However, the industry as a whole is aware that government regulation is never far away, so media owners such as newspapers, TV and radio stations and internet sites comply with ASA rulings, which means that an advertiser who ignores the ASA may well find that there is nowhere for the ads to appear. So far, this sanction has proved very effective and, provided everyone acts in a gentlemanly manner, there is no reason why it should not continue to do so.

(ASA, 2012)

The example above tells us how **not** to be customer oriented: in the short term, these firms have obviously been fairly successful by using questionable tactics, but in the longer run they will suffer from poor word-of-mouth and customer defection. This is in addition to any penalties or restrictions imposed by the regulators.

> **Exam tip**
>
> Some of the case studies you will be given may well depict firms which lack a customer orientation in some way. You may want to consider, in each case, what the firm might do to become more customer oriented: this will often give you a clue as to how to answer the question.
>
> Students frequently lose marks because they do not go beyond the immediately obvious: when asked to outline a particular theory and apply it to the case study, they will often describe the theory and then recommend the company to consider the implications. This is not a sufficient answer: you are supposed to do the thinking, not pass the buck to a senior manager! You should always relate your answer directly to the case study: someone working for the firm should, on reading your recommendations, have a clear set of instructions to follow.

7 Segmentation, targeting and positioning

Although segmentation, targeting and positioning are not part of the Marketing Essentials syllabus, and you will not be expected to answer questions about these aspects of marketing, it may be helpful to have a brief outline of what they are since they are fundamental to the concept of meeting customer need.

7.1 Segmentation

> **Key term**
>
> **Segment**: a small part of a larger market to be targeted.

Segmentation is the process of dividing the overall market into groups of people with similar needs. For example, the car market comprises a very large number of different types of people: in Western Europe and the United States it might be considered to be the entire population. Within that overall market, however, there are many subgroups: people who need a small, economical car for city driving, people who need a luxury car, people who need a car for long-distance driving (sales people, for example), people who need a car with off-road capability and so forth. It would be impossible to produce one car that would suit all these different people, so manufacturers divide the market into segments, each with similar needs and wants.

Segments are typically defined by demographic factors (age, wealth, family life stage, etc), by geographical factors (climate, terrain, country of residence), by behavioural factors (the way people use the product, purchase behaviour, etc) or by psychographic factors (attitudes to the company and product category, specific fears or desires, personal motivations). No single segmentation factor is adequate, though – for example, segmenting a market by age is extremely unreliable since people do not always 'act their age', whereas segmenting by age and by attitude can be extremely revealing.

7.2 Targeting

> **Key term**
>
> **Targeting**: the development of a marketing mix which can then be directed at a particular unique segment.

Having decided how the market breaks down, marketers are in a position to choose which segment or segments the company can serve best. This decision, the **targeting** decision, is made by matching up what the company is capable of doing, against the needs and wants of the segment. In many cases, a segment which would be very profitable (or which would be strategically important) has to be passed up because the company cannot meet the needs of the segment. In other cases, segments which have been ignored by other, perhaps larger, firms are easily served by the company. In general, the more tightly defined the segment is, the more their needs converge and the more likely it is that customers will be prepared to pay a premium price for the 'ideal' product.

7.3 Positioning

> **Key term**
>
> **Position:** how organisations and customers see a product in comparison with other similar products.

Finally, **positioning** is the process of communicating the brand to the target customers in such a way that they can easily recognise where it fits with competing products. Positioning may be achieved in terms of price, quality, reliability, availability, exclusiveness or any of several hundred factors. Sometimes brands are positioned in psychological terms: whether a particular brand of trainers is 'cool' or not will determine its position, and some people are certainly loyal to particular motor manufacturers, switching between different models as their needs change.

In Figure 1.3, the overall vehicle market is shown as breaking down into a number of product categories. A company with a particular capability in producing off-road vehicles might segment its market as landowners (farmers, etc), recreational drivers, such as mountain climbers or canoeists who may need to drive their equipment and friends to remote locations, and fashionable city dwellers who like to drive a big four-wheel drive vehicle. The respective positions for the product are shown: note that each end user will have a different idea of what is a desirable position for their purchase.

Figure 1.3 Segmentation, targeting and positioning

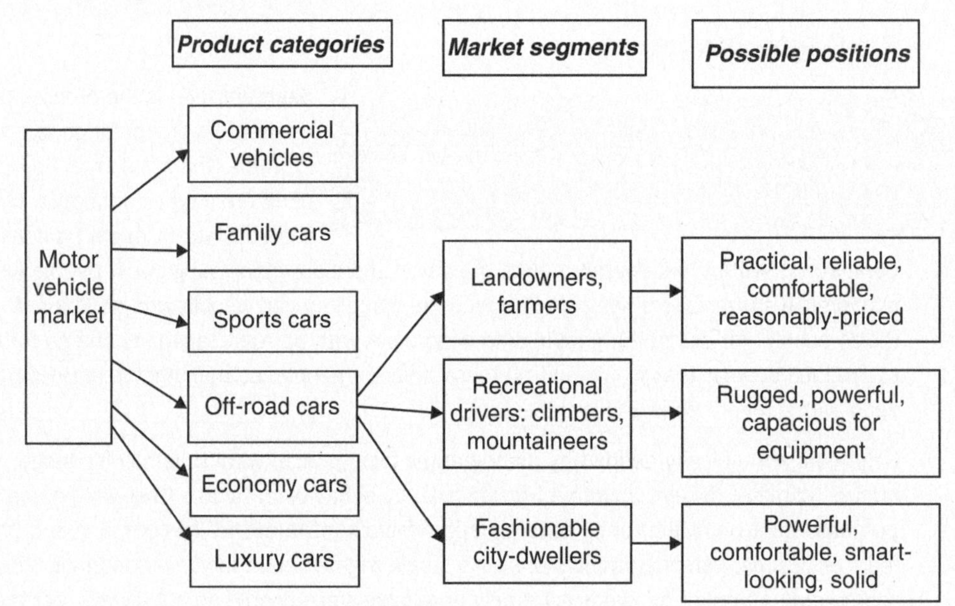

ACTIVITY 1.4

Thinking about your firm's customers, how would you describe the typical customer? If your customers are consumers, are they male or female, old or young, rich or poor? Or are there other characteristics that would best describe your typical customer?

If you are in a business-to-business environment, is your typical customer a large firm, a small firm, an end user of the product, an intermediary who sells your product on? Are they in high-tech industries, low-tech industries, or a mixture? Importantly, do the buyers you deal with have something in common?

If you can answer these questions, and develop a picture of your typical 'best customer', you have a great deal more chance of recognising similar characteristics when you are looking for new customers.

8 Summary

Marketing is a young discipline: it has its roots in economics, psychology, sociology, salesmanship and many other areas, but it has gone through a rapid evolution to reach the current state. As a dynamic process of continual re-invention, academic marketing has paralleled developments in day-to-day practice, moving the profession from a somewhat dubious commercial practice to a means by which people meet their daily needs and life aspirations.

CHAPTER ROUNDUP

- Marketing is about taking a view of the market place.
- A market can be almost anywhere: from the local market of your local village shop, to the global market in which giants such as the energy producer BP operate. It could also be in the not-for-profit arena, such as the market in which the UK's NHS operates.
- Using the tools and ideas around communications and relationships ensures everyone in an organisation is driven by the same thing – customers' needs.
- Create change and with change will come impact. Those impacts have to benefit the organisation and its community.
- It is important to understand that everyone including staff, colleagues and customers has the same desire to have their needs fulfilled effectively and efficiently.

FURTHER READING

Blythe, J. (2008) *Essentials of Marketing.* 4th Edition. Harlow, Prentice Hall. Chapter 1.

Blythe, J. (2009) *Principles and Practice of Marketing*. 2nd Edition. Andover, Cengage. Chapter 1.

Brassington, F. and Pettitt, S. (2006) *Principles of Marketing.* 4th Edition. Harlow, Prentice Hall. Chapter 1.

Jobber, D. (2009) *Principles and Practice of Marketing.* 6th Edition. Maidenhead, McGraw-Hill. (Jobber approaches the definition of marketing in a somewhat different way which does not fit the CIM syllabus.)

Kotler, P. *et al* (2008) *Principles of Marketing* 5th edition FT Prentice Hall. Chapter 1.

The CIM Code of Practice

National broadsheet newspapers

Marketing magazine

Product-based magazines in your organisation's area of specialism

REFERENCES

ASA (2012) http://www.asa.org.uk/ [Accessed on 21 June 2012].

BT (2012) http://www.btplc.com/Thegroup/RegulatoryandPublicaffairs/Codeofpractice/BTPeople/BTpeople.htm [Accessed on 21 June 2012].

CIM (2012) http://www.cim.co.uk [Accessed on 21 June 2012]. (For CIM code of practice).

CIM (2012) The Benefits of Marketing in the NHS. http://www.cim.co.uk/training [Accessed on 21 June 2012].

Dibb, S. *et al* (2005) *Marketing: Concepts and Strategies.* 5th edition. Houghton Mifflin.

Docstoc (2012) Introduction to Marketing Concepts. http://www.docstoc.com/docs/88189332/mk1-Marketing---Introduction-to-Marketing-Concepts [Accessed 21 June 2012].

Encarta Dictionary: English (UK) Microsoft 2000.

Garg, N. *et al* (2007) The Influence of Incidental Affect on Consumers' Food Intake. *Journal of Marketing*: Vol. 71, No. 1, pp. 194-206.

Kirby (2012). http://www.kirby.com/Portals/0/corporate_jobs.html [Accessed on 21 June 2012].

Kotler, P. *et al* (2010) *Principles of Marketing*. 5th edition. FT Prentice Hall.

OFT (2012) http://www.oft.gov.uk/ [Accessed on 21 June 2012].

Smith, P. *et al* (1996) *The Multimedia Marketing Consortium CD Rom Series*. 3rd edition. London Guildhall University, Manchester Metropolitan University and University of Central Lancashire

Michelin Group (2012). http://www.michelin.co.uk/about/involvement [Accessed on 21 June 2012].

Tesco plc (2012). Annual Report and Financial Statements 2011. http://ar2011.tescoplc.com/ [Accessed 21 June 2012].

The Times (2012). Growing a business by developing products and markets. http://businesscasestudies.co.uk/beiersdorf/growing-a-business-by-developing-products-and-markets/beiersdorfs-growth-strategies.html [Accessed 21 June 2012].

QUICK QUIZ

1 Which of the following is true?

A In a transactional marketing environment, quality is the responsibility of everyone in the firm.

B In a relationship marketing environment, there is a high emphasis on customer service.

C In a transactional marketing environment, the focus is on the long term.

2 Which of the following is a stage in marketing evolution?

A Product orientation.

B Orientation on product benefits.

C Quality control.

3 Which of the following is true?

A Product orientation came before production orientation and after sales orientation.

B Sales orientation came after production orientation but before marketing orientation.

C Production orientation came after product orientation and before sales orientation.

4 Lack of committed leadership:

A Creates production orientation.

B Hinders marketing orientation.

C Promotes sales orientation.

5 Common goal setting is an example of:

A Marketing's ability to generate cross-functional coordination.

B Production orientation.

C Relationship marketing.

6 Define marketing

ACTIVITY DEBRIEFS

It is the intention with the majority of these activities to facilitate thoughts and ideas on how you might best fit the marketing theory into the real world, your world. We are all affected by marketing, at home, at work or in the wider environment so it is important you have the opportunity to relate the theory within the chapter to your own experiences.

Activity 1.1

1. Having low costs coupled with high prices must have made Tesco very profitable in the 1950s and the early 1960s. Why would Jack Cohen have lobbied for the abolition of Resale Price Maintenance? Cohen saw that he had a clear competitive advantage, because his supermarkets had a lower cost base than traditional corner shops and therefore he could undercut other shops. Removing price controls would therefore benefit him in the long run – as indeed has proved to be the case. Providing customers with better value for money (which does not necessarily mean lowest possible prices, of course) is always advantageous.
2. Presumably Tesco's various customer-focused innovations cost money. Why not simply cut prices even further? Price is not the only way to compete. Most people do not buy the cheapest – they buy products which represent best value for money. Providing extras such as the 'one in front' policy creates a better value proposition, at relatively low cost to the firm – the value to the customer is vastly greater than would be the tiny reduction in prices the company could make if it did away with the policy.
3. Why have three separate own-brand labels? The separate own-brand labels exist to provide for the needs of different segments of the market. Price-sensitive customers use value brands: people seeking value for money look for the ordinary Tesco brand, and people seeking something luxurious might buy the Tesco's Finest. The Finest brand does not actually compete head-on with national brands in the way that the ordinary Tesco brand does.
4. What is the difference between the trading-stamp system and the loyalty-card system? What advantages do loyalty cards have for customers and for Tesco? Loyalty cards have the major advantage that they enable Tesco to record individual customers' purchasing patterns. This allows Tesco to plan better for meeting customer needs and also to target special offers and promotions more accurately. From the customer's viewpoint, the cards are much more convenient, and having special offers which are accurately targeted reduces the amount of junk mail the customer receives.
5. Why stock a range of organic products as well as ordinary products? Stocking organic products enables Tesco to meet the needs of a health-conscious group of people: at the same time, organic products tend to be more expensive, so the majority of Tesco's customers currently prefer the cheaper factory-farmed products

Activity 1.2

You can also look for these mission statements online and then compare and contrast different organisations, and decide if the customer is at the heart of what they try to achieve.

Activity 1.3

You will find that many barriers are similar to those within the text, however there maybe different blocks in your organisations.

Activity 1.4

Targets, segments and position can be seen from an organisational point of view or customers. You can look at this and consider products that you and your friends purchase: are you a similar age, live in the same area of the city, do similar leisure activities and so on. All of this builds a picture of a target segment which has needs that are satisfied by a particular product which is positioned correctly. For example, Nike trainers are targeted at particular age ranges and are sold in particular shops and promoted by particular sports people.

QUICK QUIZ ANSWERS

1 B. Customer service is crucial in developing customer relationships.

2 A. The other two are aspects of relationship marketing.

3 B. The correct order is production, product, sales, marketing and societal.

4 B. Production orientation and sales orientation have nothing to do with leadership styles: they are strategic positions.

5 A. Setting common goals is necessary to coordination of departments.

6 Common sense applies.

CHAPTER 2

The nature and scope of marketing

Introduction

The marketer's perspective will need to look at many different aspects of the organisation, from the products we make or offer through to the major drivers of that organisation. This chapter will begin to explore these ideas from a historical point of view and will look at organisations that continue to succeed without apparently using the marketing mind set.

We will look at various markets – are we a business selling to another business? If so, what difference does that make to us? If we sell to consumers should we act differently to those who sell to other organisations? We need to understand who leads the organisation and why they lead in a particular direction. The organisations that recognise the importance of the customer and how that adds value to the organisation will be successful in the longer term, developing a marketing approach that puts the customer at the centre of everything they do to achieve the goals and aspirations of the organisation's stakeholders, whoever they may be. Finally, we will look at what makes a marketing organisation and how the leaders should lead such an organisation to success.

After working through this chapter and reading around the subject you should be able to:

- Demonstrate how marketing can affect an organisation's structure
- Explain the cross-functional role of marketing in an organisation
- Explain the impact of marketing activities on consumers, society and the environment: marketing ethics
- Describe internal marketing within an organisation

Topic list

Syllabus references

1.4	Identify and evaluate the factors that may make market orientation difficult to achieve within the organisation: ▪ Lack of committed leadership and vision ▪ Lack of customer knowledge ▪ Lack of infrastructure eg technology ▪ Autocratic leadership ▪ Conflict between marketing and other functions ▪ Preference for production or sales focus ▪ Transactional approach to business
1.5	Explain the cross-functional role of marketing and its importance to organisational performance: ▪ The importance of internal relationships and information sharing ▪ The setting and achievement of common and realistic goals ▪ Establishing common information and control systems ▪ Establishing clear company policies in relation to products, branding, production, etc ▪ The role of marketing as an internal service provider for other business departments ▪ Contribution of marketing to the development of the business strategy
1.6	Evaluate the impact of marketing actions on consumers, society and the environment, and the need for marketers to act in an ethical and socially responsible manner: ▪ Ethical codes of practice for marketers (CIM Code of Practice) ▪ Corporate Social Responsibility as a cultural value ▪ Corporate citizenship – upholding the law and behaving responsibly ▪ Social awareness of key marketing issues relating to social causes ▪ Societal marketing
1.7	Explain the significance of buyer-seller relationships in marketing and comprehend the role of relationship marketing in facilitating the attraction and retention of customers: ▪ Benefits of customer retention ▪ Drawbacks of customer defection ▪ Relationship management in B2B and B2C ▪ The link between degrees of customer loyalty and long-term organisational stability and growth ▪ The role of technology in enhancing or undermining relationships and thereby affecting retention

1 Marketing's cross-functional role

▸ Exam tip

Candidates often fail to acknowledge the degree to which marketing acts as a co-ordinating force within the firm. If the firm is market-orientated and customer-centred, everyone in the firm should be looking for ways to improve the customer experience. This means that their activities will co-ordinate around customer satisfaction – provided, of course, everyone is clear about what the customers need and want.

This is where the marketers come in as the co-ordinators of the firm's activities around customer need. Of course, not every firm is truly customer oriented, so this may not always work out, but you will be expected to think like this in the exam

Provided the firm does develop a **marketing orientation**, marketing will have a role in co-ordinating all the activities of the firm at every level. Each department, and indeed each individual, should be carrying out his or her role with the customer's welfare in mind. The co-ordinating role manifests itself in the following ways:

> **Key term**
>
> **Marketing orientation**: where a business focuses on customer needs and wants to build long term relationships.

- **Information is shared** between departments, and interdepartmental relationships are facilitated. For example, market-oriented firms often have a single customer database which contains all the information about any given customer. Non-market-oriented firms often have a separate database for the salesforce, another for the invoicing department, another for the shipping department and so forth. Integrating the databases improves the level of customer service dramatically.
- **Common goal setting**. Since everything is driven by customer need, the firm can set goals which are measured according to customer-based outcomes. For example, the firm might decide that it needs to reduce customer complaints by 90% and ensure that complaints are satisfactorily dealt with within 48 hours. Since any department in the firm might be subject to a complaint, this type of target will be applied universally.
- **Clear company policies** can be established regarding products, branding, production, delivery and so forth. All of these impinge on customer satisfaction, and all of them cut across every department in the organisation.
- **Marketing becomes a service provider**. The marketing department should be offering services to all departments; for example, providing information about the market to engineers developing new products, advising the finance department on the best way to approach slow payers, talking to the delivery people about providing a better service for customers and so forth.
- **Marketing contributes to strategic planning. Strategy** in business is about **developing competitive advantage.** Marketing offers the opportunity to develop competitive advantage through superior customer value, and although there may be other ways of developing advantage (eg by reducing costs dramatically), a good understanding of customer need is difficult to copy: customers are almost always prepared to pay more for a better product or service.
- **Internal marketing** becomes an important aspect of the marketing function.

ACTIVITY 2.1

List the people from other departments who are affected by what the marketing people in your firm do. Which people are adversely affected by marketing activities? Which are affected positively by what marketing does?

How might you lessen the impact on those adversely affected, bearing in mind their own needs, both in their jobs and as individuals, and also bearing in mind the need for marketing to achieve its own objectives? How might you win them over to your cause?

THE REAL WORLD

Legoland

This case study illustrates how customer orientation acts as a co-ordinating theme for a company's activities and as a central focus. It also shows how resistance to marketing (in this case, the resistance comes from retailers) can be addressed.

Fifty years ago, the children's toy market was invaded by a little plastic brick with eight studs on it. The studs enabled the bricks to stick together, and soon millions of children were playing with Lego – the old wooden building bricks that children had played with for centuries were doomed to remain at the bottom of the toy cupboard.

Lego has moved on from strength to strength – the Legoland theme park in Denmark was followed by another one in the United Kingdom, at Windsor, to the west of London. Lego brand was extending beyond its core business – and the man in charge of licensing the Lego brand, Karl Kalcher, had even bigger ideas in store.

In 1999, Kalcher opened the first Lego store in Britain, at the Bluewater shopping complex in Kent, not far from the Channel Tunnel. Kalcher is a champion of innovative thinking in marketing, something which has led to his becoming a Fellow of the United Kindom's Chartered Institute of Marketing. He is famous for saying 'There's no such thing as children. It doesn't mean anything.'

This statement sounds a little odd from a man whose company targets the 0–16 age group, but in fact what he says makes perfect sense: there is a vast difference between a 3-year-old and a 12-year-old, and even between a 3-year-old and a 5-year-old. Kalcher says that there are only consumers – each with a separate personality and separate needs.

Lego Licensing licenses watches, clothing, the Lego Island CD-ROM and of course the Legoland theme parks. The Lego group plans to become the leading brand among families and children, which means doing a lot more than moulding eight-stud plastic bricks. The Lego store is set to help in this bold ambition. The store is designed to be as user-friendly as possible for its diminutive customers – the store adheres to the 'Lego values', and these were referred to throughout the design and construction of the store. Beginning with the store front, Lego decided that the company's heritage lay in design and construction – so the store front is designed around the colours and proportions of the Lego bricks. Lego is a toy, so the interior of the store is a high-touch environment – customers are actively encouraged to touch things and play with things, but since Lego is also an educational toy, much of what happens in the store is also educational. For example, there is a 'rocket-race' game in which children have to memorise a number in order to make the rocket fly. Many of the displays are at children's eye level, so that children can use the store without adult intervention (until it comes time to pay, of course).

Finally, the Lego store has impressive giant Lego models in the window area, which, according to Lego's retail boss Paul Denham, creates the 'wow' factor. Kalcher believes that, in creating the store, he is setting a standard of innovation that retailers alone would be unable to aspire to. He believes that it is up to the brand owners to invest time and trouble in extending the brand into new areas such as retailing: traditional retailers are, in effect, unable to achieve these standards.

Not unnaturally, retailers in the area objected strongly to the establishment of the Lego store. As long-term Lego stockists, they felt that their loyalty had been betrayed, and they feared that Lego would also undercut them on price. In fact, these fears proved groundless. Kalcher explains why: 'The Lego store is essentially about creating a superior standard for our brand, in the eyes of the consumer. This will promote the esteem of our products for all retail customers.' Kalcher could be confident in making this statement – sales were actually boosted in retailers near Lego's Minneapolis store and near Legoland Windsor. And as regards price cutting, the Lego stores are stand-alone franchised outlets – they operate under the same constraints as any other retailer, so they have to show a profit, which means no price-cutting.

Lego has come a long way in 50 years, but it has a reputation for quality and for getting it right – so much so that, even before there was any hint of Lego opening a store at Bluewater, the developers had used Legoland Windsor as a benchmark for designing the entire shopping centre. Lego now has 80% of the world's construction toy market and expects to build even further successes around the other elements of the brand.

(Lego, 2012)

ACTIVITY 2.2

Consider the Lego example above.

1. What is Lego doing that most of its competitors are not doing?
2. Lego's consumers are children, but the customers are the parents. How does Lego address this?
3. What is the co-ordinating role of Lego's approach?
4. How is Lego using its marketing philosophy to expand the business?

2 Internal marketing

2.1 Aims of internal marketing

Internal marketing is the use of the tools of marketing to create a suitable organisational culture, usually one which places the customer at the centre of what the firm does. Internal marketing should aim to achieve the following outcomes:

- **Encourage an atmosphere of pride**. This might involve highlighting the achievements of individuals (perhaps as Employee of the Month) and publicising these to others in the organisation, or perhaps empowering innovative staff to become agents of change.
- **Provide suitable vehicles for innovation**. Communication channels should be established which enable innovative ideas to be disseminated and discussed across departmental boundaries. Weblogs, discussion forums and newsletters can be powerful in achieving this type of outcome.

- **Improve lateral communication**. Encouraging joint project teams and working groups, encouraging interdepartmental social events and exchanging people between departments on temporary secondments wherever possible will help here.
- **Cut down layers of hierarchy**. Empowering staff at 'grass roots' level will mean that customer needs will be met more efficiently, especially in the case of complaint handling. Employees tend to feel more motivated if they have more control over what happens in the firm.
- **Increase the available information** about company plans and projects. Obviously there will be some plans which will be commercially sensitive, and of use to competitors, so not everything can be publicised to staff. However, it is clearly beneficial if staff understand how the company plans to achieve its strategic objectives, and internal marketing will help in ensuring that everyone knows which direction the firm is going in. This will reduce errors and duplication of effort as well as ensure that everyone is aware of what they should be doing at any given time.
- **Ensure that the leadership is aware of its limited perspective**. Senior managers can easily lose touch with the day-to-day reality of work at the 'grass roots' level. Even though most of them will have worked their way up from the lower ranks, they may be unaware of how the environment has changed. Internal marketing should help to facilitate communications between people working with customers and senior managers at the top of the firm.

2.2 Tools of internal marketing

Internal marketing uses similar tools to customer-based marketing. It begins by recognising that the exchange between employer and employee goes far beyond simply exchanging hours or work for money: there is considerable emotional labour involved in the workplace. People talk about their work when they go home, feel involved with the organisation, feel proud when their organisation does something they approve of and feel ashamed when their organisation does something they do not approve of.

Typical internal marketing tools are as follows:

- **Internal newsletters.** These can take the form of notice boards, e-mail attachments or even a simple A4 sheet of paper with the latest company information on them.
- **Staff magazines.** These can be glossy magazines with articles about employees, articles of general interest and even advertising – employees who want to sell unwanted goods, invite people to a social event or even publicise their out-of-office hobbies might want to advertise. Often these advertisements will be the main reason for staff reading the magazine, so these can be a powerful addition to the staff magazine.

- **Staff meetings.** Meetings can often be extremely boring, but a meeting between staff members and senior managers to raise issues, hand out praise or simply communicate new policies can be a powerful tool. Such meetings can be conducted in an informal manner – the organisation might provide a buffet or arrange for the meeting to be held in a conference room away from the firm. Both these techniques reduce the barriers between senior managers and staff.
- **Team-building exercises.** These can be particularly important when inducting new people into the organisation. The company can set up games or challenges to encourage people to understand each others' approach to problem solving or can form groups such as quality circles across departmental boundaries to work on specific projects.
- **Awards for employees.** Employee of the Month awards are often used, but small prizes or gifts for exceptional performance can be offered at any time, particularly if a staff member has facilitated a successful new idea. Some firms have suggestion schemes which pay cash rewards for successful ideas – many motor manufacturers do this, as it is often the case that a production line worker will recognise a recurring problem much faster than a design engineer who rarely works on the line.

Internal marketing is an important, and sometimes neglected, aspect of marketing. Helping to build a successful, dynamic corporate culture is a key factor in creating a successful, dynamic corporation

3 The impact of marketing on society, consumers and environment

▸ **Exam tip**

You are likely to be asked a specific question on ethics or societal marketing (see below) and it is likely that you will gain marks by bearing in mind any ethical issues raised within case studies. In particular, you should consider the ethical issues implied by any recommendations you make in your answers.

Since you will have at least some questions with a global element in them, you will need to consider ethics in a global sense, not just in terms of your own country's morality.

Anybody who works in marketing has had the annoying experience of being accused of **creating needs**, **persuading people to buy things they do not need or want** and of **being anti-environmentalist**. Business generally has a bad reputation in some quarters, and marketers often bear the brunt of people's complaints about the system.

▸ **Key term**

Corporate Social Responsibility (CSR):the theory that organisations should consider the community and society in which they work as well as customers and profits.

In recent years, the concept of **corporate social responsibility (CSR)** has come to the forefront of business thinking, particularly for marketers since they are at the interface between the firm and its customers. Corporate social responsibility implies that firms should behave ethically and responsibly, avoiding damage to the environment or to society at large. For marketers, this view has become encapsulated in the concept of societal marketing. **Societal marketing** questions whether the marketing concept is sufficient in a world of resource shortages, pollution problems and poverty.

▸ **Key term**

Societal marketing: considers that organisations should achieve their objectives by undertaking their activities in a sustainable way in the long term and support the well-being of the society in which they function.

Societal marketing aims to balance the needs of consumers, society and the company so as to meet the corporate and consumer needs without damaging the interests of society at large. The balance is difficult to maintain – as the example below shows.

THE REAL WORLD

BP

This example illustrates the complexity of dealing with ethical issues at a practical level. At first sight, this is a clear case of corporate negligence – but identifying the organisation responsible, and possibly even who the victims are, might not be so simple.

British Petroleum, now known as BP PLC, is a global oil and gas company with headquarters in London. BP's history is full of discoveries, since 1908 when oil was found in a rugged part of Persia after a long and difficult search. It is now the third-largest energy company and fourth-largest company in the world measured by revenues; and is one of the six oil and gas 'supermajors' companies on the globe. BP is in every area of the oil and gas industry, including exploration and production, refining, distribution and marketing, petrochemicals, power generation and trading.

BP has operations in over 80 countries and produces around 3.8 million barrels of oil equivalent per day.

As well as a large investment into renewable energy activities, including in biofuels, hydrogen, solar and wind power. BP currently invests over $1 billion per year in the development of renewable energy sources. However BP's track record of corporate social responsibility has been reported as being 'mixed'. The company has been involved in a number of major environmental and safety incidents and received criticism for its political influence. This culminated recently on 20 April 2011, when the Deepwater Horizon drilling rig exploded in the Gulf of Mexico, killing 11 workers and causing an oil spill that soon got the press describing it as 'the worst environmental disaster in US history'. Since this time many differing activities have been undertaken. BP has struggled to stem the leak and then look to clean up the oil as it washed ashore along the Gulf Coast, from the fragile Louisiana wetlands to the white sand beaches of Florida, as well as endeavouring to clean up the BP brand and try to distance BP from the worst oil spill in US history. Reports suggest that poor leadership and a poor cement used by BP and its contractors have been the major contributors to the problems that continue to stalk BP.

It is reported that BP was ultimately responsible for rig safety, with Transocean, their subcontractor, responsible for safe operations and worker safety. It is clamed that BP tried to save time and money at the cost of safety, Transocean operated normally despite the hazards, it said. "Multiple causes, involving multiple parties, including Transocean and Halliburton" were to blame; BP said "It took three months and highly complex undersea engineering effort to plug the well and stop the oil flow".

However a report, issued by the The Bureau of Ocean Energy Management, Regulation and Enforcement and the US Coast Guard Joint Investigation Team, echoes previous reports in concluding that multiple factors contributed to the disaster. The explosion was the result of poor risk management, last-minute changes to plans, failure to observe and respond to critical indicators, inadequate well control response, insufficient emergency bridge response training by companies and individuals responsible. As well as labelling BP as ultimately responsible for the safety of the rig, the report continues to blames Halliburton for conducting a poor cement job to seal the well that failed in the run-up to the blast.

The report was commissioned in April 2010, just days after the explosion at the rig; the report also offers recommendations to improve the way the offshore drilling industry is regulated.

A number of other reports have been published in the wake of the oil spill, including The Oil Spill Commission and even BP, who have published their own which appear to try to limit any legal ramifications for BP and others, although they could lead to more charges against BP by the US government. In December 2010, the US Department of Justice sued BP and eight other companies for billions of dollars in damages from the spill. The lawsuit asked that the companies be held liable without limitation. These reports are also likely to be combed through by the differing company's legal teams who are working at lawsuits, the Deepwater Horizon has brought about a huge legal battle involving all the different companies looking to sue each other.

For example, in April 2011, a year after the blow-out at the Macondo well, BP sued Transocean for $40bn (£25.3bn) in damages – the start of a long legal battle to spread the costs of the clean-up that, until then, had been covered by BP alone.

Transocean spokesman Brian Kennedy told the BBC that while the company agreed with some of the report's conclusions, they took "strong exception to criticisms of the Horizon drill crew, nine of whom perished fighting to save their fellow crew members and the rig, for the actions they took in the face of such an unprecedented emergency". Halliburton and BP have also filed several lawsuits against each other - over the issue of the faulty cement seal, defamation and the concealment of vital information that could have prevented the disaster. This appears also to have given some respite to the BP brand and allowed the re-building of customer perception of the global icon.

As the case shows, BP has paid out substantial compensation, as have many of their partner organisations as well as the Government of the USA. For BP paying out any more may be a violation of the trust their shareholders have placed in the company: after all, it is not the Board of Directors' own money, but belongs to the shareholders, which is why they continue to pursue the other organisations involved in the spill . Legally and morally, the company believes itself to be in the right – but this does not help the people who have suffered, and continue to suffer, with the seafood still being a problem apparently, as a result of the spill. This is further complicated by the decision of BP to continue to sponsor the British Museum, the National Portrait Gallery, the Royal Opera House and Tate Britain, pledging £10m over the next five years. Each of the four institutions already has a long standing partnership with BP - most stretching back more than 20 years.

The societal marketing concept remains an issue which excites considerable academic and practitioner debate, since it expands the role of marketing to include everybody in the world, not just customers and consumers. There is a question about whether companies are justified in using shareholders' money for social purposes and a question about where to draw the line: should companies simply stay within the law and rely on government to set the appropriate rules, should companies and trade organisations (such as CIM) set codes of practice or should managers and directors obey some higher moral code?

(BP, 2012)

THE REAL WORLD

Bribery and Big Business

This case study is about bribery and the conflict between managing shareholders' money to best effect on the one hand and taking a moral stance on the other. Bribery is clearly endemic in some business cultures, while in others it is regarded as seriously immoral, which adds to the problem.

Lockheed is one of the world's largest aircraft manufacturers and therefore conducts business throughout the world. Though primarily a military aircraft manufacturer (producing the F1-11 fighter and the Galaxy transport plane), Lockheed also produced the TriStar commercial aircraft, until 1983, when the company left the commercial aircraft business permanently.

In 1976, Lockheed revealed that it had paid out over $22 million in 'sales commissions' to foreign Government officials, including $1 million to Prince Bernhard of the Netherlands in exchange for doing business with Lockheed. Although there was some doubt at the time as to whether these were bribes or payments extorted by the officials under threat of cancelling orders, several senior Lockheed executives were forced to resign, and a shocked US Government passed legislation outlawing such practices even when they occurred outside the United States.

Unfortunately, the legislation seems to have done little to prevent bribery from happening. Lockheed has been fined (in 1995) for bribing the Egyptian government, General Electric was fined for diverting funds from the Military Aid Program to finance the sale of aircraft engines to Israel and in 2000 Boeing was fined for exporting arms to Turkey. It seems that the only way to do business in some countries is to pay 'commissions' or to 'grease the wheels' even if this does violate the law. In fact, the US Government even ignores its own policies on the issue of corruption, by continuing to give contracts to these companies – but of course they have little choice in practice, unless they took the bizarre step of placing defence contracts with foreign suppliers.

Ultimately, the morality of bribery is not in question, even in countries where it is rife. Bribery is immoral and in most cases illegal. It is damaging to the business, to the countries where it happens and to the people who give and accept the bribes. Yet it still goes on, because immediate gain often outweighs long-term disadvantages – especially when the stakes are as high as they are in the aircraft industry.

(Lockheed, 2012)

ACTIVITY 2.3

Consider the Lockheed example above.

1. Why should not Lockheed continue to offer bribes in countries where this is normal business practice?
2. How might governments stop bribery from happening?
3. Is bribery an appropriate use of shareholders' money?
4. Why is bribery damaging?

> **Key term**
>
> **Ethics**: put simply, ethics describes a code of behaviour considered to be right or wrong.

> **Exam tip**
>
> If you are using an American textbook, or one of the adaptations of American textbooks which are around, you will usually find that there is a separate chapter on ethics. You may notice that the ethical issues raised do not always coincide with what you would regard as important ethical issues – this is a demonstration that ethics may have different emphases in different cultures.

Business morality is driven by three main influences (see Figure 2.1):

Figure 2.1 Drivers of business morality

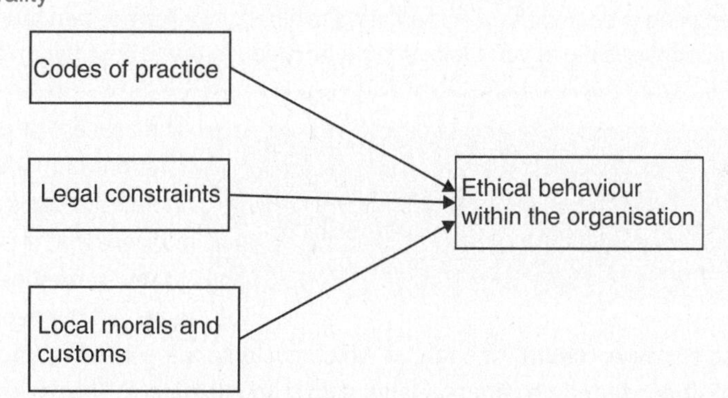

- **Codes of practice such as the CIM code**. These are voluntary sets of rules drawn up by trade or professional bodies and are policed by the trade bodies themselves. They do not usually have a legal status, but they would certainly be taken into account in the event of any legal action taken by an outside party. Sanctions against violators can include having membership of the body cancelled, which may or may not have serious effects — but would certainly be embarrassing.
- **Legal constraints**. Corporate citizenship involves upholding the law and behaving responsibly, so firms need to be aware of the legal implications of their actions. This can be complex for companies operating globally, since they not only have to take account of different laws in different countries, but also have to work within different legal systems (eg the American system and the Japanese system are entirely different, so that contracts have an entirely different status and meaning in each country). For this reason, international contracts usually specify which jurisdiction will be used for settling any disputes.
- **Local morals and customs**. This is, again, a minefield for the global company, since morality is not universal (as the Lockheed case study shows). What is moral does not necessarily equate to what is legal, further complicating the issue – this is yet another potential source of conflict within the firm, as the legal department concentrates on legality while the marketers consider wider moral and cultural issues.

> **▸ Exam tip**
>
> You will be expected to understand the social issues surrounding business activities, so you should read some of the anti-business, anti-global, anti-marketing literature. You should also be aware of the activities of pressure groups such as Greenpeace and Friends of the Earth: since these are regularly reported in the news, you should try to stay abreast of developments. Visiting their websites will allow you to understand their point of view – but remember that websites only ever give one side of the story!
>
> A general point here is that you are studying for a vocational qualification: you should always be applying what you have learned to what you read in the newspapers or online.

ACTIVITY 2.4

Obtain copies of some trade codes of practice. If you have one for your own industry, compare it with the CIM code of practice or with other codes of practice. What are the similarities? What are the differences? What sanctions can be applied to violators?

In the case of comparing the CIM code with the industry code, are there any areas where there might be conflicts, that is, points at which following one code would bring you into conflict with another?

To what extent do you think codes of practice are actually followed in the real world?

4 Relationship marketing versus transactional marketing

> **▸ Exam tip**
>
> Because relationship marketing is so important in marketing thinking, it is likely to pervade any exam question even if this is not specifically stated. Any recommendations you make should be made in the light of trying to establish customer loyalty.

> **▸ Key term**
>
> **Relationship marketing**: the development and management of a long-term relationship with customers, suppliers and distributors; moving from attracting to retaining.

The concept of **relationship marketing** has been at the forefront of marketing debate for the last 20 years or more. The basis of relationship marketing is the concept that it is **cheaper**, **easier** and **more profitable** to **retain existing customers** than it is to **recruit new ones**, so the general aim of relationship marketing is to minimise customer '**churn**' (the rate at which customers are lost to competitors and replaced by new ones) and to establish a long-term business relationship with customers. This is very different to the transactional approach which considers one transaction at a time, with high levels of customer churn, always searching for the next new customer and therefore never having a long-term relationship with the customer. This can be a high cost model of business and may also be very short term.

ACTIVITY 2.5

Anybody working in marketing quickly becomes aware that some customers just are not worth keeping. They are troublesome, are expensive to deal with or simply do not spend enough money to be worth the effort.

Find out what your company does to retain customers. Are there mechanisms in place for recovering defecting customers? If so, what discrimination is made (if any) between customers who are worth recovering and those who should be allowed to go because retaining them would be too expensive or troublesome? If there is no system for retention, what could be done to develop such a system? How would you discriminate between customers who are worth retaining and those who are not?

Relationship marketing has the following drivers:

- **Retaining customers is cheaper than recruiting new ones**. This is debatable: much depends on the relative costs of retention and acquisition, but for firms where acquisition costs are high this would certainly be true. Usually, this will be the case if the value of goods is high, or in the case of business-to-business transactions.
- **Customer defection is damaging to the company**. If customers leave, they may do so as a result of dissatisfaction, in which case they are likely to generate negative word-of-mouth publicity. Also, if they continue to buy similar products, they will be helping to fund a competitor.
- **Customer loyalty leads to long-term stability and growth**. If we have a core of loyal customers, it is much easier to predict revenues, and recruiting **new** customers will lead to growth.
- **Technological advances** allow firms to keep much more detailed information about customers and enable marketers to **determine (and meet) customer needs more effectively**. For example, in Victorian times shopkeepers would know their customers personally, but for a modern supermarket chain this would be impossible without using computers and loyalty cards.
- **Customers should be judged on their lifetime value**, not just on the value of the individual transaction. The danger here, especially in business-to-consumer markets, is that the firm may tend to target younger people, ignoring older consumers who probably have more money. Lifetime value is a key concept in relationship marketing: a customer who spends relatively little but remains loyal for many years is likely to generate a great deal more revenue and profit for the company than a customer who spends a large amount, but quickly defects to a competitor.
- **Small changes in retention rates have large effects on future revenues**. The research evidence for this is strong – quite a minor improvement in retention, as little as 1%, has been shown to increase a firm's value by around 5% (Gupta *et al*, 2004). Other studies have shown similar benefits – a study undertaken by the Cumberland Bank in the United States showed that a 5% improvement in retention of the bank's top customers added 4% to the bank's profitability.

Having said that, not every customer is worth retaining, and not every firm finds that the benefits outweigh the costs of building the relationship.

Exam tip

It is worthwhile familiarising yourself with the arguments against relationship marketing: the jury is still out on the effectiveness of the approach, especially in terms of business-to-consumer situations. For relationships to work, both parties need to be prepared to adapt: many firms are unable or unwilling to do this, and certainly few consumers are prepared to.

In practice, establishing and managing relationships require a different mindset from that used in a traditional, transactional approach. Table 2.1 makes the comparison between **relationship marketing** and **transactional marketing**.

Table 2.1 Transactional marketing *vs.* relationship marketing

Transactional marketing	Relationship marketing
Focus on single sale	Focus on customer retention
Orientation on product features	Orientation on product benefits
Short timescale	Long timescale
Little emphasis on customer service	High emphasis on customer service
Limited customer commitment	High customer commitment
Moderate customer contact	High customer contact
Quality is the concern of the production department	Quality is the concern of all

(Christopher, M. *et al*, 1991)

Relationship marketing has generally been more successful in business-to-business markets than in business-to-consumer markets. There may be several reasons for this. Some are as follows:

- **Business needs change a great deal more slowly than consumer needs.** A consumer who is loyal to a baby product such as Pampers will not need the product once the baby is out of nappies, so the maximum lifetime value of the customer is probably around 2 years. Of course lifetime value for such things as nappies can be extended when more babies are born and when parents discuss their experiences with other parents.
- **Consumers see little benefit in establishing a relationship with a supplier**, whereas a business buyer gains a great deal from establishing a good working relationship with suppliers.
- Good relationships depend on **goodwill** and **trust**, and consumers tend not to trust businesses.

THE REAL WORLD

União Digital Periféricos LTDA

This case study illustrates the difficulty of maintaining good customer relationships over long distances and in conditions where the infrastructure might be poor. This company has needed to be innovative in its approach to relationship marketing.

In 1989, Brazil opened its doors to trade liberalisation. Until then, many imports had been so heavily taxed that they were effectively excluded from the ailing Brazilian economy: in the case of computer imports, this restriction almost proved fatal. When American and Japanese computer systems arrived in Brazil, the country's own systems were so far behind the times that the economy was severely affected.

In the intervening years, however, Brazil has made incredible progress in catching up with computer technology. This has opened up a huge market for components and software – and União Digital Periféricos LTDA has taken full advantage of the rapid growth in demand. The company concluded distribution agreements with Compaq, Flextronics Semiconductors, OPTi Inc. and many other multi-national and global firms. In 2000, the company set up a joint venture with Nokia to establish a seamless remote connection system providing secure connections between the internet, intranets and extranets: the system operates nationwide for remote business, and the solution was expected to cost around $20 million. União Digital is now among the largest distributors of electronic components in South America, distributing throughout the Mercosul countries.

União Digital supplies a complete range of products for LAN and WAN and (given the rapid growth of computer-based systems in Brazil over the last 15 years or so) now supplies, or has supplied, virtually every major company in Brazil. The company always adds value to its products – it supplies training, system design and after-sales technical assistance. This level of service is important in a country where computer literacy has only recently been on the agenda.

Brazil is the largest country in South America – as large as the United States or Australia, with a population of 140 million, Brazil is also the industrial powerhouse of the continent, particularly in the South. This means that União Digital has a problem retaining its relationships with customers who may be thousands of miles from the company's São Paulo base. To help solve the problem, União Digital called in international business consultants BearingPoint to revamp the company's website with the express purpose of improving customer retention and relationships.

BearingPoint reconstructed the already-effective União Digital website in order to increase the personalisation and one-to-one marketing capability of the site. The site allows customers access to news and information which is tailored to the customer's precise profile – this eliminates the need for customers to plough through masses of irrelevant information in order to find the particular information they need. BearingPoint used its alliance with Cisco Systems to carry out the project.

As one of the key features of the solution, União Digital has incorporated its new price policy, whereby pricing varies by client and is based on individual purchasing volumes, future opportunities, technical certification and reseller's performance. In addition, resellers will have the ability to publish their own marketing information through the União Digital website. The website will also be integrated with Cisco Systems' website to allow clients to purchase and configure Cisco products from the União Digital website.

BearingPoint was originally KPMG Consulting, but after acquiring the Andersen consultancy business, the name was changed and the new company was formed. The company's worldwide perspective, and its ability to bring numerous international alliances to bear, was crucial in its thinking on União Digital. BearingPoint has a large network of suppliers and customers (some of whom are both, at different times) and was able to use its network to develop a creative and effective solution for União Digital.

In a society where personal relationships are important, União Digital has managed to create an impressive set of business relationships. The company is able to use its website to support and even build on those relationships – the key to its long-term success in a growing market.

ACTIVITY 2.6

Consider the União Digital example.

1 Why are relationships so important for União Digital?

2 Why would the company use the impersonal medium of a website to improve its relationships rather than spend more effort and money on personal contacts via salespeople?

3 What role did BearingPoint's relationship marketing have in the process?

4 How might União Digital further improve its relationship marketing?

5 What are the specific advantages for União Digital in retaining customers?

Undoubtedly, relationship marketing has a great deal to offer, and the general thinking behind it is the basis for key account management, database marketing and much of the direct marketing that you will learn about later in the course. Making it work in practice is, however, somewhat more problematical.

Many marketers think that providing a good product and a good back-up service is enough to create customer loyalty, whereas in fact this is far from being the case. The purpose of relationship marketing is to establish a **true dialogue** with customers, so that they become '**locked into**' the supplier. On a small scale, restaurants and some retailers such as family butchers establish relationships with regular customers. This has nothing to do with offering lower prices or better food than competitors, but it has everything to do with knowing the customer's name, knowing their individual tastes and preferences and knowing their likely spending power. A butcher who can greet a customer by name, tell him or her that a special cut of meat will be available and sometimes do a special deal for a customer will create loyalty. Likewise, a restaurateur who can offer a customer 'the usual, Mr. and Mrs. Smith?' will generate a sense of being 'a friend in the business' rather than someone who is simply looking to show a profit.

The difficulty for relationship marketers is to translate this **small-business capability** into a **large-business scenario**. Major supermarkets create this sense of dialogue by offering loyalty cards. At first, the data collected from loyalty card records was used to promote products that the customer currently was not buying. This proved counter-productive, because people have many reasons for not buying something, but it usually boils down to one overwhelmingly obvious reason – they do not want the product. Supermarkets then went on to **analysing customer purchases** and offering items which were specifically tailored to the individual; for example, promoting home-baking products to someone who has shown, by his or her purchasing pattern, to be keen on baking at home.

Small gifts can be helpful, but in general firms do well to show that they have a sympathy for the customer and are looking for ways to make life easier. For example, before Christmas 2011, The Co-oporative retailer provided a range of Christmas-based products with a range of **promotional prices**, such as mince pies, bottled beer and potatoes as 'buy one get one free', instead of using these at the end of January, the supermarket sent them out so that people could take advantage of them at Christmas, which is of course an expensive time of year for most people. Having these offers enabled consumers to have more choice when they undertook their Christmas shopping.

ACTIVITY 2.7

Make a list of your best customers. This should be about 20% of your customers overall (if you work in a B2C company this may be difficult to assess, of course). Approximately how much of your firm's sales do these customers account for?

Now calculate what would happen if they defected to your competitors. How would your company survive? Could it survive?

Finally, think about what you would need to do to ensure that each of these customers remains with your firm. What can you do for each of them, individually or collectively, that would tend to lock them into your company?

5 Summary

Marketing is therefore a complex set of activities which all organisations must consider as an important element of their business planning. However, marketing can and should give competitive advantage, increase customer value and is an organisational goal. It is a creative and dynamic element of the organisation which is embedded in 'common sense'.

CHAPTER ROUNDUP

- Bringing everything together to achieve success is fundamental to marketing orientation.
- Marketing organisations are driven by the customer.
- Leaders of these types of organisation have differing styles of management.
- It is important that the customer is at the centre of the organisation and it therefore becomes a marketing lead and orientated organisation.

FURTHER READING

Blythe, J. (2008) *Essentials of Marketing*. 4th Edition. Harlow, Prentice Hall. Chapter 1.

Blythe, J. (2009) *Principles of Marketing.* 2nd Edition. Andover, Cengage. Chapter 1.

Brassington, F. and Pettitt, S. (2006) *Principles of Marketing*. 4th Edition. Harlow, FT Prentice Hall. Chapter 1.

Jobber, D. (2009) *Principles and Practice of Marketing*. 6th Edition. Maidenhead, McGraw Hill.

Kotler, P. *et al* (2008) *Principles of Marketing, 5th edition*, FT Prentice Hall. Chapter 1

Woodruffe, H. *Service Marketing.* Pitman Publishing. Chapters 1 and 2. (Gives an insight into service ideas and marketing.)

The CIM Code of Practice

National broadsheet newspaper

Marketing magazine

Product-based magazine in your organisation's area of specialism

REFERENCES

BP (2012) http://www.bp.com/bodycopyarticle.do?categoryId=1&contentId=7052055 [Accessed on 21 June 2012].

Christopher, M. *et al.* (1991) *Relationship Marketing*, Oxford: Butterworth-Heinemann.

Dibb, *et al*. (2005) *Marketing: Concepts and Strategies*, 5th edition, Houghton Mifflin.

Gupta, S. *et al* (2004) *Valuing customers*. Journal of Marketing Research 2004;41(1):7–18.

LEGO (2012) http://www.legoland.co.uk/ [Accessed on 21 June 2012].

Lockheed Martin (2012) http://www.lockheedmartin.co.uk/ [Accessed on 21 June 2012].

QUICK QUIZ

1. Internal customers are......?
2. What exchange process occurs in the museum market?
3. List three social elements to the marketing role within any organisation.
4. Illustrate where marketing should sit within a marketing-orientated organisation.
5. What product do accounts and human resources departments have to sell and to whom?
6. Why is it important to satisfy customers and/or consumers?
7. Has there got to be a monetary exchange to ensure marketing is important?
8. Is marketing an organisational function?
9. Name an excellent marketing-orientated organisation that you know.

ACTIVITY DEBRIEFS

It is the intention with the majority of these activities to facilitate thoughts and ideas on how you might best fit the marketing theory into the real world, your world. We are all affected by marketing, at home, at work or in the wider environment so it is important you have the opportunity to relate the theory within the chapter to your own experiences.

Activity 2.1

You could consider accountants, human resources assistant, forklift driver, post room assistant or work experience colleague. Everyone should be affected by marketing, but some may find it difficult to understand and therefore see it as adverse.

When thinking about lessening the impact on those adversely affected, consider the definition of marketing and try to satisfy their needs.

Activity 2.2

Legoland

1. What is Lego doing that most of its competitors are not doing? Lego is appealing directly to its young customers by means of opening stores that are customer-friendly for children. It is also using parallel distribution: most toy manufacturers operate through retailers, but Lego also sells direct to the consumers.
2. Lego's consumers are children, but the customers are the parents. How does Lego address this? Because the children make their wishes known to their parents, Lego seeks to involve the parents in the process by means of the theme park. Parents bring their children to the park as a way of entertaining them and enjoying a day out, but they are then exposed to the educational and creative advantages of the toy.
3. What is the coordinating role of Lego's approach? Lego seeks to coordinate everything the firm does through the theme park idea. The franchising, production, licensing and distribution deals all rely on the fundamental view that children are individuals.

4 How is Lego using its marketing philosophy to expand the business? Lego extends the business via franchising and licensing deals, thus increasing the number of products which can be bought bearing the Lego brand. Considering the needs of its customers (the parents) and the consumers (the children) are the driving forces behind this approach.

Activity 2.3

Bribery and Big Business

1 Why should not Lockheed continue to offer bribes in countries where this is normal business practice? Lockheed should not offer bribes because it leads to a spiralling effect – the more companies offer bribes, the more they come to be expected. The company would be better occupied in seeking to stamp out bribery and compete on a level playing field.

2 How might governments stop bribery from happening? Governments do have the option of imposing large fines or imprisonment on people who accept bribes, but they can also impose sanctions on companies who offer them. An effective method is to allow people who accept bribes to keep the money provided they tell the authorities about the bribery.

3 Is bribery an appropriate use of shareholders' money? Bribery can be appropriate in the sense that shareholders' interests are best served by corporate growth: however, in the long term, bribery will push up costs.

4 Why is bribery damaging? Bribery ultimately results in poorer quality firms prospering, with consequent damage to consumer interests. This is apart from the effects on the morals of the people giving and receiving bribes.

Activity 2.4

This depends on your own research.

Activity 2.5

You can also look at purchases you make and consider how the organisation looks to retain your custom, ie loyalty cards, iPhone Apps, SMS texting and many other activities

Activity 2.6

União Digital Periféricos LTDA

1 Why are relationships so important for União Digital? União Digital operates in a culture where personal relationships are important. The company also has to deal across very large distances: many of the firm's agents operate far from the company and may not therefore be as assiduous in looking after the company's interests as they might be were it not for the close relationships involved.

2 Why would the company use the impersonal medium of a website to improve its relationships rather than spend more effort and money on personal contacts via salespeople? Websites offer an excellent way to maintain contact over very long distances, at relatively low cost. Paying salespeople to cover the territory of South America would be prohibitively expensive: it could easily take more than a day's travel to visit a single customer.

3 What role did BearingPoint's relationship marketing have in the process? BearingPoint's own network of suppliers, and especially its close relationship with Cisco Systems, enabled the company to develop a complete system for União Digital. An essential element of developing networks is to have access to a wide range of firms.

4 How might União Digital further improve its relationship marketing? União Digital might improve its relationships by continuing to consult its customers, by meeting with customers at every opportunity (eg at exhibitions and trade shows). The company should also consider customer win-back tactics.

5 What are the specific advantages for União Digital in retaining customers? União Digital would face exceptionally high costs in recruiting new customers due to geographical distances. Recruitment is likely to be largely undertaken by salespeople rather than by direct mail or other means: salespeople are expensive in such a widespread geographical area.

Activity 2.7

This depends on your own research.

QUICK QUIZ ANSWERS

1. Anyone in the organisation who provides a service to another department or group of people, for example finance department and distribution or retailing.
2. Individuals offer time, knowledge, leisure, pleasure and skills for no direct payment (many museums are free in the UK), in return customers gain new knowledge, skills and information as part of a leisure activity which they pay for indirectly as part of the taxation system.
3. Communications, understanding shareholders, community involvement, development of a co-ordinated approach and acting ethically and morally.
4. Everywhere – it should have influence across every element of the organisation.
5. They will have their services such as finance and budgeting or invoicing and human resources could provide recruitment and selection to other departments in the organisation.
6. So that they come back again, paying for products generates profits, satisfied customers do not complain and feel their taxes have been well spent (NHS).
7. No. Not-for-profit, charity or government services should still aim to achieve satisfaction.
8. Yes and no, it should be part of the organisation's DNA but will also have a functional role such as promotional activities, customer information and so on.
9. This is very personal – name one and explain how they make you feel so good.

Section 2:

Planning within the marketing context (weighting 25%)

This section accounts for 25% of the marks for the module, so (like Section 1) it should account for about 10 hours of study time in total for the average student. If you do less than this, you will need to be exceptionally bright, or you will lose marks! You need to read around the subject, read the course textbook and think about what you are reading – what you learn is not only about passing the exams, it also prepares you for a successful career in marketing.

CHAPTER 3

Planning within the marketing context

Introduction

This chapter looks at putting marketing into the organisational context – what does the organisation want to achieve and how will we measure success? Marketing is all about making plans and seeing how those plans progress into the future. This chapter will answer some basic business questions regarding the particular business you are in and will explain how you can go about using scarce resources to gain a competitive advantage.

A marketing plan must be created to meet clear objectives. Objectives can be related to many things such as market share or sales, or even an understanding of a particular health issue such as smoking. Longer term objectives can be broken down into small attainable targets which can be achieved over time and measured against as time moves on.

The marketing audit should be seen as the 'launchpad' for the marketing planning process – it gives a level of control and allows for monitoring in the future. This chapter will describe its elements in some detail: the marketing audit will ask 'where are we now?'; the strategy will look at 'where we wish to be in the future' and 'the tactics to help us get there'. As part of this we must create objectives that are clear road signs on the journey. This chapter starts your journey towards understanding how marketing actions and resources can be used together to achieve the organisation's overall objective whatever that might be.

After working through this chapter and reading around the subject, you should be able to:

- Explain the importance of objectives, the processes for setting them and the influences upon them.
- Identify the various possible organisational objectives.
- Show how marketing planning is crucial in a market-oriented organisation.
- Describe the stages of the marketing planning process.
- Explain the concept of the marketing audit.

Topic list

Syllabus references

2.1	Explain the importance of objectives, the processes for setting them and the influences upon them: ▪ Objectives as a basis for determining future direction, consistency, motivation and measurement ▪ Objectives as a basis for determining achievement ▪ SMART objectives (Specific, Measurable, Achievable, Realistic, Timebound) ▪ Internal and external influences on setting objectives
2.2	Identify the different types of organisational objectives: ▪ Profit ▪ Sales/revenue ▪ Marketing ▪ Growth eg market share ▪ Technical – technology innovation ▪ Survival ▪ Ethically and socially responsible
2.3	Evaluate the importance of the marketing planning process to the market-oriented organisation. Using a marketing plan as a means of: ▪ Delivering strategies and achieving objectives ▪ Implementing a marketing project ▪ Monitoring of timeline progress against schedule ▪ Managing implementation ▪ Resource management (human and physical) ▪ Financial management ▪ Measurement of successful implementation
2.4	Explain the different stages of the marketing planning process: ▪ Corporate objectives/business mission ▪ Marketing audit ▪ Setting business and marketing objectives ▪ Marketing strategies ▪ Marketing tactics/mix decisions ▪ Implementation ▪ Monitoring and control
2.5	Explain the concept of the marketing audit as an appraisal of: ▪ The internal and external environment ▪ Organisational strengths, weaknesses, opportunities and threats ▪ Organisational competences and capabilities ▪ Organisational resource versus an organisation's capacity to deliver ▪ Competitor analysis

1 Setting objectives

1.1 Aims and objectives

> **Key term**
>
> **Strategy**: gives an overview of an organisation's future, based on analytical and evaluative processes, and sets out objectives to be achieved.

First, we need to distinguish between an **aim** and an **objective**. An aim is simply a statement of something we would like to do: for example, the firm might aim to be the best-respected in the industry, or we might aim for our promotional campaigns to be more memorable. These are not objectives. An **objective is an aim which is measurable**, that is, we have some means of

knowing that we achieved the objective. Statements such as 'we wish to sell as much as possible' are aims, not objectives, because we have no real way of knowing how much 'as much as possible' actually is.

Objectives are the building blocks of **strategy**. They are the basis for determining future direction, consistency, motivation and measurement of performance.

THE REAL WORLD

Michelin

This case study looks at the effects of objective setting in a major company. The co-ordinating effects of setting appropriate objectives derived from clear vision is illustrated well by Michelin's approach.

In 1889 two brothers, André and Edouard Michelin, embarked on one of the great human and industrial adventures of our times: one that shaped and continues to drive progress in modern means of transport, through constant innovation. From the invention of radial tyres to that of PAX System, and from the first gastronomic guide to the steel wheel, Michelin has played an active role at every stage of the automotive adventure.

The approach aims to measure and reduce the gap between the Group's values and their implementation. To a large extent, it takes existing practices from the Michelin culture and translates them into management principles. Driven by a constant will to innovate, it helps to provide a long-term response to issues pertaining to mobility and to the sustainability of the company.

Following internal audits carried out in 2002, they published the Michelin Performance and Responsibility Charter. The Charter explains their values, in order to help us better implement them and it specifies their responsibilities toward their different stakeholders: customers, shareholders, employees, industrial and commercial partners, public authorities, media and local communities.

Michelin is committed to an approach of balanced and responsible long-term development, and the progress it makes is to be measured over time. We have therefore chosen to publish the Michelin Performance and Responsibility Report every two years. In the years between, they set out the performance of our key indicators in an interim summary document.

To better fulfil Michelin's mission of driving a constant innovation to provide long-term responses to sustainable mobility throughout the world, it launched, in 2002, the Michelin Performance and Responsibility Charter, which clearly states the Five Respects as their core values, with the objective of the implementation of these values in its worldwide operations. The implementation of the Five Respects not only facilitates better understanding and practice of its corporate mission, it also contributes to the sustainable development of the company itself. The Five Respects are:

1. Respect for customers
2. Respect for people
3. Respect for shareholders
4. Respect for the environment
5. Respect for facts.

By setting objectives, Michelin gives itself a sense of purpose and direction. This provides a framework around which to create its plans. With an overall plan in place, Michelin can set particular targets and monitor its progress towards reaching them. Targets can vary from a customer and/or shareholder focus to a zero-accident target within the workplace. Having a sense of direction and a coherent, overall plan is particularly important to a global organisation like Michelin, which produces many different product lines worldwide.

Based on Michelin's Five Respects, it established a formal framework for the organisation's day-to-day activities.

Michelin's mission in more detail is 'to make a sustainable contribution to progress in the mobility of people and goods by constantly enhancing freedom of movement, safety, efficiency and pleasure when on the move.'

Michelin intends to achieve its goals through:

- Constant improvement of its products 'technical performance and its tyre-related services' quality
- Development of new technologies or products to support sustainable mobility
- Looking at the future modes of transport and ways of transition towards sustainable mobility
- Enabling customers to demonstrate behaviours and positive attitudes towards road safety and environmental issues.

Any organisation must be based on a sound economic footing in order to achieve its mission. As such, Michelin intends to remain the world number one in tyres.

Having overall aims brings a sense of direction to everything Michelin does. These are translated into particular objectives:

- Growth in sales, market share and product reliability
- Increased safety at work, training, diversity
- Improved operating margin and return on assets
- Development of end-of-life tyre recovery
- Increased number of sites with a certified environmental management system
- Maintaining manufacturing cost per tyre.

Wherever possible, Michelin expresses its particular objectives which can be easily measured and monitored. For example, some of its sales objectives are to achieve:

- A 10% operating margin on all sales.

Michelin intends to achieve these mainly by growing faster than the market in the attractive segments that it has chosen, developing its positions in high-potential regions, reducing overheads and increasing flexibility and productivity.

(Michelin, 2012)

ACTIVITY 3.1

Consider the Michelin example.

1. Why would Michelin look at the Five Respects as part of its overall mission?
2. How do the objectives relate to mission?
3. How will Michelin's management at local level arrive at the objectives?
4. How realistic are Michelin's overall plans?

Exam tip

You will often be asked to make recommendations for future action for a firm. You will gain marks if you think in terms of setting objectives for your recommendations, because this will make them more concrete.

For example, if you are asked to suggest ways in which a firm might enter an overseas market, it is of no help to say 'the firm should investigate the local culture further'. A recommendation would include an objective such as 'the firm should commission a local agency to report on the acceptability of the firm's products, the report to be completed within 3 months. The report should also indicate the size of the potential market, stated as a percentage of the population'. Put this way, the senior managers have a solid course of action to follow.

1.2 SMART objectives

An objective should be **SMART**, that is, it should be:

- **Specific**. This means that it should be possible to state it in precise terms, in such a way that it cannot be confused with any other action. If an objective is not clearly stated, it becomes open to interpretation by those who have to carry out the necessary actions to achieve it. In some cases this simply leads to misunderstanding and wasted effort, but in more serious cases it can leave the way open for people to work to their own agendas, using the objective as a way of justifying their actions.
- **Measurable**. There should be some kind of numerical or other measure to quantify the objective. Without this, we cannot know whether the objective has been achieved. Over-achievement can be as serious as under-achievement: sometimes over-achieving a sales objective leads to problems in meeting demand, which can result in a loss of goodwill towards the firm. For example, a flying school which

over-achieves its objectives for attracting new customers might find that it does not have enough aircraft and instructors to meet the demand, leading to disappointment among the would-be aviators.

- **Achievable**. If an objective cannot be achieved, there is little point in setting it. Objectives which are perceived by employees and others to be unachievable will simply be ignored: worse, employees will have less respect for management as a result and be less likely to believe in future objectives.
- **Realistic**. Following on from the criterion of being achievable, an objective needs to make sense within the context of the firm's situation and strategy. If the objective does not connect with other objectives in the strategy, it is unlikely to be achieved, and even if it is achieved it will not contribute anything to the firm's success.
- **Timebound**. There should always be a point at which the managers can say that the objective has not been achieved. If there is no timescale, people can continue to try for the objective indefinitely, which is of course a pointless state of affairs.

For example, if we have an aim that our promotional campaigns should be more memorable, this can only become an objective if we are able to map it against SMART, perhaps as follows:

- **Specific**. We would like 30% of respondents to name our brand in an unaided recall test.
- **Measurable**. We will be commissioning a market research organisation to carry out the recall test.
- **Achievable**. Our campaign last year resulted in 20% unaided recall, so this campaign should be able to improve on that.
- **Realistic**. 30% unaided recall is well within what other brands in our portfolio have achieved, and we would expect this brand to achieve this if it is to remain in the portfolio.
- **Timebound**. We are allowing a 3-month time frame for the campaign to have its effect.

Obviously, there will be a degree of overlap between the various SMART factors, but if even one of them is not present the objective is not viable.

Exam tip

Within your own work environment or working day, try analysing your day's objectives against SMART factors. This will help you remember them more clearly and will also provide you with suitable examples if you are asked to comment on your own company in an exam.

You will almost certainly be expected to know the SMART factors by heart, so learning them by rote is a good idea!

Without objectives there can be no **strategy**. Objectives determine the overall direction of the firm and also determine tactics, since they are the guidelines by which junior managers make decisions. Each decision has to be made on the basis of whether it brings the firm (or the brand, or the department) nearer to achieving the stated objective.

THE REAL WORLD

Mercedes-Benz

This case looks at a number of differing ways in which a global brand in the automotive industry looks to continue its development by identifying a new target market and setting a goal to achieve sales to that market.

Mercedes-Benz set its sights on the younger generation of drivers at the 2012 Beijing motor show where it unveiled for the first time one of its smallest cars intended for the American market.

Built around the older A-Class from the European market, the new four door 'coupé' from Mercedes-Benz has been officially named the CLA. The smaller, but still luxurious, incomer from Mercedes-Benz is doubtless meant to introduce a new, younger generation to the brand. Its higher fuel economy may also help the company meet the US government's overall mileage requirements and attract individuals who have an awareness of environmental issues that come with owning a car. The CLA is expected to have many features normally reserved for larger cars, including radar-based collision-avoidance system, for example.

At the same time the new CLC will have its unveiling on the other side of the Pacific. The CLC, also known as the Concept Style Coupé, will be on display in Los Angeles at an art festival; an event featuring Mike D from the New York-based hip-hop group the Beastie Boys. The multidisciplinary art show will feature visual art, music, food and, it would appear, at least one car. The festival is sponsored by Mercedes-Benz, which chose the CLC as its representative piece of artwork for the show.

Add to these activities a four-week campaign that features Marie, a fictional character, who finds herself trapped driving a Mercedes-Benz C63 AMG Coupé model in Street View. Participants watching the four-minute 'Escape the Map' video online are asked to help Marie escape via a series of interactive challenges developed to build relationships with the younger web-based market.

At the end of the task, the call to action requires the potential customer to give their mobile number to Marie by entering it into Marie's telephone. They immediately receive a phone call from Marie thanking them for their help and are entered into a competition to win a C-Class coupé.

An additional set of media such as TV, print, outdoor and social media activity has been put into place to promote the web-based film promotion.

David George of Mercedes-Benz has been quoted as saying, "Escape The Map" is a bold brand-sharpener – it presents Mercedes-Benz as a vibrant, fresh, aspirational premium brand – and shows people a new side to one of the most prestigious companies in the world.'

Consider this against a backdrop of longstanding innovation and creativity. The company continues to push the boundaries of automotive engineering, creating a succession of truly iconic vehicles. As vehicle segments become less clearly defined, opportunities arise to develop entirely new vehicle types, such as the highly acclaimed CLA – its first ever four-door coupé.

Gorden Wagener is one of the youngest design chiefs in the automotive industry, and is the champion of bold, radical styling, which should attract the younger driver. He has said 'A Mercedes has to have a certain presence; it should look like a luxury car. We have a long history of the brand and we have to respect that history.'

So clearly Mercedes-Benz has set its stall out to attract a new and younger target audience to their brand. Its objective is to maintain its historic luxury image but also to gain market share in a new age profile.

(Mercedes-Benz, 2012)

ACTIVITY 3.2

Consider the Mercedes-Benz example.

1 Why might Mercedes-Benz have revised its target market?
2 How does this new objective relate to the existing vision of Mercedes-Benz?
3 Why might Mercedes-Benz management have looked at this new objective?
4 In your opinion how realistic is their new objective?

According to McKay (1972) there are only three basic marketing objectives: **to enlarge the market, to increase share of the existing market** or **to improve profitability within the existing market share**. This somewhat simplistic view of objectives can be expanded to provide more concrete objectives: for example, enlarging the market can be carried out by bringing out new products aimed at a new group of customers, or by developing the existing products in order to reach new customers. These objectives can themselves be broken down further into developing existing end-use markets, or opening up new end-use markets. In each case, new objectives can be set.

In some cases, complexity in the problems facing the firm will lead to difficulties in setting objectives, because each possible solution to the problem simply creates another problem. Such complex problems are called wicked problems, because they have no definitive solutions.

Obviously, the vast majority of problems are 'tame' ones which have a fairly straightforward set of solutions. Only occasionally do managers have to tackle wicked problems, and they are usually solved at high levels in the organisation.

ACTIVITY 3.3

When considering current world problems, it is easy to see how actions have an impact on other elements within the global market. To illustrate this and to bring it a little closer to home let's consider actions and impacts in your own work life.

You arrive late for a team meeting:

1. List who it will affect.
2. List what impact it will have on the local organisation.
3. List what other elements of the organisation this will impinge upon.
4. List the customers, both internal and external, that may be affected.

You can use the same four questions with different problems; what you will usually find is that many of the same individuals and problems will occur whatever the problem was that started the issue. Every problem impinges on every other problem and person until there is no solution that does not result in a worsening of the situation somewhere in the process.

2 Internal and external influences on objectives

Objectives cannot be set in a vacuum. Any manager needs to take account of the environment within which the firm operates. We have already seen that objectives that are perceived by staff as impossible or unrealistic will simply not be attempted, but equally an objective that does not take account of the realities of the external environment will not be achievable.

2.1 Internal influences

Internal influences include the following:

- **Corporate culture**. This is the set of beliefs and behaviours shared by the members of the organisation. Corporate culture can only partly be influenced by management: typically it builds up from grassroots level. Internal marketing has some role in developing an appropriate corporate culture.
- **Resource constraints**. This is not only about money: resources also include staff knowledge and experience, and company assets such as patents, plant and equipment, premises and so forth. No company operates with infinite resources, so there will always be constraints and limitations, no matter how urgent or tempting the objective might be.

- **Aspirations of staff members**. Internal politics and career structures may affect the feasibility of corporate objectives. Employees primarily consider their own agendas – no one is going to damage his or her career simply to meet a corporate objective set by senior management.

The type of organisation itself may have an influence on what type of objectives might be set. For example, in business to business (B2B) environments long-term relationships might be important. In a not for profit (NFP) organisation it may be survival in the face of governmental and economic cutbacks. In business to consumer (B2C) it might be about market share or increased sales.

As a general rule, staff members need to buy into any changes management tries to make to the corporate culture: in part, this is a problem for human resources departments (who may be able to recruit people who are already sympathetic to the culture) and in part it is a function of internal marketing, which will be covered in more detail in other chapters (Figure 3.1).

Figure 3.1 Internal influences

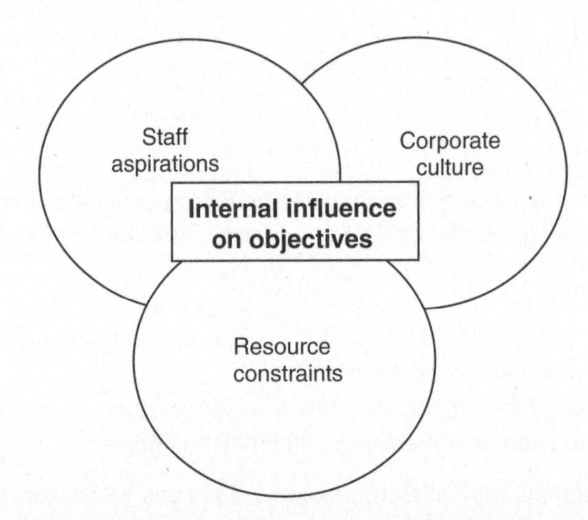

THE REAL WORLD

Aer Lingus

This example illustrates the importance of getting employees 'on side' and developing an appropriate corporate culture.

During late 1999, Aer Lingus ran a series of magazine advertisements in which they emphasised the friendliness of their staff. Much was said in the advertising about the warm welcome that Irish people traditionally give to strangers, but the most telling point was the headline: 'we don't spend money teaching people to smile at our customers. We just hire nice people to begin with.'

Although these advertisements were ostensibly aimed at the travelling public, their effect on the staff themselves was considerable. Aer Lingus staff (especially those with direct contact with passengers) felt rewarded for their efforts in being friendly to customers and felt encouraged to continue to do so: for an employee, the acknowledgement in the advertising was a clear indicator of expected behaviour. As a way of encouraging an appropriate corporate culture, as well as promoting a unique selling proposition in an industry which has few differentiators, the advertisements were a great success.

(Aer Lingus Group plc, 2012)

The Aer Lingus example demonstrates how a firm can develop an appropriate corporate culture by using a suitable recruitment policy.

2.2 External influences

External influences include the following:

- **Competitors**. Any objective needs to take account of possible competitor responses, as well as current competitor behaviour. Competitors are not always predictable, but it is important to remember that they

will always respond to any major changes in your own firm's marketing, so planners need to consider what possible retaliation might be in store and have responses ready. In some cases plans might be adapted or dropped altogether in order to minimise or negate competitive retaliation.

- **Customers**. As in any question of marketing, objective setting should start with the customers. Knowing what customers want, knowing what they might want in future and knowing what they will find less interesting in future are, of course, crucial issues, but for objective setting it can be equally important to identify new groups of customers who might benefit from the company's product offerings.
- **Government and legislation**. Objectives obviously need to be legal, but they should also be ethical, within the cultural context of the society in which the firm operates. For large firms, some objectives might provoke a government response, even if the action is currently within the law.
- **Technological advances**. This means more than just IT and communications – a technological advance could also mean a new drug on the market, a new way of making concrete, a new genetically modified crop or any number of other technical breakthroughs. The Real World item about the Atkins diet illustrates a technical change which affected several industries.

THE REAL WORLD

The Atkins diet

This example illustrates how an environmental change – in this case a fashionable diet– can affect firms dramatically.

During 2003, the revolutionary Atkins diet suddenly became the 'diet of choice' of over 4 million British people. Despite warnings from some quarters that the diet was actually dangerous, its proven ability to help weight loss ensured its popularity among the large numbers of obese Britons raised on fish and chips and Mum's treacle pudding.

The Atkins diet advocates eating large amounts of protein foods and very little carbohydrate. Originally published in 1972, the diet received a tremendous publicity boost after actress Jennifer Aniston and former Spice Girl Victoria Beckham both claimed to have used it successfully. Meat sales grew by 11% and sales of some fruits (the ones allowed by Atkins such as watermelons and raspberries) also soared by as much as 64%. The Waitrose supermarket, mainly based in wealthy southern England, saw a 16% increase in meat sales, which a spokeswoman for the firm attributed to Atkins.

On the other hand, sales of bread and potatoes showed corresponding declines. The decline was steady – of the order of 1–2% per annum, but it was enough to have the bakers worrying. John White, the director of the Federation of Master Bakers, said, 'one can speculate as to the reasons, but personally I have no doubt that Atkins has had an impact. We can only hope that it's a fad that will pass.'

The Flour Advisory Bureau signed up model Denise van Outen to star in commercials promoting flour products. The British Potato Council spent £1 million on a makeover for the humble spud, and plans were laid for the potato, rice and flour industries to band together to meet the threat of Atkins.

Other diet products also felt the pinch. Roche's anti-obesity drug, Xenical, suffered a 16% drop in sales and Slim-Fast (a Unilever product) also showed a sharp decline. As 2004 started, however, some relief was on the horizon in the form of the South Beach Diet. Perhaps a new diet fad would replace Atkins in the public consciousness and save the carbohydrate industry.

Since 2004, the South Beach Diet has also gone the way of all fad diets, and although carbohydrates still have a bad name, people are beginning to realise that more exercise and less eating is probably the main way we have of losing weight. Dr. Atkins died in April 2003 from a head injury sustained when he slipped on an icy street: two years later his company filed for bankruptcy protection under the United States' Chapter 11 legislation. By that time less than 2% of Americans were on the Atkins diet, down from a peak of 11% in 2003. The global food industry may have breathed a sigh of relief – but sooner or later another dietary idea will come along!

The example on Benidorm, below, shows how planning can go wrong, even when carried out carefully: a failure to recognise the consequences of short-termism, allowing any and all developments, is a major contributor to the failed dream. The planners also failed to take sufficient account of the market environment, which was rapidly changing as the Northern European economies became wealthy enough for most people to afford foreign holidays.

THE REAL WORLD

Benidorm

This example illustrates the potential problems which can arise even when everything is well-planned. External factors can easily disrupt the best-laid plans.

During the 1960s, town planners in Spain had the idea of creating a quiet respectable resort for the wealthier middle classes of Europe, foreseeing (correctly) that these people would have large disposable incomes and would be prepared to spend increasing amounts of their money on leisure, particularly as air travel became more widely available. The intended image of the resort was that of a peaceful town with an old quarter at its heart and upmarket, comfortable hotels around it.

The chosen area for the new resort was a small fishing village of 2,000 people, located about half an hour from the nearest airport, in an area with little in the way of natural resources apart from fairly constant sunshine all the year round. In 1958, the village mayor decided to hold a song contest to establish the town's reputation and to encourage the kind of respectable, middle-class arts lovers the town needed to feed its fledgling tourist trade and fill its hotels. The contest was a runaway success, mainly because the first contest spawned a major hit, over 70 versions of which were recorded worldwide. The resultant publicity would have put the town on the map even if the contest had never run again.

Unfortunately, although the publicity put the town on the map and started the developments rolling, the image of a quiet resort for the wealthy never materialised. The result of the careful planning was Benidorm – now widely regarded as the epitome of rampant overdevelopment and used as a byword for appalling resorts even by people who have never been there. The existing beach is excellent, but is now topped up with sand shipped in from the Sahara: acres of high-rise hotel and apartment development run for several miles along this seafront, and the original village is almost invisible. The original 2,000 inhabitants have been supplanted by hotel workers, waiters, bar-owners and the like from all over Europe, and the resort is capable of coping with 5 million visitors a year. Maybe the original planners of Benidorm are not unhappy with the outcome – the town is nothing if not prosperous – but as a demonstration of the way things can turn out unexpectedly, Benidorm takes some beating!

ACTIVITY 3.4

Consider the internal and external environment of the firm you work for. What company objectives can you identify which are unpopular with staff? Which can you identify which are popular? What do you think will happen when these objectives are attempted?

What external factors might have led to these objectives being set in the first place?

Often, objectives which are going to be unpopular with staff have come about because of overwhelming external issues. In some cases these external factors are not known to the staff concerned, which of course makes the introduction of unpopular policies incomprehensible.

ACTIVITY 3.5

Most people talk to their colleagues about work and where they think the organisation is going. Make a list of what you think are the shared beliefs of your company, based on conversations with your colleagues.

To what extent do these match with the 'official' beliefs stated in the corporate mission statement? How might you change the actual beliefs within the firm? Which beliefs would you need to change in order to improve the performance of the organisation?

3 Categories of objectives

Marketing objectives are usually derived from the wider corporate objectives. In the case of a truly marketing-orientated firm, corporate objectives and marketing objectives should be almost identical: but most firms are not as marketing orientated as this, by any means.

3.1 Corporate objectives

Corporate objectives are strategic statements of where the organisation's senior management thinks the organisation should be. Objectives can be grouped as follows:

- **Financial objectives**. These relate to sales, profits, return on investment, balance sheet issues and so forth.
- **Philosophical objectives**. These might encompass such factors as the core values of the organisation, a desire to be the biggest or the best or the most caring or (of course) customer orientation.
- **Qualitative objectives**. These are to do with service levels, the desire to be innovative or perhaps the desire to be respected as a good employer.

There will often be trade-offs in corporate objectives, since all organisations have limited resources and therefore cannot do everything they might want. The following is a list of possible conflicts in setting objectives (Weinberg, 1969):

- **Short-term profit versus long-term growth**. Going for a quick profit is likely to sabotage longer-term steady growth, because the firm will launch products too soon, over-pressure customers to place orders now rather than later, and cut back on long-term investments in research and brand building.
- **Profit margin versus market positioning**. Investment in brand building and positioning the brand is likely to cost money, which of course affects the profit margin: likewise, some positions (eg a low-price position) will involve reducing margins so as to offer low prices.
- **Direct sales effort versus market development**. Making quick sales may well involve tactics such as strong sales promotions, which will affect people's perception of the brand in the longer term.
- **Penetrating existing markets versus developing new ones**. Gaining greater sales from existing markets will take resources away from moving into new markets and vice versa. Penetrating existing markets is likely to require brand extensions or new products aimed at existing customers, whereas developing new markets (eg export markets) will require companies to promote heavily in those markets.
- **Profit versus non-profit goals**. Almost all non-profit goals (eg becoming the best employer) will impinge badly on profit goals.
- **Growth versus stability**. Following a growth strategy will inevitably result in disruptions within the firm as new management jobs are created and new responsibilities emerge. Stability has the advantage of being less risky, at least in the short term.

- **Change versus stability**. As with growth, any other change will destabilise the company. On the other hand, firms which do not change in response to changes in their environment will eventually become obsolete.
- **Low-risk versus high-risk environments**. Firms choosing a low-risk environment are likely to find that they earn relatively low returns: likewise, firms in a high-risk environment may earn more if everything goes well, but could equally lose a great deal more if things go wrong.

Objectives will generate a set of **sub-objectives** in most cases: these are often tactical, which means that they can be changed relatively easily. Building up the strategic objectives by reaching the tactical objectives is the way in which firms progress.

3.2 Objectives other than profit maximisation

Firms are **not necessarily entirely profit maximising**. Objectives may encompass many other outcomes (although firms will usually need to show a profit if they are to survive in the long term). The following are possible other objectives, but this list is not, of course, exhaustive.

- **Sales/revenue maximisation**. Firms may decide that maximising sales and revenue is a good way of shutting out competition and maintaining a strong presence in a competitive market. This may mean reducing profit: a firm which competes on price may sell more, but will certainly reduce profitability per unit sold and the extra sales may not compensate for this, so overall net profit may very well reduce.
- **Marketing objectives**. Some managers like to achieve high customer loyalty levels, or high levels of word-of-mouth recommendations. While these may not maximise profits, they do ensure survival: customer loyalty comes at a price, but does make the company more resistant to competitive pressure since loyal customers are (by definition) difficult to lure away. There are three generic marketing objectives: to increase market share, to increase profitability or to enlarge the existing market (McKay, 1972). Enlarging the existing market is usually only available to very large firms, and to be worthwhile the firm has to have a large enough share of the market not to have to worry about helping competitors (since competitors will gain from an overall enlargement).
- **Growth**. Often firms aim for growth rather than profit, since this again ensures survival. A growing firm will be investing more in marketing than one which is in a steady state, but the larger a firm is, the less likely it is to have to go bankrupt if business drops off – it is relatively easy to find ways of cutting back.
- **Technological innovation**. Firms such as Sony and 3M pride themselves on their technical strengths. They are very much driven by engineering talent: in the case of Sony, the company was founded by two engineers and appears to exist mainly for engineers to enjoy creating novel electronic devices. Profit is simply a way of funding their inventiveness, rather than the other way round.
- **Ethical and social responsibility**. The Body Shop is frequently quoted as a firm which has aimed for, and achieved, ethical trading as its prime objective. Fair Trade companies also exist purely as vehicles for social change and for whom profit is a necessary, but secondary, outcome.

As a general rule, most firms want to grow. This is for the following reasons:

- **Protection against competition**. If the firm becomes one of the largest in the industry, competitors find it harder to enter the market. Growing firms are able to apply more resources to the market and take away market share from their competitors.
- **Improved economies of scale**. Greater size means greater efficiency in almost everything: employees' time and skill is used more efficiently, the firm has greater purchasing power for raw materials and corporate resources (such as patents, designs and so forth) are used more intensively.
- **Better control of the distribution networks**. A growing firm represents a more attractive proposition for suppliers and distributors because it is likely to generate more business for all concerned in the future. Growing firms thus have a negotiating advantage over others in the industry.
- **More opportunities for career advancement**. Managers and employees of a growing firm have more opportunities for promotion, which means greater motivation and productivity. Also, having worked for a company which has grown is something which looks good on a manager's CV.

Growth is therefore a common aim, even if it is not quantified as an objective.

Clearly firms need to survive, but in most cases companies have many objectives other than profit maximisation. Sometimes these are enshrined in the company's mission statement. It is worth remembering that companies are run by people, each of whom has his or her own agenda, so in most cases profit is only a means to an end, not an end in itself.

3.3 Non-profit-making organisations

In some cases, organisations are entirely non-profit-making. This does not preclude them from marketing, but it does mean that they may have multiple objectives and a wide range of 'customers' since they tend to manage exchanges with a wide range of stakeholders. This obviously complicates the marketing effort, since there may well be conflicts of interest between the stakeholders.

Typical objectives for non-profit organisations might be:

- **Charitable objectives** such as helping needy people or funding research into a disease. This would be a typical objective of a registered charity such as Oxfam or Médecins Sans Frontières.
- **Persuasive objectives** such as changing attitudes towards minority groups, promoting environmentalism or supporting a political party. Organisations such as Greenpeace, CND or the Labour Party fall into this category.
- **Financial objectives** such as fund-raising. This would be a typical objective for any non-profit group, since they all require a surplus of income over outgoings if they are to survive.

Sometimes non-profit organisations have a long-term survival need, but some may only exist for a short period to achieve a specific objective (e.g. lobbying Government for a single outcome such as preventing a hospital closure or raising money for an operation for a sick child).

> **Exam tip**
>
> When dealing with case study questions, do not assume that the company is profit maximising. On the other hand, you need to remember that customer centrality does not mean simply giving everything away to customers – we still need to show a profit to stay in business and the aim of marketing is to look after customer needs, because this is the best way of getting their money off them. A great many marketers, both academic and practitioner, miss this point.

4 Using the marketing plan

> **Key term**
>
> **Marketing plan**: a document which often details the organisation's marketing intentions and activities.

The marketing plan, once it is in place, can be used in the following ways:

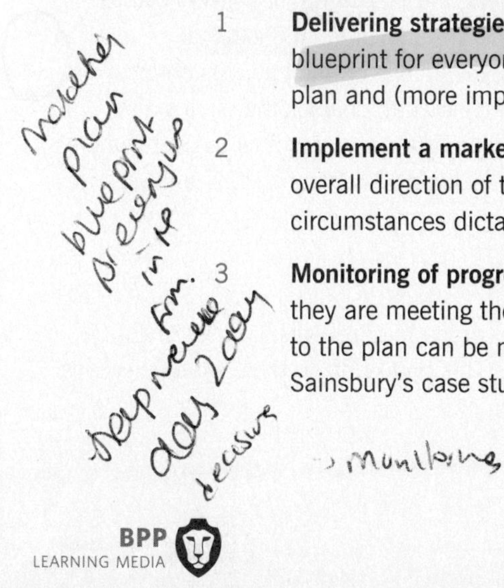

1. **Delivering strategies and achieving objectives**. If the plan is well drawn, it should provide a clear blueprint for everyone in the firm. People should be able to know exactly what to do when they read the plan and (more importantly, perhaps) should know what everyone else is supposed to be doing.
2. **Implement a marketing project**. The plan should help people make day-to-day decisions based on the overall direction of the plan. In other words, people should be able to make adjustments to the plan as circumstances dictate, without having to refer back to the senior managers.
3. **Monitoring of progress**. The plan should contain enough information to enable staff to know whether they are meeting the objectives and staying on course to meet the overall strategic outcome. Corrections to the plan can be made in the light of new information: this may mean restating the objectives (see the Sainsbury's case study).

4 **Managing implementation**. Staff should be aware of what needs to be done and when, and of course what other people will be doing and when. Deviations from plan should be obvious, and it should be straightforward for staff to make adjustments: clearly, someone will need to be in overall control, at least from a monitoring viewpoint, to remind people of target dates and deadlines.

5 **Resource management**. The plan should enable managers to direct people, money and materials towards achieving the objectives. It should also enable planners to obtain resources which the organisation does not currently have.

6 **Financial management**. The plan should enable long-term financial planning, in terms of both incoming revenues and outgoing expenditure.

7 **Measurement of success**. The plan should enable managers to celebrate over-achievement or analyse under-achievement. Achieving objectives is satisfying and motivating for all concerned, which is another reason for ensuring that objectives are attainable: persistent failure to reach objectives is damaging to staff morale.

> **Exam tip**
>
> If you are asked to draw up a marketing plan, or even to outline some recommendations, be clear about exactly what you want people to do. You should also include monitoring and evaluation systems, with timescales, so that people can see what went wrong if the plan is not achieved. Remember that planning is one thing – achieving outcomes is another.
>
> Many students lose marks by not making solid recommendations. You should be specific in what you are telling people to do – if you are asked for recommendations, say something that people can act on.

5 Stages of the planning process

Planning goes through distinct stages, as follows:

Stage 1 **Corporate objectives are set**

These are the overall strategic objectives set by the directors of the firm. They may or may not be customer oriented, depending on the orientation of the firm, but almost all corporate objectives will rely on marketing to a greater or lesser extent. The corporate objectives may be very long term or relatively short term.

Stage 2 **Marketing audit**

> **Key term**
>
> **SWOT analysis**: Strengths, weaknesses, opportunities and threats are widely used to assess the current situation in an organisation.

This is a snapshot of the company's current situation: there is more on this later in the text. Essentially, it covers everything the marketing managers need to know about the firm's internal and external environments, including competitors, customers, available resources and current activities and commitments. The marketing audit enables the planners to understand where the company is now, an important piece of information when deciding how to get to where we want to be. There are many models that can be used at this stage including SWOT and PEST analyses to name just two.

Stage 3 **Setting business and marketing objectives**

These objectives are set in terms of meeting the overall corporate objectives, so they might be seen as sub-objectives (ie tactical rather than strategic). This breaks down the overall objectives into manageable chunks for each department to handle.

Stage 4 **Marketing strategies**

Strategy is about where we are going rather than about how we get there. Strategy is therefore concerned with determining where we should be as a firm and is usually (though not always) considered in terms of competitive position. The marketing strategy is aimed at meeting corporate objectives: in a completely market-oriented firm there will be little or no difference between corporate strategy and marketing strategy, but in most firms there is a distinction.

Stage 5 **Marketing tactics/mix decisions**

Tactical decisions revolve around choosing the appropriate combination of marketing tools to achieve the overall strategic outcome. Tactical decisions are usually much easier to reverse or fine-tune than strategic decisions, since strategic decisions usually involve a lot of people doing diverse thing towards the strategy. There is more in Unit 3 about using the marketing mix to achieve tactical outcomes.

Stage 6 **Implementation**

To an extent this is the moment of truth: putting the plan into action often reveals its flaws very quickly. Implementation is often carried out by more junior staff: it is helpful if they can be given the whole picture, in terms of the strategic plan, so that they are able to understand the purpose and intent of their part of it.

Stage 7 **Monitoring and control**

Having systems in place to check whether we are deviating from the plan is essential: having feedback systems which will allow us to make adjustments easily are also important. The systems should, ideally, enable managers to correct problems before they become too large.

> **Key term**
>
> **Marketing planning process**: builds the organisation's strategy using all the fundamental analyses to form marketing tactics for the future.

> **Exam tip**
>
> You should learn this process by heart. There is a strong chance that you will at least be asked to repeat it and explain it, but you will in any case be asked to apply it. Forgetting a stage is a quick way to lose marks.
>
> A good way to remember the process is to think of it as going on a journey. First decision is where you want to end up (corporate objectives). Then you need to know where you are starting from (audit). Next you decide how you are going to get there (marketing strategies and tactics). Next is to go on the journey (implementation) and finally check that you are still on the right course (monitoring and control).

> **Key term**
>
> **Monitor and control**: when objectives are set, measures must be included. Monitoring checks the progress of a plan. Control takes action if the plan is not on track.

6 The marketing audit

▸ **Key term**

Marketing audit: a systematic and comprehensive review of the organisation's current marketing activities and capacity.

The **marketing audit** provides us with a quick overview of what the current situation is in terms of our marketing. The audit is shown in Table 3.1: you should note that this version of the audit is probably not exhaustive, but it does provide the main headings and can be used as a checklist.

ACTIVITY 3.6

Carry out a marketing audit of your own firm or one that you are familiar with. This will probably take some time and you will need to ask a lot of people a lot of questions: you may find that some information is confidential and therefore not available to you.

You will note that the process is time consuming and often meets with obstruction: How could you reduce the time frame and encourage people within your firm to co-operate with the process? What information systems are already in place, or could easily be adapted, to generate the information more quickly for you?

▸ **Exam tip**

You will not be expected to remember the entire audit, but you will be expected to understand its importance and know how it is used. Many students, when asked to discuss the audit, only use (and quote) a SWOT analysis (strengths, weaknesses, opportunities and threats). Although this is *part* of the audit, it is by no means sufficient for setting objectives. Try to bring in other aspects of the audit in your answers whenever you can, to demonstrate a wider understanding.

The most obvious aspect of the audit to keep in mind is that it is comprehensive: very few of the organisation's activities are omitted and it covers all the relevant external factors.

Table 3.1 The marketing audit

The marketing audit process should have two key roles in an organisation, it should check where the organisation is today and of course where it came from to get to this latest position.

Areas	Coverage	Business/elements	Issues to be assessed
Internal environment	Internal environment – gathering information about the culture, social & economic factors inside the organisation itself	Marketing strategy	An organisation has a vision and focus. What are the objectives, do they link to the organisation's overall objectives and how? Does the organisation have the resources to achieve the objectives set?
		Marketing organisation	The organisational structure and the individuals involved need the skills and commitment to achieve objectives. How effective is the communication, can the plan be implemented and is there the capacity?
		Marketing systems	Systems in place to collect, analyse, communicate and act upon information provided from research and organisational activities. Control systems in place to measure success.

Areas	Coverage	Business/elements	Issues to be assessed
		Marketing productivity	Organisational information of effective and efficient use of resources, cost control, profits and benefits of activities undertaken.
		Marketing functions	Review the organisation's marketing mix. All elements must be assessed to ensure they achieve desired outcomes for both customers and organisation. Product – PLC/BCG Place – Effective distribution to customers Price – Review and assess strategies Promotion – Is the mix right
Micro or task environmental audit	Market environment – looks at all aspects of the internal marketing activities, the market, customers and competition.	Suppliers/distribution	Availability, capacity & polices. Channels their efficiency, level of growth and potential in the future. Look at support services such as agencies, warehousing or transport.
		Markets	Major and minor, growth, changing. Performance of differing markets and within the market segments.
		Customers	Who are they, what are their needs and wants? How do they perceive quality, price and service?
		Stakeholders/public	How and what should we communicate, importance and influence?
		Others, such as the media and pressure groups	Organisations need to be mindful of what these groups could be communicating about them and how they may affect their future plans.
Macro environmental audit	External environment – looks at all elements outside the organisation's control, but that may influence the organisation and how it does business.	Political	How society and the market may change due to politicians' and government's priorities. They may use laws and economics to set new rules.
		Economic	The state of the economy will affect markets and customers. Key to this will be inflation, unemployment, interest rates, taxation, credit and exchange rates. Locally this will also include wages, labour, income and spending power.
		Social	How society evolves. Key areas would be living standards, attitude to business, employment types, cultural changes and development of socio-economic groups.
		Technological	How technology affects the way the market acts. This could include communications, provision of goods and services, production methods and customer purchasing habits.
		Environmental	The 'green issues' such as how we obtain raw materials, buying habits and the link between monetary value and human activity

Areas	Coverage	Business/elements	Issues to be assessed
		Legal	Can be linked to political. This concerns how we do business and the rules and regulations imposed on organisations in particular geographic areas or countries.

Basically, the audit is used to appraise the following aspects of the firm:

- The **internal and external environment**. This means determining what resources we have at our disposal and what is out there in the external environment for us to deal with.
- **Organisational SWOT**. This is necessary but not sufficient: SWOT analysis is only the beginning of the process and is in any case a subjective and inaccurate tool.
- **Organisational competences and capabilities**. This is about what are able to do, in terms of our skills and internal resources: SWOT analysis looks at our strongest capabilities, but we also need to consider everything that we can do competently. We do not have to be the best at everything to be able to do things competently, in other words.
- **Organisational resource versus capacity to deliver**. Our resources are a large part of our capacity to do what we say we are going to do – although the effectiveness with which we use those resources is also crucial. The main issue here is that we should not promise anything we cannot deliver, since this destroys good will and creates negative word of mouth.
- **Competitor analysis**. We always need to remember that our competitors are not standing still. They have their own plans which will affect us, and they are very likely to respond to anything we do, especially, if it threatens their own plans.

The audit does have some 'health warnings' attached to it. First, it only provides a snapshot: by the time the full audit has been carried out, the situation may well have changed anyway, so it only provides a backward view. Second, it is not an objective tool. It does require judgement and even guesswork. Third, it will not make the decisions for you – it is only a way of generating and organising information, and to an extent focusing on the managers' thinking.

Having said all that, the audit is an excellent starting point for objective setting and also (if carried out regularly) a good way to monitor progress. It also has the major advantage of focusing management thinking – conscientiously carried out, the marketing audit provides managers with an unrivalled opportunity to consider every aspect of the firm's situation before making decisions.

THE REAL WORLD

Amway and the internet

This case shows how companies need to adapt their objectives and behaviours in the light of changing circumstances, whether externally generated (technological change like the internet) or internally generated (such as rapid growth).

In 1959, Rich DeVos and Jay Van Andel founded Amway, operating out of the basements of their homes. The partners were ex-servicemen who believed in the American way – hence the name of the firm. Amway operated then, and operates now, by encouraging people to found their own businesses to sell Amway products.

The products range from household cleaning materials through to cosmetics and all are sold by individuals operating from their own homes. Amway products are not available in retail shops and most of the individuals selling them deal only with their friends, work colleagues and families.

The system is relatively straightforward. Amway sells the products to individuals (called Independent Business Owners or IBOs) who then have two responsibilities. First, they sell products on to final consumers and, second, they recruit more people to become IBOs. Recruiting more IBOs means that the recruiter moves up the Amway hierarchy and earns commission based on the new recruit's sales levels. This system, known as multi-level marketing (MLM), means that Amway has automatic growth built into it, and so by 1980 the firm's turnover passed the billion-dollar mark – no mean achievement in only 20 years.

By 2004 the company had 3.3 million IBOs in 80 countries worldwide, with little sign of the growth slowing down. However, several changes in the company's marketing environment were apparent.

First, many other multi-level marketing operations had come into existence since 1959. These included several hundred companies marketing 'miracle cure' products of dubious efficacy. Reputable and honest multi-level marketing companies represented competition for Amway, not for products but for recruits. The dishonest and disreputable companies represented a more insidious threat – they gave multi-level marketing a bad name, putting off many people who might otherwise have had successful careers with Amway.

The second problem arose because of a rash of schemes which looked like multi-level marketing but in fact were not. These schemes paid commission for recruiting people, so that the main activity for a member was finding unsuspecting victims to offload over-priced goods onto. These pyramid schemes, as they are known, had little or no intention of selling products to end consumers. Recruits were encouraged to pay for large stocks of product, and the only way they could recoup their losses was to find someone else to sell the stock to. Many people lost their life savings in such schemes, which provoked governments worldwide to introduce strict legislation regarding all schemes involving individuals recruiting other individuals. This meant that Amway had to adapt its systems to respond to government restrictions in all the countries within which it operates.

A third problem became apparent in the late 1990s, with the rapid growth of the internet worldwide. The main advantage (for consumers) of buying from Amway is the convenience of obtaining the products directly from a friend, neighbour or work colleague, thus avoiding a trip to the shops. The internet represented both an opportunity and a threat for Amway, since online purchasing operates 24 hours a day, 7 days a week, but on the other hand the company was well-placed to take advantage of e-commerce, since it already had worldwide distribution systems in place.

For Amway, constant growth was therefore going hand-in-hand with a constant need to adapt to the trading environment.

Amway needed to overcome the slightly seedy reputation that MLM had acquired. To do this, the firm put in place an unprecedented support programme for its IBOs. Group leaders go on paid training programmes in various parts of the world; they are invited to spend a day at one or other of the Amway centres, to see how the company operates. Amway IBOs are not required to keep stocks of the products: they only have a small stock of samples, which is in fact the only financial commitment they have to the firm. IBOs attend regular meetings at which their enthusiasm is pumped up – sometimes in an almost cult-like manner, though this is not a million miles away from sales meetings held throughout the business world.

Amway also has a strictly enforced code of conduct regarding ethical practices in the business – and those who break the code are ejected from the company. The company has also been instrumental in agreeing an international ethical code for all multi-level marketing companies and in setting up procedures for punishing those who violate the code.

The company sponsors events and contributes to community development programmes in many parts of the world – everything from a clean-up campaign in Latin American slums through to sponsoring a youth basketball competition in China. Overall, Amway seeks to establish its credentials as a corporate good citizen and respond to the environmental shifts in its business world.

(Amway, 2012 and *The Times*, 2012)

ACTIVITY 3.7

Consider the Amway example.

1. What were the objectives of DeVos and Van Andel in setting up Amway?
2. How are objectives communicated to the workforce?
3. How have technological influences affected Amway?
4. What have been the cultural and social influences on Amway's business practices?
5. How has legislation affected the firm?

7 Summary

This chapter has introduced the main aspects of marketing planning. You will be covering all of this in more detail later in the course, but it is useful at this stage to have a good grasp of how planning works in order to understand the marketing mix decisions introduced in the next section.

Basically, managers set a wide variety of objectives, not all of which are concerned with profit. They set these objectives within the context of the firm's internal and external environments, and they can use the marketing audit to assess (a) environmental issues and (b) what the firm is currently doing about them

CHAPTER ROUNDUP

- The planning process combines the organisation's overall marketing strategy with an analysis of the environment in which it operates.
- We must review an organisation's strengths, weaknesses, opportunities and threats together with competitive advantages and identified target segments.
- The process should culminate in a set of marketing programmes or mixes which achieve the overall goals of the organisation.
- Objectives are varied and could include profit, shareholder value, community achievement or a healthier nation. All should be achievable with plans in place.

FURTHER READING

Blythe, J. (2008) *Essentials of Marketing*. 4th Edition. Harlow, Prentice Hall. Chapter 10.

Blythe, J. (2009) *Principles of Marketing.* 2nd Edition. Andover, Cengage. Chapters 2 and 10.

Brassington, F. and Pettitt, S. (2006) *Principles of Marketing*. 4th Edition. Harlow, FT Prentice Hall. Chapter 21.

Jobber, D. (2009) *Principles and Practice of Marketing*. 6th Edition. Maidenhead, McGraw Hill. Chapter 2.

Kotler, P. *et al* (2008) *Principles of Marketing.* 5th edition. FT Prentice Hall. Chapter 3.

National broadsheet newspaper

Marketing magazine

Product-based magazine in your organisation's area of specialism

http://www.businessballs.com/freebusinessplansandmarketingtemplates.htm: This site gives advice and a template for planning.

http://www.websitemarketingplan.com/marketing_plan2.htm: This website offers a wide range of articles on improving your marketing planning.

http://www.bplans.co.uk/sample_business_plans.cfm: This site has a large number of templates for all kinds of businesses: unfortunately, it is American, which means that the plans would need considerable adaptation, but they do offer 'worked examples'.

REFERENCES

Aer Lingus Group plc (2012) http://www.aerlingus.com/Corporate/Current_Report/chairmans.pdf [Accessed on 21 June 2012].

Amway (2012) Your own business http://www.amway.co.uk/CMS/opportunity/your-own-business [Accessed 21 June 2012].

Bronsell, A. (2011) Mercedes targets younger audience with 'bold' online film. http://www.brandrepublic.com/news/1103591/ [Accessed on 21 June 2012].

McKay E.S. (1972) *The Marketing Mystique*. New York. American Management Association.

Mercedes-Bens (2012) http://www.mercedes-jacksonville.com/ [Accessed on 21 June 2012].

Mercedes-Benz (2012) http://www2.mercedes-benz.co.uk/content/unitedkingdom/mpc/mpc_unitedkingdom_website/en/home_mpc/passengercars/home/passenger_cars_world/innovation_new.html [Accessed May 2012].

Michelin Group (2012) http://www.michelin.co.uk/about/involvement [Accessed on 21 June 2012].

The Times (2012) The Times 100 Business Case Studies http://businesscase-studies/by-topic/ [Accessed 21 June 2012].

QUICK QUIZ

1 What does SMART stand for?

A Specific, memorable, actionable, repeatable and timely.
B Specific, measurable, achievable, realistic and timebound.
C Specific, meaningful, active, reliable and teachable.

2 Which of these is correct?

A Enlarging the market can be carried out by increasing profitability.
B Increasing profitability will increase market share.
C Enlarging the market and increasing profitability are basic categories of marketing objective.

3 Which of the following is true?

A Aspirations of staff members are part of the external environment.
B Corporate culture is dependent on staff 'buying in'.
C Resource constraints are irrelevant to the internal environment.

4 Technological breakthroughs are examples of:

A External influences.
B Resource constraints.
C Competitive forces.

5 Which of the following is true?

A Corporate objectives come before the marketing audit but after setting the objectives.
B Objectives are set after the marketing audit but before the marketing strategies are decided.
C Marketing strategies are set before the objectives and after the marketing audit.

ACTIVITY DEBRIEFS

It is the intention with the majority of these activities to facilitate thoughts and ideas on how you might best fit the marketing theory into the real world, your world. We are all affected by marketing, at home, at work or in the wider environment so it is important you have the opportunity to relate the theory within the chapter to your own experiences.

Activity 3.1

Michelin

1 Why would Michelin look at the Five Respects as part of its overall mission?
It gives everyone a focus to achieve and the regional management structures can produce individualised objectives which can be specific to a particular element of the global organisation. But importantly, the local emphasis to achieve meets both local and global outcomes.

2 How do the objectives relate to mission?
The objectives come directly from the mission statement the company seeks to increase revenue and profit but in a sustainable and environmental way. However it also ensures that all the major elements of the stakeholders are respected and achieved – environmental, shareholder value and employees respected.

3 How will Michelin's management at local level arrive at the objectives?
It is that the objectives and mission has been driven by the company as a whole, they have looked at the local management and provided the Five Respects to support the efforts at a local level.

4 How realistic are Michelin's overall plans?
Looking at the global economy over the last few years Michelin has continued to grow, the ability to look at differing regions and markets has been fundamental to this success. Once again linking back to the mission, with the Five Respects and localised objectives they have continued to succeed in markets such as Far East motor trade, airplanes such as Airbus A380 and continue to produce over 150 million tyres and 10 million maps per year.

Activity 3.2

1 It is hoped that younger drivers will become loyal to the brand at an early stage and therefore that their lifetime value will be higher.

2 The company's new objective is to gain customers within the younger driver market, however it still maintains its overall vision to 're-invent' the car. Design for luxury and achieve shareholder value by increased sales in an embattled market.

3 With car sales under pressure across the globe and new cars difficult to shift because of the economic climate as well as pressure from the 'green' lobby, Mercedes-Benz needed to expand and continue to sell. What better way than into a new market of younger drivers who traditionally would not be a Mercedes-Benz driver or customer.

4 This is a very new experience for Mercedes-Benz and we will have to wait and see. However from a marketing objective point of view the company has very clear goals and can identify measurements of success, as well as the monitoring and controlling aspects of the process as they move towards their final aim.

Activity 3.3

Some consequences and impacts of your arriving late could be:

1 The other members of the team

2 The team may not achieve its local targets

3 The organisation may not achieve its overall objective

4 The customer purchasing the products may be let down and manufacturing staff may be laid off because sales reduce.

Activity 3.4

The answer depends on your own research; however, this activity could also be related to government's objectives to reduce debt because of the global financial crisis. Governments may look to cut services; this may lead to a lessening of debt, but may have an detrimental impact on education, defence or social services for example.

Activity 3.5

This depends on your own research. Consider finding mission statements in company reports and as a customer of the organisation decide how you feel they are doing in achieving their goals.

Activity 3.6

This depends on your own research.

Activity 3.7

Amway

1 What were the objectives of DeVos and Van Andel in setting up Amway? DeVos and Van Andel appear to have had an ethical or socially responsible driver for setting up Amway. The company was started on the basis of an ideal – the American Way of being self-sufficient and enterprising – and the founders not only believe in this themselves, but wanted to encourage other people to believe in it. Obviously, the new company needed to be profitable in order to survive – and the aim of growth is another strong element in Amway's objectives – but the main element is the founders' joint vision of a worldwide group of entrepreneurs creating an independent living for themselves.

2 How are objectives communicated to the workforce? The company communicates objectives in two main ways: first, its group leaders are sent on regular training courses at which company policies are promoted and the corporate culture is strengthened and, second, the IBOs are invited to regular 'pep talk'-type meetings at which enthusiasm for the Amway ethos is engendered. The company also communicates its strict code of ethical conduct in writing to IBOs and group leaders.

3 How have technological influences affected Amway? The main technological influence on Amway has been, of course, the internet. This has made shopping from home extremely easy and convenient, which was of course Amway's main advantage over traditional retailers. Amway needs to respond to this either by offering its products online (which would harm the interests of the IBOs) or by allowing IBOs to have their own websites (which might well dilute the brand values). Simply ignoring the internet is not an option – the company's products would be forced into direct competition with other mainstream brands available through online retailers.

4 What have been the cultural and social influences on Amway's business practices? Cultural and social influences include the need for foreign cultures to buy into the 'American way' of entrepreneurship and independence – something which is alien to many cultures. For many people, there is an ethical problem in selling to friends and family, and there is of course a cultural problem in acting independently or (in some cases) of going into business at all. Amway has responded to some of these issues by demonstrating its credentials as a good corporate citizen – its strict code of practice, its community development programmes and its sponsorship of worthy events help to make people feel good about the company. This has helped to overcome the tarnished image of multi-level marketing.

5 How has legislation affected the firm? Legislation has affected the firm seriously in many ways. The advent of pyramid schemes has caused governments to introduce legislation, but because each country has taken a different approach to tackling the problem, Amway has had to set up different systems in different countries, which creates major problems in terms of global corporate policy. Legislation concerning product formulation has been less of a problem, but still represents a potential threat, especially as environmental concerns become more important and governments might be expected to ban certain ingredients.

QUICK QUIZ ANSWERS

1 B is correct. The others are invented.

2 C is correct. Enlarging the market cannot be carried out by increasing profitability (although the reverse might be true) and likewise increasing profitability will not increase market share (again, the reverse might well be true).

3 B is correct. Aspirations of staff members and resource constraints are both part of the internal environment.

4 A is correct. Technological advances may come from competitors and may alter the resource constraints, but they are part of the external environment.

5 B is correct. The order is as follows:

- Corporate objectives are set
- Marketing audit
- Setting business and marketing objectives
- Marketing strategies
- Marketing tactics/mix decisions
- Implementation
- Monitoring and control

Section 3:

The marketing mix (weighting 50%)

This section is the largest in the Marketing Essentials unit, accounting for 50% of the overall marks. It should therefore take you about 20 hours to study, including reading around the subject and carrying out the various exercises and tests. You may be studying alone or you may be part of a class: either way, you do need to put in about that much time!

The marketing mix is about the tactical tools marketers have at their disposal, so it is central to what they do in their day-to-day work. It is important to have a good grasp of it if you are going to succeed in your marketing career, and of course it is certain to come up at least once in the exam. The likelihood is that it will be relevant to more than one question, so it is worth understanding the concept as well as learning the elements of it.

CHAPTER 4

The marketing mix

Introduction

The marketing mix is the fundamental building block of marketing – without the marketing mix, nothing can be achieved. In the last chapter we looked at the marketing audit, 'where are we now?' and the strategy, 'where do we want to be in the future?'. The marketing mix is the means to achieving that goal. It brings together many aspects of the plan and the tools we use to develop the strategy to achievement.

The marketing mix involves getting the right product in the right place for customers to pay the right price with the right communication for them – a synergy.

Over the next chapters we will look in detail at the **4Ps** of the **marketing mix** (**product**, **price**, **place** and **promotion**) which are the simple requirements to satisfy need; how much we need to be paid to achieve satisfaction; where that satisfaction is available; and, finally, how we must communicate that these elements are available.

We will also develop the marketing mix to the **7Ps**: including **people**, **process** (how customers go about the exchange) and **physical evidence** (what the customer comes away with in their hand once the exchange has taken occurred).

After working through this introduction to the marketing mix and undertaking some additional reading, you should be able to:

- Identify the key elements of the marketing mix
- Demonstrate how the marketing mix can come together to achieve organisational objectives
- Explain the synergy between the differing elements of the marketing mix.

Topic list

Syllabus reference

3.14	Explain the concept of developing a co-ordinated approach to the marketing mix, as a means to satisfying customers' requirements and competing effectively: ▪ Designing a mix which is compatible and co-ordinated effectively ▪ Being mindful of the target market, their needs and expectations ▪ Being mindful of tactical competitive activities ▪ Being mindful of the impact of other elements of the marketing mix

1 The marketing mix

> **Key terms**
>
> **Marketing mix**: the core of marketing. It is traditionally expressed as either the 4Ps (product, price, place and promotion) or 7Ps (the 4Ps plus people, process and physical evidence).
>
> **Services**: a set of benefits which satisfy needs and wants but are not tangible – they are intangible and non-physical such as travel, medical care or consultancy.

The **marketing mix** is the basic set of tools marketers have available to carry out **tactical marketing**. The mix is generally thought of as being like the ingredients in a recipe – they need to be combined in the correct proportions and at the correct time if the overall result is to be a success. As in a recipe, one ingredient cannot substitute for another – they all work together to produce a result. The proportions of the mix necessarily need to be different according to the product type, corporate resources and, of course, the consumers' characteristics.

1.1 The 4Ps

The basic mix elements were originally thought to be as follows.

1.1.1 Product

> **Key term**
>
> **Product**: an item that satisfies a customer's needs and/or wants, eg a car.

This is the bundle of benefits the firm offers to the customer, and is the element which is intended to meet people's needs. The product is not necessarily physical – it could be a service, and indeed most products contain elements of both service and physical.

1.1.2 Price

> **Key term**
>
> **Price**: the monetary value given to a product/service, eg money spent on a car.

This is the total of what the firm expects the customer to do in return. Price goes beyond the amount the company receives – it also includes other costs the consumer has to pay, such as the cost of learning to use the product, the cost of switching from their existing product, the cost of installation and so forth.

1.1.3 Place

> ▸ **Key term**
>
> **Place**: where the product/service is available, eg the dealership used in the purchase.

This is the location where the exchange takes place – the retail store, through the mail, in cyberspace, etc. Place decisions involve thinking about physical distribution (shipping and delivery) as well as about finding the most convenient location for customers to buy the product.

1.1.4 Promotion

> ▸ **Key term**
>
> **Promotion**: how we communicate the other Ps to customers, eg advertising which enable you to find the car and dealership.

This is the subgroup of mix elements which the marketer uses to communicate the total offer to the customer. Promotion is itself divided into a promotional mix, and new ways of communicating are being added.

This categorisation of mix elements proved to be inadequate, as it has only limited application to service products: since services now comprise the bulk of marketing in the developed world, extra mix elements need to be considered. This led to the development of the 7Ps.

1.2 The 7Ps

The additional 3Ps that make up the 7Ps are as follows:

1.2.1 People

> ▸ **Key term**
>
> **People**: those individuals involved in making or selling the product/service, eg sales people, reception staff, mechanics and so on.

These are the 'front-line' staff who deliver the service benefits to the customer, for example, the chef, waiters and waitresses in restaurants or the legal personnel in a law firm. For the customer, these people are perceived as the suppliers: their attitudes, behaviour and skills are the products the customer is buying.

However anyone within an organisation that may interact with the customer will need to understand the importance of the customer to that organisation and endeavour to offer excellent customer service.

1.2.2 Process

> ▸ **Key term**
>
> **Process**: the activity that customers will go through to obtain the product/service. For example, discussing needs and wants, agreeing a price, arranging a loan agreement and the collection of a new car .

ProcessThis is the system by which the product benefits are delivered. A self-service restaurant differs in process from an à la carte restaurant, for example. Process not only defines part of the product, but also has implications for the cost base of the supplying company. In many businesses, ordering online has streamlined the purchase process, and many service companies operate online booking systems (airlines, hotels, some restaurants, ferry companies and so forth).

1.2.3 Physical evidence

> ▸ **Key term**
>
> **Physical evidence**: the tangible record or representation of the provision of an intangible service, eg a bunch of flowers to thank the customer for their custom.

Physical evidence This is the tangible aspect of the service delivery. The décor, the tablecloths, the menus and so forth in a restaurant are all evidence of the service being delivered: in some services such as insurance, glossy brochures or imposing office buildings provide physical evidence. From a consumer's viewpoint, physical evidence is useful in judging the expected quality of the service provision.

> ▸ **Exam tip**
>
> If you are asked to discuss the marketing mix of a service business, remember that you are being asked for all seven elements, not just the last three. You will definitely lose marks if you do not discuss product, price, place and promotion if asked to comment on the marketing of, say, a retail store.
>
> You should also remember that the product consists of the benefits the retailer supplies – this is not necessarily the same as the physical products they sell. In other words, what the retailer supplies is convenience, a pleasant in-store atmosphere, reassurance of quality and perhaps even some prestige if the retailer is an upmarket one.
>
> Finally, almost all products have both a service element and a physical element – the 7P model covers all products, therefore, not just those which we normally define as 'service' products.

1.3 Physical vs service products

Many academics regard the distinction between **physical products** and **service products** as artificial, since most products contain elements of both: generally speaking, current thinking is that all products are somewhere on a continuum between physical and service elements, with some products containing a higher service element than others. Having said that, if a product is close to the 'service' end of the spectrum, the marketing mix will emphasise different elements more than would be the case for a product near the 'physical' end of the spectrum, and consumer behaviour will be different in each case.

In Figure 4.1, an insurance policy represents an entirely service-based product. There is no physical existence at all (apart from the policy document, which has no intrinsic value except as physical evidence). A meal in an expensive restaurant is mainly composed of the service element – the waiters, the chefs, the ambience, etc – but there is a physical element in that there is actually some food. A computer with a support package is much more of a physical product, but the support service may represent quite a large proportion of the price and could be a very large proportion of the value the consumer gets from the product. A ready meal bought in a supermarket has some service element (since it has been prepared by someone and is offered for sale in a retail outlet) but is mainly a physical product. A box of vegetables is almost entirely physical – only the delivery element is a service. Finally, a bag of building sand is entirely physical, with no discernible service element.

Figure 4.1 The product-service continuum

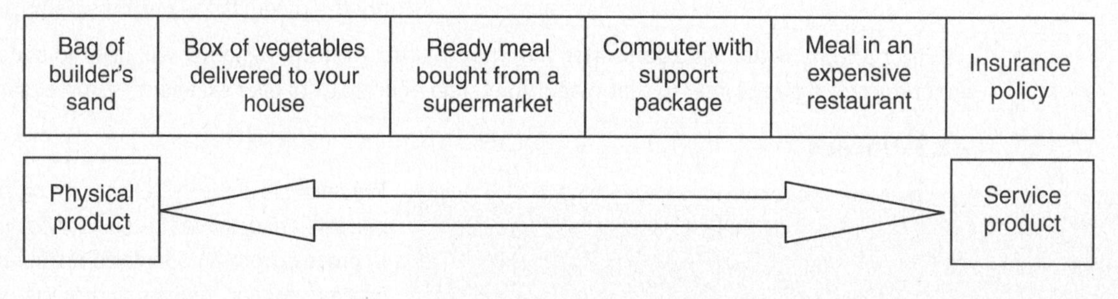

> ▸ **Exam tip**
>
> Although the elements of the marketing mix need to be learned individually, each element impinges on every other element. In practice, you cannot consider the elements in isolation, so you need to cultivate the habit of thinking how an adjustment to one element will affect all the other elements.
>
> In particular, many of the elements overlap – price, for example, conveys an impression of quality, which is part of the product benefit and also part of the promotional mix. Likewise promotion might be considered as part of the product: owning a well-known and well-regarded brand (such as Nike or Rolex) conveys very real benefits to the customer.

THE REAL WORLD

Screwfix Direct

Screwfix Direct is an excellent example of how, in the modern business environment, there is a requirement to offer elements of both the 4Ps (Product, Price, Place, Promotion) and 7Ps (as per the 4Ps, but add People, Process, Physical Evidence) to ensure your business is successful. Screwfix may be selling a physical product in many cases, but needs the level of service to continue to compete in the market.

Based in Yeovil in Somerset, Screwfix originally started life in 1979 as the Woodscrew Supply Company. The company's first catalogue consisted of a single page, solely dedicated to screws. In 1987 this was increased to a four-page version offering hardware to do-it-yourself and trade professionals and going by the name of Handimail. The first catalogue to be produced in the name of Screwfix Direct appeared in 1992. This led to an increase in turnover to £4m, and a move into larger premises, but still in Yeovil. This was to herald a period of significant growth and in 1998 turnover had virtually doubled, year-on-year, to £28m.

The first website, www.screwfix.com, was launched in 1999, just five months prior to the company being acquired by Kingfisher plc. which continued with an organisational philosophy of providing high-quality, low-cost, building, maintenance and refurbishment items to the trade. In January 2000, Screwfix achieved a turnover of £58m and introduced next-day deliveries within mainland UK. Turnover first exceeded £100m in January 2001 and, following further expansion across the business, Screwfix announced sales of £185m in 2002.

With a reconstructed website in 2002, making it more interactive, secure and quicker and easier to use, they were rewarded by the accolade of E-tailer of the Year. In 2004, turnover continued to increase, growing to £221m. By 2005, the company was ready to trial a new Trade Counters concept. The first such store was opened in Yeovil, and was hugely successful. Many more Trade Counters were opened across the UK in the months and years that followed. Today, the company's turnover has increased to £490m, of which nearly 25% is generated online. It holds in excess of 4m customer records, and employs approximately 3,300 people at its 146 Trade Counters. Deliveries are now co-ordinated from two main distribution centres, based in Stafford and Trentham.

In November 2000 Screwfix Direct sponsored the 'Building Blocks' weekends on Discovery Home & Leisure television and was the first-ever to carry a phone number. This took advantage of the relaxation in the Independent Television Commission sponsorship regulations to display the direct response telephone number on sponsorship bumpers throughout the weekend. This was a real breakthrough for Screwfix Direct, maintaining its view of direct-response advertising.

Screwfix is recognised as being "where the trade buys" and promising a fast, reliable service. Screwfix is the UK's leading multi-channel supplier of thousands of high quality fixings and fastenings, hand tools, power tools, plumbing and electrical supplies, kitchens and bathrooms, landscaping and outdoor products, safety products and workwear, and building supplies.

In 2009 it launched Plumbfix and Electricfix, specialist stores dedicated to the plumbing and electrical trades, which gave the company the opportunity to develop specialist catalogues and special prices in these markets, and to change the environment to meet the needs of these building specialisms. There are Plumbfix and Electricfix stores linked to some of the company's highest profile branches. Screwfix continues to develop its offer of fast, reliable service and will also be looking to extend its range of low cost, leading brand name items for the building trade. Screwfix continues to introduce innovative items aimed at helping these trades to work smarter and faster, saving money and making each application simpler and easier. This goes alongside developments and improvements to its store coverage, catalogue and website.

(Screwfix, 2012)

Over the next few chapters we will consider each of the elements individually. Always keep in mind that the elements of the mix do not operate in isolation – each one affects the others, in the same way as each ingredient in a recipe affects the flavour or texture of every other ingredient.

Exam tip

Whenever you are asked to consider changes to one element of the promotional mix, you should try to think about how the other elements will be affected: you will gain marks if you can explain these effects and come up with answers for how to handle such changes.

CHAPTER ROUNDUP

- The 7Ps of the marketing mix should not be considered in isolation if they are to satisfy customers' needs.
- Without understanding the importance of synergy to achieve satisfaction of customer needs in the marketing mix, we cannot move forward.
- Without synergy, the process is likely to fail and the organisation will be unsuccessful in achieving its overall objectives.
- As we change and develop each element of the mix the end result will change. Change one small element and the whole mix needs to be reviewed. This is a fundamental aspect of marketing that you must grasp at this stage.

FURTHER READING

Since the marketing mix is such a large part of practical marketing, the reading tends also to be comprehensive. For more detail on the mix elements:

Baker, M. J. *The Marketing Manual*, Butterworth Heinemann. Chapter 7.

Blythe, J. (2009) *Essentials of Marketing.* 4th Edition. Harlow, Prentice Hall. Chapters 1, 6, 7, 8 and 9

Blythe, J. (2008) *Principles and Practice of Marketing.* 2nd Edition. Andover, Lengage. Chapters 1 and 12–22.

Brassington, F. (2008) and Pettitt, S. (2006) *Principles of Marketing.* 4th Edition. Harlow, Prentice Hall. Chapters 7–19.

Kotler, P. (2008) *et al Principles of Marketing.* 5th Edition. FT Prentice Hall. Chapters 13–22.

Jobber, D. (2009) *Principles and Practice of Marketing.* 6th Edition. Maidenhead, McGraw-Hill Chapters 8–17.

http://www.myoffers.co.uk: This website directs users to many sales promotions, providing a useful set of examples.

http://www.advertisingarchives.co.uk: This site contains advertisements going back over a hundred years.

http://http://brand.blogs.com/mantra/2005/02/lovehate_brand_.html: This is a chat room for people to post their messages of love or hate about brands. It offers some interesting insights into what goes wrong with brand messages.

http://www.strangenewproducts.com

National broadsheet newspaper

Marketing magazine

Product-based magazine in your organisation's area of specialism

1.1.3 Place

> **Key term**
>
> **Place**: where the product/service is available, eg the dealership used in the purchase.

This is the location where the exchange takes place – the retail store, through the mail, in cyberspace, etc. Place decisions involve thinking about physical distribution (shipping and delivery) as well as about finding the most convenient location for customers to buy the product.

1.1.4 Promotion

> **Key term**
>
> **Promotion**: how we communicate the other Ps to customers, eg advertising which enable you to find the car and dealership.

This is the subgroup of mix elements which the marketer uses to communicate the total offer to the customer. Promotion is itself divided into a promotional mix, and new ways of communicating are being added.

This categorisation of mix elements proved to be inadequate, as it has only limited application to service products: since services now comprise the bulk of marketing in the developed world, extra mix elements need to be considered. This led to the development of the 7Ps.

1.2 The 7Ps

The additional 3Ps that make up the 7Ps are as follows:

1.2.1 People

> **Key term**
>
> **People**: those individuals involved in making or selling the product/service, eg sales people, reception staff, mechanics and so on.

These are the 'front-line' staff who deliver the service benefits to the customer, for example, the chef, waiters and waitresses in restaurants or the legal personnel in a law firm. For the customer, these people are perceived as the suppliers: their attitudes, behaviour and skills are the products the customer is buying.

However anyone within an organisation that may interact with the customer will need to understand the importance of the customer to that organisation and endeavour to offer excellent customer service.

1.2.2 Process

> **Key term**
>
> **Process**: the activity that customers will go through to obtain the product/service. For example, discussing needs and wants, agreeing a price, arranging a loan agreement and the collection of a new car .

ProcessThis is the system by which the product benefits are delivered. A self-service restaurant differs in process from an à la carte restaurant, for example. Process not only defines part of the product, but also has implications for the cost base of the supplying company. In many businesses, ordering online has streamlined the purchase process, and many service companies operate online booking systems (airlines, hotels, some restaurants, ferry companies and so forth).

1.2.3 Physical evidence

> **Key term**
>
> **Physical evidence**: the tangible record or representation of the provision of an intangible service, eg a bunch of flowers to thank the customer for their custom.

Physical evidence This is the tangible aspect of the service delivery. The décor, the tablecloths, the menus and so forth in a restaurant are all evidence of the service being delivered: in some services such as insurance, glossy brochures or imposing office buildings provide physical evidence. From a consumer's viewpoint, physical evidence is useful in judging the expected quality of the service provision.

▸ Exam tip

If you are asked to discuss the marketing mix of a service business, remember that you are being asked for all seven elements, not just the last three. You will definitely lose marks if you do not discuss product, price, place and promotion if asked to comment on the marketing of, say, a retail store.

You should also remember that the product consists of the benefits the retailer supplies – this is not necessarily the same as the physical products they sell. In other words, what the retailer supplies is convenience, a pleasant in-store atmosphere, reassurance of quality and perhaps even some prestige if the retailer is an upmarket one.

Finally, almost all products have both a service element and a physical element – the 7P model covers all products, therefore, not just those which we normally define as 'service' products.

1.3 Physical vs service products

Many academics regard the distinction between **physical products** and **service products** as artificial, since most products contain elements of both: generally speaking, current thinking is that all products are somewhere on a continuum between physical and service elements, with some products containing a higher service element than others. Having said that, if a product is close to the 'service' end of the spectrum, the marketing mix will emphasise different elements more than would be the case for a product near the 'physical' end of the spectrum, and consumer behaviour will be different in each case.

In Figure 4.1, an insurance policy represents an entirely service-based product. There is no physical existence at all (apart from the policy document, which has no intrinsic value except as physical evidence). A meal in an expensive restaurant is mainly composed of the service element – the waiters, the chefs, the ambience, etc – but there is a physical element in that there is actually some food. A computer with a support package is much more of a physical product, but the support service may represent quite a large proportion of the price and could be a very large proportion of the value the consumer gets from the product. A ready meal bought in a supermarket has some service element (since it has been prepared by someone and is offered for sale in a retail outlet) but is mainly a physical product. A box of vegetables is almost entirely physical – only the delivery element is a service. Finally, a bag of building sand is entirely physical, with no discernible service element.

Figure 4.1 The product-service continuum

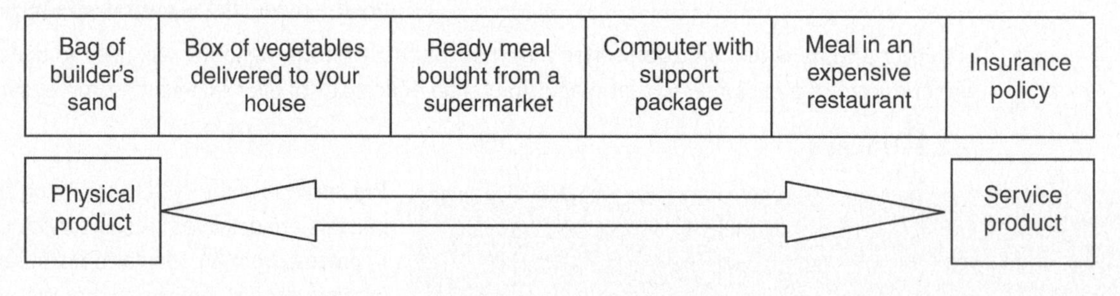

▸ Exam tip

Although the elements of the marketing mix need to be learned individually, each element impinges on every other element. In practice, you cannot consider the elements in isolation, so you need to cultivate the habit of thinking how an adjustment to one element will affect all the other elements.

In particular, many of the elements overlap – price, for example, conveys an impression of quality, which is part of the product benefit and also part of the promotional mix. Likewise promotion might be considered as part of the product: owning a well-known and well-regarded brand (such as Nike or Rolex) conveys very real benefits to the customer.

THE REAL WORLD

Screwfix Direct

Screwfix Direct is an excellent example of how, in the modern business environment, there is a requirement to offer elements of both the 4Ps (Product, Price, Place, Promotion) and 7Ps (as per the 4Ps, but add People, Process, Physical Evidence) to ensure your business is successful. Screwfix may be selling a physical product in many cases, but needs the level of service to continue to compete in the market.

Based in Yeovil in Somerset, Screwfix originally started life in 1979 as the Woodscrew Supply Company. The company's first catalogue consisted of a single page, solely dedicated to screws. In 1987 this was increased to a four-page version offering hardware to do-it-yourself and trade professionals and going by the name of Handimail. The first catalogue to be produced in the name of Screwfix Direct appeared in 1992. This led to an increase in turnover to £4m, and a move into larger premises, but still in Yeovil. This was to herald a period of significant growth and in 1998 turnover had virtually doubled, year-on-year, to £28m.

The first website, www.screwfix.com, was launched in 1999, just five months prior to the company being acquired by Kingfisher plc. which continued with an organisational philosophy of providing high-quality, low-cost, building, maintenance and refurbishment items to the trade. In January 2000, Screwfix achieved a turnover of £58m and introduced next-day deliveries within mainland UK. Turnover first exceeded £100m in January 2001 and, following further expansion across the business, Screwfix announced sales of £185m in 2002.

With a reconstructed website in 2002, making it more interactive, secure and quicker and easier to use, they were rewarded by the accolade of E-tailer of the Year. In 2004, turnover continued to increase, growing to £221m. By 2005, the company was ready to trial a new Trade Counters concept. The first such store was opened in Yeovil, and was hugely successful. Many more Trade Counters were opened across the UK in the months and years that followed. Today, the company's turnover has increased to £490m, of which nearly 25% is generated online. It holds in excess of 4m customer records, and employs approximately 3,300 people at its 146 Trade Counters. Deliveries are now co-ordinated from two main distribution centres, based in Stafford and Trentham.

In November 2000 Screwfix Direct sponsored the 'Building Blocks' weekends on Discovery Home & Leisure television and was the first-ever to carry a phone number. This took advantage of the relaxation in the Independent Television Commission sponsorship regulations to display the direct response telephone number on sponsorship bumpers throughout the weekend. This was a real breakthrough for Screwfix Direct, maintaining its view of direct-response advertising.

Screwfix is recognised as being "where the trade buys" and promising a fast, reliable service. Screwfix is the UK's leading multi-channel supplier of thousands of high quality fixings and fastenings, hand tools, power tools, plumbing and electrical supplies, kitchens and bathrooms, landscaping and outdoor products, safety products and workwear, and building supplies.

In 2009 it launched Plumbfix and Electricfix, specialist stores dedicated to the plumbing and electrical trades, which gave the company the opportunity to develop specialist catalogues and special prices in these markets, and to change the environment to meet the needs of these building specialisms. There are Plumbfix and Electricfix stores linked to some of the company's highest profile branches. Screwfix continues to develop its offer of fast, reliable service and will also be looking to extend its range of low cost, leading brand name items for the building trade. Screwfix continues to introduce innovative items aimed at helping these trades to work smarter and faster, saving money and making each application simpler and easier. This goes alongside developments and improvements to its store coverage, catalogue and website.

(Screwfix, 2012)

Over the next few chapters we will consider each of the elements individually. Always keep in mind that the elements of the mix do not operate in isolation – each one affects the others, in the same way as each ingredient in a recipe affects the flavour or texture of every other ingredient.

Exam tip

Whenever you are asked to consider changes to one element of the promotional mix, you should try to think about how the other elements will be affected: you will gain marks if you can explain these effects and come up with answers for how to handle such changes.

CHAPTER ROUNDUP

- The 7Ps of the marketing mix should not be considered in isolation if they are to satisfy customers' needs.
- Without understanding the importance of synergy to achieve satisfaction of customer needs in the marketing mix, we cannot move forward.
- Without synergy, the process is likely to fail and the organisation will be unsuccessful in achieving its overall objectives.
- As we change and develop each element of the mix the end result will change. Change one small element and the whole mix needs to be reviewed. This is a fundamental aspect of marketing that you must grasp at this stage.

FURTHER READING

Since the marketing mix is such a large part of practical marketing, the reading tends also to be comprehensive. For more detail on the mix elements:

Baker, M. J. *The Marketing Manual*, Butterworth Heinemann. Chapter 7.

Blythe, J. (2009) *Essentials of Marketing.* 4th Edition. Harlow, Prentice Hall. Chapters 1, 6, 7, 8 and 9

Blythe, J. (2008) *Principles and Practice of Marketing.* 2nd Edition. Andover, Lengage. Chapters 1 and 12–22.

Brassington, F. (2008) and Pettitt, S. (2006) *Principles of Marketing.* 4th Edition. Harlow, Prentice Hall. Chapters 7–19.

Kotler, P. (2008) *et al Principles of Marketing.* 5th Edition. FT Prentice Hall. Chapters 13–22.

Jobber, D. (2009) *Principles and Practice of Marketing.* 6th Edition. Maidenhead, McGraw-Hill Chapters 8–17.

http://www.myoffers.co.uk: This website directs users to many sales promotions, providing a useful set of examples.

http://www.advertisingarchives.co.uk: This site contains advertisements going back over a hundred years.

http://http://brand.blogs.com/mantra/2005/02/lovehate_brand_.html: This is a chat room for people to post their messages of love or hate about brands. It offers some interesting insights into what goes wrong with brand messages.

http://www.strangenewproducts.com

National broadsheet newspaper

Marketing magazine

Product-based magazine in your organisation's area of specialism

REFERENCES

Screwfix (2012) http://www.screwfix.com/jsp/help/pressoffice.jsp [Accessed on 21 June 2012].

QUICK QUIZ

1 Define synergy.

2 Describe the marketing mix in two words.

3 What would be the basic mix?

4 What would be the extended mix?

5 A bag of apples purchased from a supermarket would have which elements of the marketing mix?

QUICK QUIZ ANSWERS

1. The working together of two or more elements to produce an effect, greater than the sum of the individual parts or greater than the sum of the individual effects.
2. The ingredients.
3. Product, price, place and promotion.
4. People, process and physical evidence.
5. Product, place, people, price, promotion, physical evidence and process.

CHAPTER 5

The marketing mix – product

Introduction

A product is anything that has tangible benefits and intangible benefits to the customer. This could be anything from the top speed of a car to the enjoyment of making a donation to a charity. Marketing is all about putting those benefits into a bundle that will be valued by customers.

This chapter will start by looking at product types and what they do at their simplest level. A car is a mode of transport and so is a train, so why do people own cars but sometimes use a train? We will then look at the life of products as they are born, live and die over time and why that might be important to us as marketers. We will also develop the ideas around how new products come into the market and why. There is also the notion of what a brand is, why it exists and what benefit it brings to the customer and, of course, to the organisation. The development and building of brands, product portfolios and ranges are both part of the satisfaction of need.

Finally, we will look at how new products are accepted by customers over time. Why are there still individuals who do not own a mobile phone or use a computer? Why do some customers feel it is not important to have the latest model of an existing product? It is about bringing together a bundle of benefits that satisfies the needs of the customer.

After working through this section, and carrying out the associated reading, you should be able to:

- Explain the principles of product planning
- Explain the product life cycle
- Explain the importance of introducing new products and services
- Explain the new product development (NPD) process
- Explain the adoption of service and products in terms of customer characteristics

Topic list

Syllabus references

3.1	Explain and illustrate the principles of product and planning: ▪ Branding ▪ Product lines/ranges (depth and breadth) ▪ Packaging, eg sustainability, design, eg recycling ▪ Service support
3.2	Explain the concept of the product life cycle, (PLC) and its limitations as a tool for assessing the life of the product/services: ▪ Development ▪ Introduction ▪ Growth ▪ Maturity ▪ Decline ▪ Obsolescence ▪ Limitations including failure of the product to succeed/no measurable outcome
3.3	Explain the importance of new products and services into the market: ▪ Changing customer needs ▪ Digital revolution ▪ Long-term business strategies
3.4	Explain the different stages of the process of new product development: ▪ Idea generation ▪ Screening new ideas ▪ Concept testing ▪ Business analysis ▪ Product development ▪ Test marketing ▪ Commercialisation and launch
3.13	Explain the process of product and service adoption explaining the characteristics of customers at each stage of adoption: ▪ Innovators ▪ Early adopters ▪ Early majority ▪ Late majority ▪ Laggards

1 Elements of the product

▸ **Key term**

Product: an item that satisfies a customer's needs and/or wants, eg a car.

A **product** is anything that satisfies the needs and wants of the customer; a product is a bundle of benefits, therefore, which can take the form of a physical item (such as an ice cream) or a service which may have some elements of physical outcome but which generally you cannot touch: they are intangible, a car service for example. From a customer's viewpoint, it is the *benefits* that are important: we, as consumers, are only interested in how the product will improve our lives, not in what it is made of, where it came from, how it was developed or anything else about it. If we do not believe that the product will improve our lives, no amount of persuasion will change our minds.

ACTIVITY 5.1

Thinking about the organisation you work for, make a list of the benefits your products provide to the people who buy them. This is easy if you work for a manufacturer or a service business like a restaurant or pizza delivery company – but not so easy if you work for a training company or a charity.

If you work for a non-profit organisation like a charity, you need to define who your customers are. If you answer that it is the beneficiaries of the charity, you would need to explain what they are providing to you as their part of the exchange. Beneficiaries are often not providing anything in the exchange process – so maybe it is the people who give money to the cause who are the real customers. In that case, what benefits are you providing for them? What might you do to add value, so that they are more likely to give to your charity rather than another one?

Whatever your organisation, you need to provide benefits if you are to receive money. The next problem would be to work out what features the product must have if it is to provide the benefits you have identified.

Competitors continually offer new products, and at the same time our own products become outdated, old-fashioned and (eventually) obsolete. Therefore, developing new products becomes extremely important for any firm, since companies must offer something different from competing products if they are to win customers. Products can be studied at different levels, as explained by Levitt (1986) when he outlined the total product concept.

The basic core product is what is offered by all companies in the market – for example, a car will carry the driver, his or her luggage and passengers, and take them from one place to another via the road system. All cars provide these benefits as a minimum: this is the **core or generic product**. Moving beyond this is the **expected product**, which is the core product plus features that the average person would reasonably expect to see. In the car example, people would expect the car to have a radio, a heater, windscreen wipers and so forth. Few cars would lack these basic features (although there was a time when windscreens were an optional extra, and even quite recently radios were not standard in cars). The **augmented product** includes features and benefits which distinguish the product from its competitors: for example, the car might have an automatic engine cut-out when the car is stationary or might have windscreen wipers which sense when it is raining. Finally, the **potential product** has all the features and benefits anyone could want or need. In fact, no products fit into that category because there are so many potential needs – and it would probably be unwise to try to offer such a product to the market, since the cost would be prohibitive.

Table 5.1 Types of products

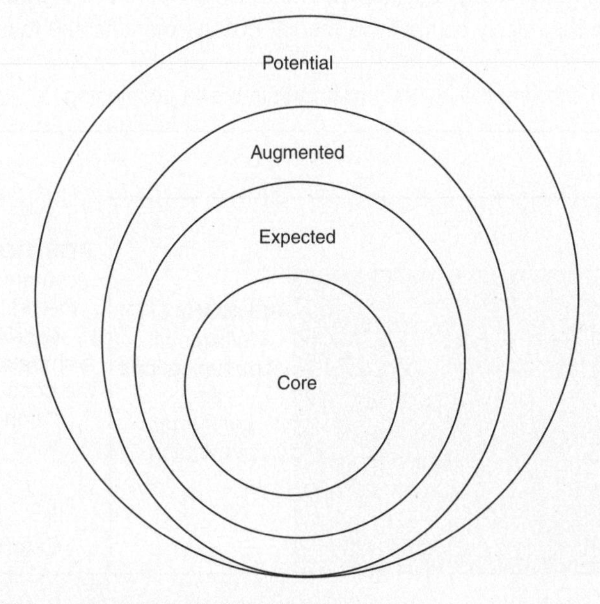

Core - benefits transport: a car

Expected - basic features of a car: an engine, wheels and gears

Augmented - added features to make the car different to the competition: environmentally friendly engine, alloy wheels and automatic gear box

Potential - tries to achieve everything for every customer

Elements of the product include the following.

1.1 Branding

> **Key terms**
>
> **Core product**: the benefits that all products would have in a particular group – all cars, for example, are forms of transport.
>
> **Expected product**: those features which are required to achieve the basic core product benefits – a car, for example, will have an engine, wheels and so on.
>
> **Augmented product**: those features and benefits that start to set one product apart from another – a car, for example, with a bigger engine than another.
>
> **Potential product**: how the product could develop and satisfy future needs and wants, eg new fuel systems that are environmentally friendly.

Brand is a simple, unified personality that follows a variety of activities which contribute to building a single perception of the brand in the mind of the customer. Positioning can be defined as a blend between vision, values and brand personality. Brand positioning as described by the 'Interbrand' model comprises all of the factors within the internal and external environment (see Figure 5.2). As seen in Figure 5.2 the internal factors, like brand vision are the organisation's long term goal for that brand over time, like any vision it is the view of the future and may be linked to the organisational strategy. Brand values form a part of the planned brand identity within the organisation which is a consistent approach to all elements of working and communicating. External factors, like perceived brand personality and the perceived brand positioning in relation to competitors, are how the brand is seen by consumers – the brand image.

> **Key term**
>
> **Brand**: a name, term, sign, symbol or design which identifies a particular product from others in the market.

Brand is a very good general term which covers everything from brand names, designs, trademarks, symbols, jingles, signage, colour schemes and much more. What branding can do is give an organisation a unique and distinguishing look, feel or satisfaction from a consumer point of view. Brands are now built and maintained by using all the elements of the marketing mix, especially promotional and marketing communications. Brands are seen across a wide sector of the market for all types of products and services. Today the 'lack' of brand can be identified with a number of 'no frills' items on the market, especially in the hugely competitive market of supermarkets and food.

Figure 5.2 Brand onion – cross-section showing the layers that underpin brand positioning

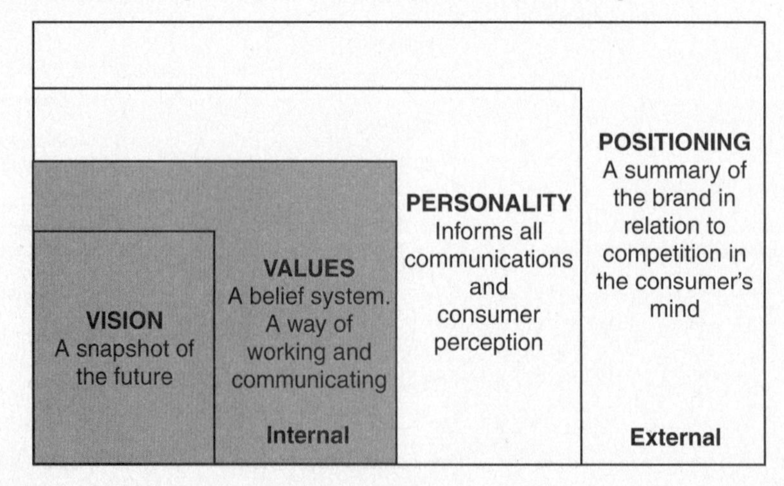

(Adapted from Interbrand, 2002)

THE REAL WORLD

Brand – Pittards

The Pittards case study is an excellent example to demonstrate how important brand and brand development is, even in a business-to-business (B2B) sector. We can see the business vision and the internal values which drive Pittards ahead in the future. The superbrands that Pittards supply understand the quality of products which build and reinforce the customer perception.

Pittards was established in 1826 and is situated in Somerset, it is a British company that uses skilled buying and high-tech production methods to produce world class leathers. Pittards produces glove leathers mainly from sheepskin and goatskin, including a range of leathers for dress, military and service gloves as well as ladies' footwear. Since the start Pittards has become a well-established brand that operates three related divisions:

- Glove leather division
- Shoe and leather goods division
- Raw material division

Glove Leather Division remains based in the South West of England. Shoe and Leather Goods Division is located in Leeds, and it makes leather for shoes and luxury leather goods mainly from UK cattle hides. Raw Materials Division is based in Scotland, and it processes Scottish sheepskins for use within the company and for sale to other non-company tanneries, for example, other factories that process leather; it operates under a differing brand name: Booth International.

Pittards is one of the UK's top 100 exporters, exporting to over 30 countries and produces quality leather products that can provide comfort, and enable sports people and those who enjoy the outdoor life to better master the elements. Being able to use sophisticated gloves and footwear gives sports professionals (eg footballers, racing drivers) a high level of control.

The sports and leisure industries generate huge revenues worldwide, and superbrands such as Nike, Adidas, Puma, Louis Vuitton operate in this most competitive market. Producers of internationally known high performance products depend heavily on their materials and components suppliers.

These suppliers are the unsung heroes that lie behind other companies' brands and their popular success. For these superbrands to be competitive they need to manufacture their products from the highest quality engineered materials. Pittards meets that need: the company is a vital business partner. Not only sports people need high quality leather. Sophisticated leather products are found in a range of other consumer industries, from hand luggage, to fashion gloves and watchstraps. High performance leathers therefore play a major role in the modern economy and in this industry Pittards is the leading brand.

Almost all of us will have come across Pittards' products, even if we haven't recognised them as such. We see them being used by leading sports players: Colin Montgomerie (gloves and footwear), David Seaman and Philip Cocu (soccer boots).

The sports shoes you wear may well have been supplied by Pittards, along with your leather watchstrap or bag. The Pittards brand seeks to develop partnerships with high quality international brands. Pittards needs to meet the demanding quality levels of these brands and this is reflected in its mission statement which reads:

'In partnership with brands Pittards aims to be the preferred supplier of high performance leather to the world leading brands of gloves, shoes, luxury leather goods and sports equipment.

We seek to achieve this aim by offering innovative leathers which are differentiated from competing products by their performance properties, quality and consistency, and which are backed by the highest standards of customer service.'

Pittards' customer is the owner of the brand, who will sell to another company e.g. a sports shop. The sports shop then sells the product to the final consumer. So Pittards offer the highest quality to its brand partners. Such as:

- Puma and Adidas require leather that is soft and lightweight enough to offer a high degree of sensitivity and comfort whilst retaining the strength, water resistance and durability demanded by professional footballers, allowing them to exhibit their skills to the full.
- Louis Vuitton, one of the world's leading brands, demands excellence in manufacturing processes. Pittards supplies the leather, using manufacturing processes that offer superior technical ability, leading-edge technology and high quality production.

- Camper, a leading Spanish shoe brand, requires leather that is engineered to offer superior comfort, water resistance, breathability and enhanced aesthetics.

To be the 'best' in the modern world, firms have to be at the forefront of technological development. Pittards' world class leather technology is a key brand differentiator. Pittards prides itself on being the brand at the leading edge of technological product development. For example, 30 years ago it began the development of WR100 technology, and over the years this has become increasingly more sophisticated. This technology is based on a detailed understanding of the fibre structure of leather. Processes are carried out which coat individual fibres to improve their performance, creating a leather-finished product that is water resistant, breathable, with a low water uptake and which allows gloves and footwear to dry soft, quickly.

Leathers treated with WR100 technology are wind and rain resistant, while at the same time allowing sweat to escape from the hands. In addition, Pittards has incorporated state-of-the-art thermal regulation technology into its leathers. This enables gloves and footwear to absorb heat from the hands and feet which is then stored in the materials. This enables the hands to stay cool, with obvious benefits to golfers, racing drivers, climbers etc.

As a global brand and being a supplier to 'high street' superbrands, Pittards is heavily involved in supporting sporting excellence, Pittards sees carefully targeted sponsorship as an important ingredient of its business activity. A good example of this is the BT Global Challenge, a ten-month Round The World yacht race in which crews fight against the prevailing winds. Pittards has been involved twice as a business sponsor of the race and with the aid of its partners has provided appropriate leather products such as gloves and footwear for this particularly demanding challenge because boats race 'the wrong way' round the world - against the prevailing winds and tides. Being involved in the race also allows Pittards to find out more about its products at 'extreme' levels, for example by investigating the impact of salt water on the leather products. Results from this research enables the company to improve the qualities of its products. In addition, Pittards directly sponsors individuals including Jeanette Brakewell, Britain's Olympic silver medallist at three-day eventing.

Recently Pittards has been associated in some joint brand communications activities with the superbrands that it supplies. A common feature of the communications was an image of an individual faced by the elements and in a difficult situation; for example, one advert had the strapline:

'it's times like these you know why you chose Puma and why they chose leather created by Pittards!

Communicating the strength of the brand through advertising and promotion, combined with the high quality of the product, premium pricing and well-organised distribution systems, all helps to give Pittards its high status as a global supplier brand.

(Pittards, 2012)

1.2 Product lines and product ranges

Marketers need to manage a portfolio of products: very few firms market only one product. The portfolio may be **broad** (a wide range of product categories) or **deep** (a range of variations on a product designed to reach all of a target market). Sometimes products need to be dropped from the range, not because they are unprofitable, but because the resources they take up can be better employed elsewhere. Portfolio management is an important part of marketing, as is new product development (NPD).

Developing and understanding the range and nature of the products within your portfolio is a fundamental activity of the marketing manager. This will enable the organisation to consider differing models, such as the Boston Consulting Group (BCG) matrix and Ansoff in the assessment of new product development and use of existing products. There are additional benefits to be gained from the appropriate management of the product portfolio in that it may reduce the range, by removing unsuccessful products, or alternatively extend the range into new markets or develop existing markets. Portfolio management also links to the wider issues surrounding organisational objectives such as resources utilisation and income and/or profit generation.

1.3 Packaging

The design of the packaging often renders products more desirable, more noticeable on the retailers' shelves and more informative in terms of product benefits. At its most basic, packaging protects the product from the environment and vice versa. Marketers also need to consider customer use of packaging and the environmental impact of different packaging options. For example, a gardener might use empty plastic soft drink bottles to

protect seedlings, or someone might use old coffee jars to store small items such as screws or nails. In some cases, packaging has become the differentiating factor for the product – some fast-food delivery services use reusable plastic containers, while others use disposable foil ones: clearly the plastic ones are more useful, and this might be the deciding factor between choosing one takeaway outlet over another. Disposal of used packaging has, of course, become a hot topic in recent years due to its environmental impact.

1.4 Service support

Many physical products have a service element, if only in terms of after-sales service or customer support helplines. This is especially true in business-to-business markets, which represent the bulk of marketing activity, far outweighing business-to-consumer marketing. Service support can often be the only differentiator a firm can offer, when rival products are similar or even identical. For example, engine oil must be similar or identical in its formula to all other engine oils, since the engine manufacturer will have designed the engine specifically to use a particular grade of oil. Oil companies cannot make major changes to the physical product, so they need to compete on service support, for example, by offering technical advice to motor mechanics or by making the product available in more convenient retail outlets.

THE REAL WORLD

Shell sponsorship Formula One (F1)

Although oil companies cannot make major changes to the physical product they need to demonstrate to their customers they are developing the product to offer better performance and offering higher levels of service. One way to achieve both of these aims is sponsorship of motorsport where they have a visual presence and they can test and develop new products which may end up in retail outlets in the future.

The 2011 season saw one win and ten podium finishes for Scuderia Ferrari's Fernando Alonso, who was consistently solid in his fight for the Drivers' World Championship. Alonso's sole win of the season at the British Grand Prix was all the more meaningful because it came at the very same track that José Froilán González clinched Scuderia Ferrari's first-ever victory sixty years previously. It was a very special win because it came at a legendary track like Silverstone, in front of a British crowd who are very enthusiastic about F1. The season also saw Shell become the title sponsor of the 2011 Formula 1 Shell Belgian Grand Prix, providing great opportunities to communicate the long-standing technical partnership with Scuderia Ferrari. The event saw Shell bring legendary Scuderia Ferrari Formula One drivers Fernando Alonso and John Surtees together to compare notes on the Spa-Francorchamps circuit. With Shell holding a multi-year agreement as title sponsor of the Belgian Grand Prix, the future looks bright for many similar success stories.

In 2012 Shell will be working on the current Shell V-Power fuel and Shell Helix Ultra lubricants, as well as the introduction of a new four cylinder, 1.6 litre power unit specification engine comprising a high pressure direct gasoline injection. These engines will deliver a 35% reduction in fuel consumption and will feature extensive energy management and energy recovery systems, whilst still maintaining current levels of performance. This once again reinforces Shell's expertise in fuel and oil development which has helped Ferrari to 12 F1A Formula One Drivers' titles and 10 Constructors' titles. The developments and learning are taken from the race track and transferred directly to products for use in every Shell customer's car.

(Shell, 2012)

THE REAL WORLD

HJ Heinz

It has been many years since Heinz had only 57 varieties. In fact, the number 57 was chosen by the company's founder, Henry J. Heinz, simply because he liked the sound of it – it had no other significance

HJ Heinz produces almost 6,000 varieties, spread across 200 brands worldwide. Food is produced and sold in eight different categories: convenience meals, condiments and sauces, infant feeding, weight control, frozen food, pet food, food service and seafood. Although the parent company is American, the British part of the company is the biggest overseas subsidiary, and many British consumers think of the company as British.

Managing such a huge range of products is by no means simple. In the United Kingdom, the Jones Knowles Ritchie packaging design company took over the account in 1997 and found a wide range of different packaging designs in place. The situation had grown up because each product had its own particular packaging problems and needs – but the situation had got out of hand, with no clear brand image being presented and a confusing message being presented to consumers.

Meanwhile, Heinz USA had decided to follow the example of its Weightwatchers brand and lose some weight. The company sold off its pet food business in 2002 and a number of its other marginal brands over the next few years. In the United Kingdom, sales of salad cream were falling – salad cream is an entirely British product, with virtually no market outside the United Kingdom. Also, healthy eating was becoming the latest fad – and for organic food, low-fat food and even low-carb food as a result of the popularity of the Atkins Diet meant that Heinz had to make a number of tough decisions.

Jones Knowles Ritchie began by linking all the different products through the Heinz Keystone design – the badge-shaped symbol which appears on all Heinz products. The agency realised that what consumers thought was important was the quality symbolised by the Heinz brand, rather than the actual product contained in the bottle or can. This still left plenty of scope for individualising the brands – the turquoise colour used for the baked beans (reputedly because it enhances the colour of the beans when the can is opened) could remain, as well as the individual graphics for the children's products such as Eazy Squirt.

Heinz' PR consultants issued a statement that salad cream might be withdrawn due to falling sales. This press release made the TV news, and amid a flurry of protests from millions of Britons who had grown up with salad cream, the threat was withdrawn. Sales rose sufficiently for Heinz to introduce an organic version of salad cream, to be sold alongside its existing traditional salad cream as well as the ever-expanding range of organic products. In February 2003, the Soil Association (Britain's leading promoters of organic food) gave Heinz an award for their organic range of foods.

In the United States, Heinz introduced 'one-carb' sauces which are low-carbohydrate sauces intended for Atkins dieters.

Managing the portfolio is, for Heinz, a constant, dynamic process. Introducing new products to meet consumer needs, cutting out products which no longer show sufficient profit, packaging products in an eye-catching manner, and responding to the rapidly changing world of nutrition are continual activities for Heinz managers. This may be why Heinz has such a solid place in the hearts and minds of consumers.

ACTIVITY 5.2

Consider the Heinz example.

1. Why would Heinz drop its pet foods range, when the products were still making money for the firm?
2. What is the importance of packaging to Heinz?
3. How has the Heinz brand developed across the range?
4. What other changes might Heinz introduce to co-ordinate the branding better?
5. Why would the company subdivide its brands into eight categories?

ACTIVITY 5.3

Find data on your company's product range, if possible going back 20 years. Which products are still available from 20 years ago? Which were viable products 20 years ago, but are now no longer offered? Why were these products dropped?

Which recently introduced products do you expect will still be around 20 years from now?

(If you work for an organisation which has not been around for 20 years, you could look at the industry as whole for this period.)

2 The product life cycle

> **Key term**
>
> **Product Life Cycle (PLC)**: a way of comparing a product to life, from conception, birth and into maturity until, of course, old age and decline.

The product life cycle is an important concept for marketers. Basically, the model states that products go through a series of stages. Each of these stages is discussed below and shown in Figure 5.3.

- **Development**. Products do not arrive fully formed: managers, marketers, engineers, designers and researchers need to consider product ideas and turn them into viable, feasible, profitable products. There is more on the development process later.
- **Introduction**. The product is launched onto the market: at first, it is likely to lose money, because the cost of developing and marketing it has not yet been recovered and sales are likely to be small at first. In many cases, products do not move on from this stage, and in fact the majority of new products fail. The losses they make have to be covered by the products which do go on to succeed.
- **Growth**. If the product is accepted by consumers, sales will rise and so will profits, although during the growth phase the product will still need considerable marketing expenditure. The growth stage can be problematic, since at any point a competing product may enter the market or some other change may occur which curtails the growth.
- **Maturity**. Sales will eventually level off, at which point the product is established in the market and will need less support: at this point, profits will be high, and the company will start to get a real return on the investment. In the maturity phase, the company will still need to promote the product (using 'reminder' campaigns) in order to fend off competitors.
- **Decline**. Sales will eventually fall off as competitors enter the market, or as consumer tastes and preferences change. During the decline phase, the product will probably still be profitable: at this point, marketers may decide to develop a 'Mark Two' version of the product or alternatively remove all support and let the product die.
- **Obsolescence**. Finally, the product will become obsolete and be withdrawn or at least dramatically downgraded. Sometimes profit can still be made from such products, since they require virtually no investment in marketing: sometimes these products can be re-launched in new markets, and in fact this was a popular tactic in the motor industry during the 1970s, when Western European car manufacturers sold obsolete designs and machine tool patterns to Eastern European manufacturers. For a while, Polish and Russian versions of Fiat designs were re-imported into the West at extremely low prices.

Figure 5.3 The product life cycle

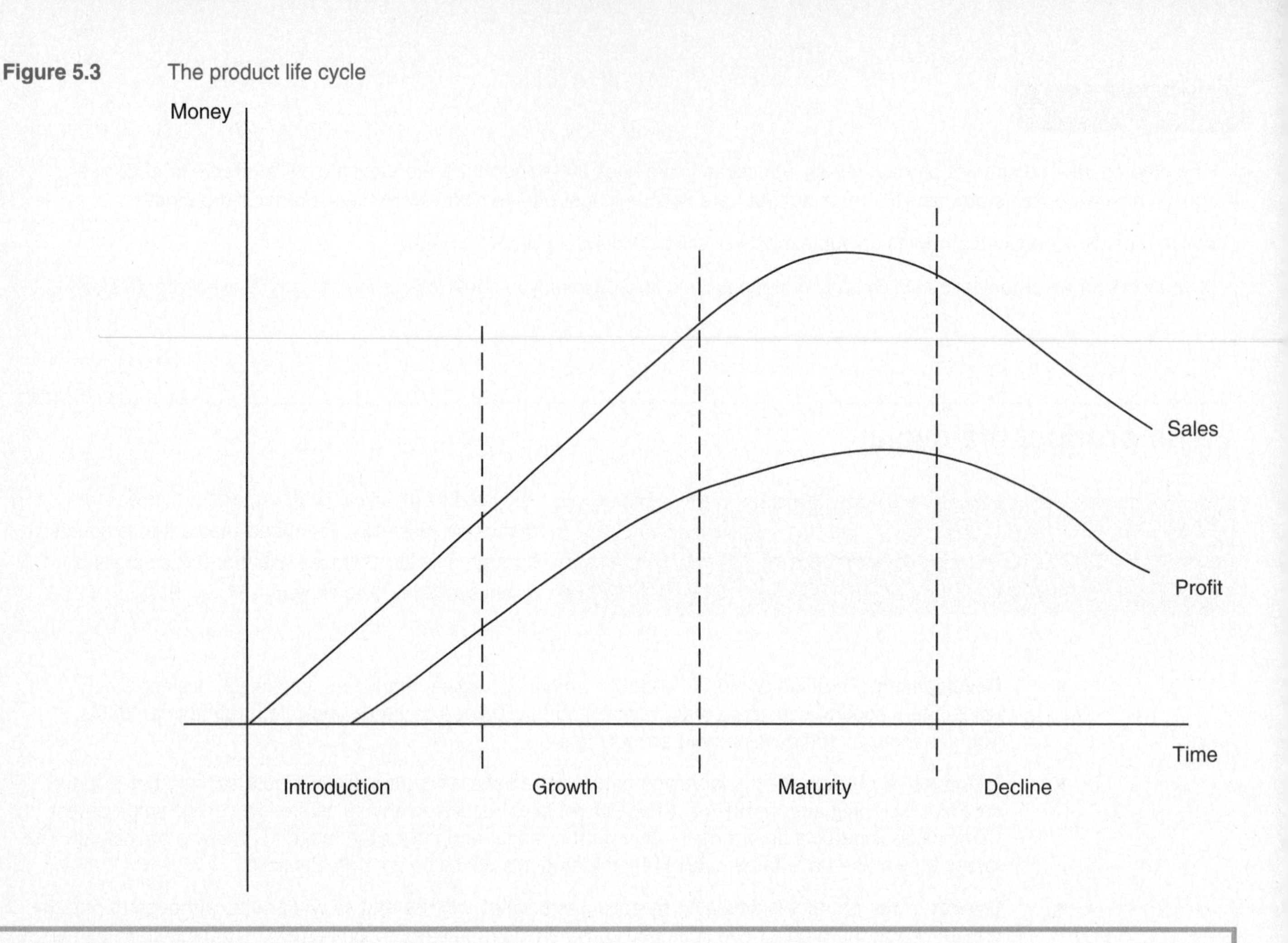

> **▸ Exam tip**
>
> You will need to learn the PLC by heart, as well as its accompanying diagram, but you need to remember that the model is far from complete. Products in decline sometimes revive, failed products sometimes never reach the growth phase and so forth.
>
> You may want to consider some products which have gone through a PLC so that you have examples to hand for the examination. For example, consider rock bands. Most have a short PLC, perhaps only 18 months or so, whereas others (the Rolling Stones, for example) seem to go on forever. What are the factors which determine this?
>
> Finally, and perhaps most importantly, you should consider what the company can do about managing the product in each of its stages. The job of a brand manager is to make decisions about the product and its promotion – and these will be different for a mature product compared with a new product, and even more challenging for a product in the decline stages.

The product life cycle is not necessarily followed by all products. Some will have regular revivals (children's toys such as the Hula hoop and the yo-yo are often used as examples), while others never really get off the starting blocks and disappear within a short time of being introduced. Others may fail initially, but be repositioned into another market and find success elsewhere. Another problem with the PLC is that outcomes are not measurable or predictable – there is really no way of knowing whether the product has reached maturity, or how long the maturity stage will last, or how long the decline phase will be or how steep the decline curve, since we have no way of predicting when a competitive response might prove too strong for the product.

The main usefulness of the PLC as a concept, and the reason it is still widely taught, is that it highlights the reason for developing new products. The PLC concept tells us that (eventually) all products will become obsolete and will disappear: a company which does not develop new products to replace those which go out of fashion or are superseded by competitors will eventually itself disappear.

▸ **Exam tip**

The PLC will almost certainly come up in the exam. You should be able to explain your product management decisions in terms of the PLC (rather than explain the PLC in terms of the case study). In other words, if you are asked to plan a campaign around a product, you should decide what stage the product is in and plan accordingly.

Decisions about advertising, for example, will be different in maturity (where the emphasis is on reminder advertising) and the introduction stage, when the emphasis will be on brand awareness. This is an example of how the 7Ps all affect each other – they are not to be treated in isolation.

THE REAL WORLD

Smith and Nephew

In 1856, a pharmaceutical chemist named Thomas James Smith opened a shop in Hull, UK. Forty years later, his nephew Horatio Nelson Smith became his business partner, and the firm of Smith and Nephew was created. Horatio was interested in developing dressings for wounds, and the business moved towards the manufacture of bandages and other dressings.

Massive expansion during the First World War (to meet the needs of wounded soldiers) took the company from 50 employees to 1,200 in only four years. In 1928, the company began development of Elastoplast, the adhesive bandage designed to compete with Johnson & Johnson's recently introduced Band-Aid bandage. Band-Aid and Elastoplast were, at the time, revolutionary products: Band-Aid, introduced in 1920, only sold $3,000 worth in its first year and was hand-made until 1924. Elastoplast was originally a cloth bandage with an antiseptic pad and adhesive edges: it was not until 1966 that the company introduced the Airstrip variant, which was a ventilated plastic adhesive strip with an antiseptic pad.

Smith and Nephew expanded by acquisition during the 1970s and 1980s, in the process of which the company acquired subsidiaries which produced medical equipment such as orthopaedic implants and continuous passive motion machines, which keep patients' joints moving after surgery in order to avoid stiffness. Smith and Nephew were thus beginning to move away from their concentration on wound management and heading into general areas of patient recovery.

This in turn led to an interest in surgery. Smith and Nephew have been at the forefront of developing endoscopy – the so-called keyhole surgery – which enables surgeons to use an extremely small incision when carrying out internal surgical procedures. Endoscopy uses miniature cameras and remote surgical instruments, and is being used more and more widely as surgeons realise the benefits of causing the minimum wound. Patients can often leave hospital the same day as their surgery and recovery times are markedly faster.

In 1999, Smith and Nephew bought out 3M's shoulder and hip implant business: the company also announced a new three-part group strategy, focused on orthopaedics, endoscopy and wound management. During 2000, this new strategy led the company to sell off its feminine hygiene and its toiletries products in a management buy-out. Elastoplast was sold to Beiersdorf AG, who also took over the distribution of Nivea in the United Kingdom. Thus Smith and Nephew pulled out of the consumer products market entirely, concentrating solely on its products for health care professionals. The company now offers over 1,000 products and continually spends on research and development to increase the range and efficacy of its products. During 2003, the company spent £67 million in R&D – 6% of the company's total turnover. Research is concentrated in the company's three strategic areas.

Graphic proof of the efficacy of Smith and Nephew's products came in October 2002. The Bali bombing killed over 200 people, but the wounds suffered by other victims were truly horrific. One young mother of two suffered 85% burns: she was treated immediately with Smith and Nephew's Acticoat dressing, and in the Sydney hospital where she was taken she was treated with Transcyte temporary skin until skin grafts could be carried out. Even five years earlier, a patient with 85% burns would not be expected to live – but this mother was discharged from hospital within a month and was able to spend Christmas with her children.

ACTIVITY 5.4

Consider the Smith and Nephew example.

1. Why would Smith and Nephew sell off its consumer products divisions?
2. Why does the company spend such a large portion of its turnover on research?
3. What stage of the PLC was Band-Aid at in during 1924?
4. What stage of the PLC was Elastoplast in when Smith and Nephew sold it?
5. To what extent are Smith and Nephew's products customer-specified?

3 Portfolio management

▸ **Key term**

Product portfolio: a range, assortment or mix of products that an organisation offers to sell.

Very few companies produce only one product. This means that most marketing managers have to deal with several products within a range, each at a different stage of the product life cycle and each with its own group of customers. Some products will be at the beginning of the life cycle, others will be in the growth or maturity stages and still others will be in decline: managers need to make decisions on what to do about each product in terms of marketing it.

Probably, the best-known portfolio management tool is the **Boston Consulting Group (BCG) matrix** (see Figure 5.4). This categorises products according to their market share and the growth rate of the market they are in. The categories are as follows:

1. A **Star** is a product with a large share of a growing market. This product will grow in sales and profits, but will need to be protected from incoming competitors, so may need a lot of marketing support.
2. A **Problem Child** is a product with a small share of a growing market. This product is problematic because it will need a lot of effort to grow its market share, but if this can be done it has the potential to become a Star. If, on the other hand, the effort fails, then a lot of investment of time and money will have been wasted, and it would have been better simply to drop the product from the range. Also referred to as **Question Marks**.
3. A **Cash Cow** is a product which has a large share of a stable market. It is probably in the maturity stage of the PLC and probably needs relatively little marketing input to maintain its position: this means that it will continue to generate income for the firm over a long period of time.
4. A **Dog** is a product which has a small share of a stable market. Dogs are not likely to be profitable and are prime candidates to be dropped from the range: however, in some cases Dogs are kept on, perhaps because they have a historical significance to the company, perhaps because sales of other products depend on them, or perhaps because some loyal customers might defect if the Dog were dropped. In any case, they require little expenditure and therefore can be 'harvested' for their remaining income.

   Researchers called Barksdale and Harris later added two more categories to the list, to reflect the possibility that a market might actually be shrinking, as follows:

5. A **Warhorse** is a product with a large share of a shrinking market. Like the Cash Cow, it is probably profitable and will certainly require very little support, since a shrinking market is probably not of interest to competitors, so it can provide good cash returns, at least in the short term.
6. A **Dodo** is a product which has a small share of a shrinking market. It is extremely unlikely to be worth keeping and will in any case eventually disappear along with its market. An example might be a product which is kept on for historical or sentimental reasons (perhaps because it has an aging, but loyal, customer group). A good example would be vinyl records.

Figure 5.4 The expanded BCG matrix

Market growth	Relative market share: High	Relative market share: Low
High	Star 	Problem child 
Low	Cash cow 	Dog 
Negative	War horse 	Dodo 

THE REAL WORLD

The rise of the Dodo – vinyl records

With Barksdale and Harris's research and additions to the BCG matrix you could argue that the vinyl record has come back from the Dodo phase and could be considered as a new rising star.

In May 2010 it was reported by the Official UK Charts Company that sales of 'old-fashioned' vinyl records rose by more than five per cent last year. In the same period CD sales fell by a fifth as global downloads increased and it is suggested that some manufacturers are threatening to halt their production of CDs and replace with good old vinyl. Even though it is seen as a small part of the total sales of music, achieving only 1% of American sales, this does account for over 3 million vinyl records being sold and this was an increase of a million from 2009.

The product maybe termed as a dodo but the recent demand has seen Amazon stock over 250,000 records. It has also seen a resurgence in the demand for record players since the teenagers of New York returned to the old vinyl recording, increasing their demand over and above those being purchased by DJs and dance music fans.

The figures quoted from 2010 may be under-valuing the sales of the vinyl records as they do not include independent small retailers, second-hand sales and those sold at gigs by the bands themselves. Bands such as The Red Hot Chili Peppers and The Courteeners have used this route to market successfully. Fans of vinyl will claim that nothing beats holding a heavy piece of plastic and the sound is deeper and richer and you cannot better the artwork and notes on the covers or sleeves.

We may not be returning to the heydays of 1979 when seven-inch vinyl records achieved 89 million sales; however, it would appear that vinyl records are gaining popularity and taking some of the market share from CDs, as it was reported in January 2012 that sales had increased once again to a 6 year high.

(Hough, 2010 and BBC Radio 4 Today, 2012)

The BCG matrix and its variants certainly provide a good way of focusing the mind on product portfolio management, but it suffers from the major drawback that it is subjective. Deciding what is a large (or small) share is a managerial judgement, nothing to do with any objective criteria, and it may be hard to judge whether a market is growing, shrinking or stable at any one time.

Having decided that a product is at a particular point on the PLC, and in the BCG matrix, managers then need to decide what to do about it. Promotion policy, distribution policy and pricing policy all are affected by this estimation. Most importantly, though, is the NPD policy.

ACTIVITY 5.5

List all the products your organisation offers. Now try to categorise them as Cash Cows, Stars, Dogs and so forth. Can you explain why the company does not simply drop Dogs and Dodos? How did you decide that those products *are* Dogs and Dodos?

Would you be able to justify your position to your boss?

4 New product development (NPD)

Key term

New Product Development (NPD): a model which looks at each stage in the development of a new product from idea to sale.

There are four main reasons for introducing new products and services:

- **Changing customer needs**. As time moves on, customers change their requirements, and new generations of consumers appear, bringing with them different ideas and needs.
- **Technological changes**. Changes in communications technology mean that many services (such as travel agencies) have been severely hit by online services. At the same time, the internet and other communications systems (such as mobile telephones and texting) have opened up new opportunities for services which could not have existed even 10 years ago. Technological change is not confined to communications and electronics, of course: a new method of making concrete could have profound effects on the construction industry, and a new diet discovery can disrupt the food industry dramatically.
- **Long-term business strategies**. New products can often put the company into new competitive positions, perhaps even against new competitors. For example, a motor manufacturer's decision to expand in the Third World might mean developing an easily maintained, reliable, cheap basic vehicle for use on poor roads in remote areas.
- **Competitor actions.** New products can often be developed to compete with existing competitors' NPD. For example, as new mobile phone platforms are designed companies will battle to develop similar platforms to compete in the same market (such as iPhone versus HTC).

NPD follows a series of stages in most cases (Figure 5.5). These are as follows:

Figure 5.5 The NPD process

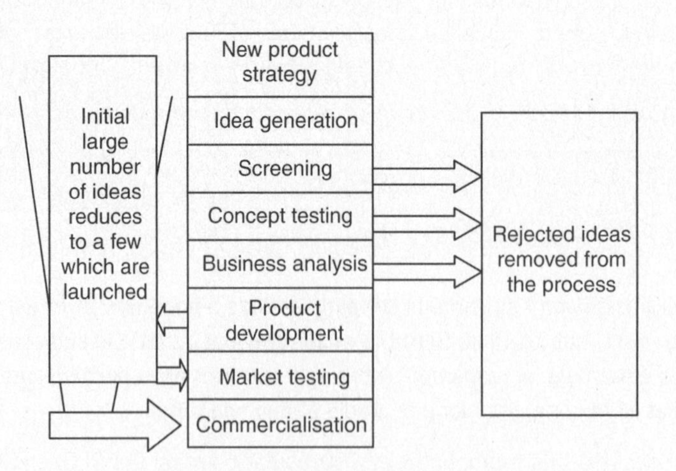

- **Idea generation**. Ideas might come from any source – customers, staff, research and development officers, senior management and so forth. Some companies have dedicated teams of people charged with the task of thinking of new ideas: such groups are often drawn from several different departments in order to take advantage of different experience, specialist knowledge and different perspectives.
- **Screening**. Ideas are discussed, and the most promising ones put forward for further development. Screening should only take place once all the ideas (however far-fetched) have been assembled. Trying to screen ideas as they are formulated tends to make people self-conscious and reluctant to offer their thoughts and also tends to impede discussion within the group. Even the worst idea might trigger a better one or be combined with a later idea to create a successful product.
- **Concept testing**. The basic idea behind each product is shown to potential customers and their comments are invited. Sometimes this can be done via formal market research; in other cases, it might simply involve informal discussions with potential customers. At this stage, there is unlikely to be any kind of prototype or mock-up: people are only being asked to comment on the basic idea.
- **Business analysis**. The degree to which the product will fit with existing products and with existing corporate strategies is assessed. Products which might harm existing sales, or which take the company in undesirable directions, will be dropped at this stage. Profitability (or at least the degree of fit with the corporate mission) will be considered at this stage, although it is unlikely that a definitive assessment can be undertaken since the costs of developing the product and manufacturing it will not be known until the engineers have carried out their part of the process.
- **Product development**. Once the business analysis shows that the product should be viable, the actual engineering process can begin. Prototypes will be produced and tested, and engineering problems will be overcome: feedback from the market will need to be considered, and competitors' products might also be tested as part of the process. Sometimes competing products are 'reverse engineered', meaning that company engineers will dismantle the competing product to find out how it has been made.
- **Market testing**. Often, though by no means always, the product will be offered to a section of the market in order to test its potential sales. This enables the company to assess the potential for the product before committing fully to it, with all the marketing and production costs entailed. In other cases, individuals might be asked to use the product and report on it: for example, a new type of house paint might be offered to several hundred people to try out, and these people might later be interviewed to find out how they found the product. The drawback of market testing is that competitors may find out about the product and prepare their retaliation before the product is established.
- **Commercialisation and launch**. Finally, the product is launched to the full market. At this point, there should be a complete marketing plan and a full commitment by the company. Even so, the majority of new products fail to recoup their development costs – there are simply too many variables for NPD to be an exact science.

Usually, these stages would be followed in the order given, but occasionally stages might be skipped or might be carried out in another sequence. In some cases, especially in volatile industries such as consumer electronics, several stages might be carried out in parallel – for example, concept testing, business analysis and even product development might overlap. In other industries, the whole process might be dramatically shortened or bypassed. For example, a restaurant might simply put a new recipe on the 'Daily Specials' board, offer it to the lunchtime customers and gauge their reaction to it. If the response is generally negative, the dish can be omitted in future, but a positive response might lead to it being added to the main menu.

Exam tip

You will certainly be expected to consider the circumstances of the company if you are asked to outline the NPD process for a case study. A pharmaceutical company might have a huge research budget with extremely long lead times – 10 or 15 years – for developing new products, while a small light engineering company might simply be told what to make by a large customer, with no real development process at all.

If you think a company will not follow the full process for some reason, simply say so in your answer and outline what you think should happen. This will show that you understand the NPD process, but can use some common sense when applying it.

THE REAL WORLD

Gillette

When King C. Gillette was 40, he was working as a sales representative for Crown Cork and Seal Company of Wisconsin. He was making a good living, but the job required a smart turn-out, including being clean-shaven. One morning he noticed that his cut-throat razor was blunt and was in fact so worn out that it would not take an edge and could therefore not be sharpened. At that point he had the flash of inspiration that has changed the world for men – he had the idea of producing a disposable blade that would simply be thrown away when it became blunt.

After some years of experimenting, he found a way to make the blades and also found a machine tool which could stamp out and sharpen the blades. Unfortunately, the cost of making the blades was higher than the price he could get for them – so this was where his sales training paid off.

Gillette realised that he could only get the production costs down if he produced blades in the millions, which meant converting a lot of men to the idea of using a disposable blade. At first, he sold the blades below cost to build up the business, but this was too slow. Then he hit on a business idea which is still used in the 21st century. He gave away the razors which held the blades in place and made his money selling the blades. Millions of the razors were handed out free, so millions of men tried the new system, and having done so very few went back to the old cut-throat razors.

By the time he was 55, Gillette was a millionaire, and the cut-throat razor was a thing of the past. Nowadays, the company he founded is a worldwide organisation, marketing items as diverse as toothbrushes and Duracell batteries.

Gillette has a history of being first to market. Following on from the launch of the world's first safety razor in 1901, the company went on to launch the following new products:

- Twin-bladed razor, 1972
- Twin-bladed disposable razor, 1976
- Pivoting head razor, 1979
- Pivoting head disposable razor, 1980
- Razor designed specifically for women – Sensor, 1992
- Triple blade razor – Mach 3, 1998
- 5 blade razor - Fusion Proglide 2006
- 5 blade razor with power - Stealth Razor 2010

Note that the rate of innovation increased rapidly after 1970. For 70 years, the company had produced essentially the same product: competition had been held off at first by King C. Gillette's original patents, but eventually competitors entered the markets anyway and began to make inroads into Gillette's position. Gillette needed to diversify – and to step up the rate of innovation.

The company's fastest growing market is oral hygiene. The Oral-B toothbrush system is a flagship brand, in both the manual and electric toothbrush categories. Gillette see their most lucrative strategy as being to encourage consumers to trade up – in world terms, most men who shave use double-edged blades. In these markets, Gillette seek to move these consumers onto better-performing twin blades or to twin-blade disposables. In mature markets, where the bulk of men are already using twin blade or disposables, the company offers triple-blade systems. Customers of Oral-B manual toothbrushes can be traded up to the electric systems, customers for zinc carbon batteries can be encouraged to switch to Duracell, and Duracell customers can be moved up to the more advanced Duracell batteries.

Overall, Gillette has a well-planned, long-standing strategic plan for NPD and diffusion. Innovation is not a haphazard process: every product has its place in the plan.

(Gillette, 2012)

ACTIVITY 5.6

1. How did Gillette develop his original idea for a disposable razor blade?
2. Why does the company innovate so much?
3. How does Gillette handle the problem of new products cannibalising sales of existing products?
4. What was the relationship between marketing and production in the case of the original blades?
5. How might trading up work in global markets?

ACTIVITY 5.7

Find out how NPD happens in your own firm, or a firm with which you are familiar. How does it relate to the standard model shown above? If it is different, do the differences make it work better or worse? What might be the reasons for senior management adopting a different approach from the standard one?

If you work for a small firm, the NPD process might well happen mainly inside someone's head – usually the boss. What are the problems with this approach?

▸ Exam tip

The adoption of innovation model (described next) parallels the product life cycle model. This is a useful way of remembering, and of understanding the processes involved in each model. The shape of the curve does differ somewhat, of course, because of repeat purchases by people who have adopted the product already.

5 Adoption model

▸ Key term

Product adoption: looks at how information and new products diffuse and spread into a market.

The **adoption of innovation**, whether of services or of physical products, is not an instantaneous process throughout the target market. Sales of products grow over a period of time, as evidenced by the product life cycle model. The delay in adoption is caused by a number of factors: word needs to get round that the product exists at all, some people are reluctant to try a new product until they have seen it in action (perhaps seen a friend using one), some people like to wait until any problems with the product have been identified and fixed, and some people are put off by the cost of switching from one product to another.

Switching cost is a key factor in adoption because it adds directly to the price. Someone considering a new product will almost certainly already have another solution that works adequately and will have to go to the trouble of learning how to use the new product, perhaps adapting his or her existing life, and perhaps have to spend money on accessories to make the new product work effectively. For example, someone buying a new mobile phone will probably already have a phone which works adequately and which might represent a considerable investment. The new phone will have new features which have to be learned, the owner's current address book will have to be transferred across, and it may be necessary to buy a new carrying case or even new software to make the best use of the phone. The company selling the new phone will have to accept that the total price the customer pays (from the customer's viewpoint) will include these extra costs. This will inevitably affect the firm's **pricing policy** (another example of the way in which the 7Ps impinge on each other – in this case, how product policy affects price).

As products spread through the market, it is possible to distinguish between the different groups of **consumers** who buy at each stage. These are generally thought to be as follows:

- **Innovators**. These people like to be the first to own a new product, and they will probably pay a premium price in order to do so. They account for around 2.5% of the target market.
- **Early adopters.** These people are eager to adopt new products and will do so once the product has been on the market for a while. They account for about 13.5% of the market.
- **Early majority**. These people like to wait until the product has been available for some time, so that teething problems have been resolved, and they have had a chance to see the product in action. They account for around 33% of the market, so that we are now at the point where half the people in the potential target market have adopted the product.
- **Late majority**. These people only buy when the majority of people already have the product. They are wary of the new product and only feel confident to buy it when it is well established. They account for a further 33% of the market.
- **Laggards**. These people are reluctant to buy anything new and will only adopt the product if they are forced to. In some cases, they do not adopt at all: they account for the remainder of the market.

The adoption sequence does not tell us much about the individuals concerned, since there is no evidence that an adopter for one category of product would be an adopter for a different category. People who do not buy the latest computer games may simply not be interested in computer games under any circumstances: perhaps the same individual spends his or her spare time listening to music and would be an eager buyer of the latest hi-fi equipment. As a predictor, the model is therefore not very helpful: it does provide us with terminology, however, and it can be useful in terms of planning the style and content of marketing communications, since we can observe the product moving through the adoption process and can tailor our appeal appropriately.

▸ Exam tip

You will be expected to know the correct terms for these adopter groups and know the order in which they adopt. If you can also remember the approximate proportions each group represents of the total market, it will gain you marks. You are likely to be asked to make recommendations about new product launches, and knowing the terminology will undoubtedly be expected of you.

Do not forget, though, that the divisions between the groups are arbitrary – they were decided on by a statistical process, not by looking at the personal characteristics of the individuals involved. Research into what makes someone want to adopt a new product is somewhat inconclusive – innovators can only really be defined by the fact that they buy new products, which is of course a fine example of circular reasoning.

THE REAL WORLD

James Dyson

When James Dyson was a 23-year-old student at the Royal College of Art in London, he designed a novel boat, the Seatruck, which was able to carry cargo at high speeds. This won a Design Council award and went on to earn $500 million in sales. Dyson later invented the ballbarrow, a wheelbarrow with a ball instead of a wheel (which made it less likely to sink in soft earth), a boat launcher using balls instead of wheels, and an amphibious vehicle for use on sand dunes and on the sea.

Eventually, though, Dyson invented the product which made him a household name – the Dyson vacuum cleaner. This cleaner was the first bagless cleaner: needing no bag, it is cheaper to own and use and never loses suction. Dyson has promoted these benefits very ably, using advertisements showing people in the familiar position of having to dismantle the vacuum cleaner to find out what is clogging it up.

Dyson's success has been based on his ability to see the drawbacks with existing products and engineer solutions. His most successful inventions (the ballbarrow, the seatruck and the vacuum cleaner) have been based on their practical advantages over existing products. The Wheelboat amphibian has been less successful – and Dyson has had many other inventions which failed to make a hit with the public. Perhaps this is because they are technically interesting, but lack a practical advantage over existing products.

Whatever the reason, Dyson continues to invent. He recently launched a washing machine which does not tangle clothes and is working on improvements to his vacuum cleaners. The inventions are not revolutionary, but they are practical and do improve the lives of millions of people – simply because they meet people's needs better than the competing products.

Products will only be accepted if they offer benefits which existing products do not have. Many new ideas have been launched, only to disappear without trace because they do not have an advantage over products which are already on the market. New products are not necessarily either new or not new: there are degrees of newness, and one of the commonest classifications is that proposed by Robertson (1967), as follows (Figure 5.6):

- **Continuous innovation.** This is a new product which follows on from a previous version and is recognisably derived from its predecessor. Heavy-duty batteries, toothpaste with a built-in mouthwash, low-calorie biscuits and squeezable ketchup bottles are examples.
- **Dynamically continuous innovation.** These products are new ways of solving old problems, but they do not make radical changes to the way people live. For example, DVD recorders do not change people's lives in the way that home video recorders did: they simply replaced the old technology with something which works better.
- **Discontinuous innovation.** These are genuine new-to-the-world products that make radical changes to people's lives. Home computers and the internet have changed the ways in which people communicate, study and work: mobile telephones have changed how people work and live. For earlier generations, the car, television, radio and aeroplane revolutionised ordinary people's lives.

Figure 5.6 Degrees of innovation

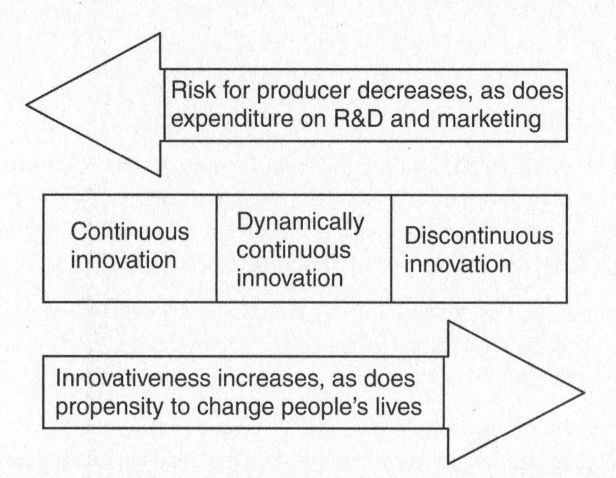

Risk for the firm increases as newness increases, but so too do the potential returns. Continuous innovation rarely leads to product failures, and it is relatively easy to research consumer acceptance of a new model of an existing product: discontinuous innovations often fail (some researchers estimate that eight out of ten do not recover their development costs) and are virtually impossible to research since most people are unlikely to recognise the advantages until they have seen other people using the product.

Discontinuous innovations are risky, but on the plus side they do offer what is called the first-to-market advantage. A company which can produce something entirely new to the world will have a long lead time to gain market share while competitors try to develop competing products: sometimes patent protection will enable such firms to capture most of a market before the patent expires or competitors find a way around it.

There are six broad types of innovation strategy, as follows:

- **Offensive.** Some firms aim to be the leading innovators in their industry (Sony is an example). Such firms seek to gain first-to-market advantage by spending a great deal of money and effort on developing new products.
- **Defensive.** Companies following a defensive strategy will usually wait until a more innovative firm has introduced a radical new product, then produce their own version of it, incorporating some improvements. This often works well because any new product on the market is almost certainly going to have some faults which the defensive company can exploit. The purpose of the exercise is to defend their own markets against the other company.
- **Imitative.** This strategy involves making almost exact copies of new products. The strategy only works if the new product has weak, or no, patent protection: this is not the same as counterfeiting, which means passing off a copy as if it were made by the brand-owning company. Counterfeiting is illegal in most countries, whereas imitation is not unless there is good patent or copyright protection.
- **Dependent.** Some companies only innovate as a result of being told to do so by a major customer. For example, a light engineering company might be contracted to produce components for a major car manufacturer and might be given an exact specification for a new component.
- **Traditional.** This strategy is not really innovative at all, since it involves re-creating old traditional designs. For example, Victorian baked potato ovens staged a comeback a few years ago: the design was traditional, but it was a new product for the companies making the ovens.
- **Opportunist.** Opportunist companies make and market new inventions as they become available, rather than having their own research and development systems. Inventors approach such companies with their ideas, taking a royalty on production as their payment.

THE REAL WORLD

Rab clothing company

This case looks at target markets and which products best suit a specialist market. It also considers the way in which specialist products can develop into new markets but still retain their unique features and benefits.

Rab is an outstanding brand in the production of high quality technical clothing and sleeping bags, suitable for extreme cold environments and high altitudes.

More than 30 years ago Rab Carrington started making sleeping bags in Patagonia, he did so to pass the time and earn some money whilst he waited for his climbing gear to be released from customs. A talented climber, Rab spent a great deal of time on new expeditions around the world during the 1970s and developed a vast understanding into what climbers and mountaineers needed from their kit. For example in 1968 in the Dolomites when other climbers were using mountaineering boots to climb, Rab was using rock boots to the summits of Phillip-Flamm and the Tre Cime.

This experience and background based in the mountaineering society has enabled Rab to design performance sleeping bags and down clothing. Rab looked first at the functions of the gear needed to achieve and then designed for that purpose. Combining his knowledge of the mountains and the skills learnt in South America he returned to Sheffield, UK to set up his first retail outlet. Rab made kit for the specialist market of mountaineers and in the mid 1980s RAB was the first manufacturer in the world to use a specialist insulation product called Pertex in the production of down sleeping bags and jackets. This legacy continued with RAB into 2010s, there is now a group of people dedicated to making products for the most extreme conditions in the world.

Their passion for the 'outdoors and long standing partnerships, with performance material suppliers' has pushed Rab's ground-breaking ethos, allowing them to always push the limits. This vision remains core to current product development; a strong focus on using functional designs and high quality fabrics to produce premium gear for mountaineering and polar travel. However it also allows the company to look at the developing 'high street' and 'fashion' market without loosing sight of their overall mission.

To that end in June 2011, Dan Fitzgerald, James Wake and Matt Balmer, visited the Cordillera Oriental range of mountains in Peru. Climbers have flocked to Peru to climb and the area caters for mountaineers with many climbing retailers, cafes and countless hostels. So many differing organisations, supply their specialist equipment to these types of trips. Rab supported this trip and the 3 man team used many items of Rab gear, including Neutrino 600 Sleeping Bags, Baltoro Alpine Jacket, Baltoro Trousers, Vapour-Rise Stretch Top, Kinetic Jacket, Extreme Down Jacket, Long Sleeve Aeon Tee, Baltoro Gloves, and Rab Beanies. Enabling Rab to once again look long and hard at the functional nature of their products and receive excellent customer feedback. This knowledge and experience will be incorporated into their new range of Vapour-Rise light weight pertex Equilibrium fabrics which will come to market in mid 2012.

(Rab, 2012)

ACTIVITY 5.8

Consider the Rab example:

1. How might Rab seek to develop its target market?
2. What might be the appeal of Rab clothing to the average person?
3. What factors enable Rab to have continued its success?
4. Why would someone buy a Vapour-Rise light weight Pertex coat?

ACTIVITY 5.9

Find three or more products from the Innovations catalogue, or from a gadget shop, or on the Strange New Products website (the URL is given at the end of this chapter).

What need does each product address? What might people be doing already to meet that need? Why is the new product better at meeting the need? What might be the costs of adopting the new product (purchase price and switching costs)? Do you think the product would be viable in the long term, and if not, why not?

CHAPTER ROUNDUP

- Products look to satisfy the needs and wants of customers.
- A product can be classified in the following ways: core, augmented, expected and potential.
- Branding a product can make the difference in competitive markets.
- All products have a lifecycle: they are designed, born, live and die over time. You should learn the stages of the PLC: development, introduction, growth, maturity, decline and obsolescence.
- Portfolios and ranges of products can hold a customer within an organisation's target for longer.
- The BCG matrix is a well-known portfolio management tool.
- Changing customer needs, technological changes, long-term business strategies and competitor actions are the four main reasons for introducing new products. The new product development model looks at each stage in the development of a product from idea to sale.
- There are several factors which influence product adoption, including the 'type' of consumer.

FURTHER READING

Since the marketing mix is such a large part of practical marketing, the reading tends also to be comprehensive. For more detail on the mix elements:

Baker, M. J, *The Marketing Manual*, Butterworth Heinemann. Chapter 7.

Blythe, J. (2009) *Essentials of Marketing.* 4th Edition. Harlow, Prentice Hall. Chapters 1, 6, 7, 8 and 9.

Blythe, J. (2008) *Principles and Practice of Marketing.* 2nd Edition. Andover, Lengage. Chapters 1 and 12–22.

Brassington, F. and Pettitt, S. (2006) *Principles of Marketing.* 4th Edition. Harlow, Prentice Hall. Chapters 7–19.

Kotler, P. *et al* (2008) *Principles of Marketing.* 5th Edition. FT Prentice Hall.Chapters 13–22.

Jobber, D. (2009) *Principles and Practice of Marketing.* 6th Edition. Maidenhead, McGraw-Hill Chapters 8–17.

Websites

http://www.berr.gov.uk/index.html: The official website of the Department for Business Enterprise and Regulatory Reform. It contains a large number of articles and statistics on innovation, as well as advice for innovative businesses.

http://www.myoffers.co.uk: This website directs users to many sales promotions, providing a useful set of examples.

http://www.advertisingarchives.co.uk: This site contains advertisements going back over a hundred years.

http://brand.blogs.com/mantra/2005/02/lovehate_brand_.html: This is a chat room for people to post their messages of love or hate about brands. It offers some interesting insights into what goes wrong with brand messages.

http://www.strangenewproducts.com

http://www.shell.com/home/content/motorsport/ferrari/formula_one_2012/

http://www.audienceswales.co.uk/client_files//default/cim_how_brands_work__3_.pdf

National broadsheet newspapers

Marketing magazine

Product-based magazine in your organisation's area of specialism

REFERENCES

BBC Radio 4 Today (2012) http://news.bbc,co.uk/today/hi/today/newsid_9687000/9687919.stm [Accessed on 21 June 2012].

Booms, B.H. and Bitner, M.J. Marketing strategies and organisation structures for service firms. J.H. Donnelly, W.R. George. (ed.). In: *Marketing of Services.* 1982, (Chicago: American Marketing Association pp47–52).

CIM (2003) http://www.audienceswales.co.uk/client-files//default/cim_how_brands_work_3.pdf [Accessed 27 June 2012].

Gillette (2012) http://news.gillette.com/about/timeline [Accessed on 21 June 2012].

Hough, R. (2010) http://www.telegraph.co.uk/culture/music/music-news/7398399/Vinyl-records-sales-rising-as-old-fashioned-albums-enjoy-a-renaissance.html [Accessed on 21 June 2012].

Levitt T. (1986) *The Marketing Imagination*. New York, Free Press.

Pittards (2012) http://www.pittards.com/discover-pittards/9/history [Accessed on 03 March 2012].

Pittards (2012). http://pittards.com [Accessed on 03 March 2012].

Rab (2012) http://rab.uk.com/about-us/expeditions-and-support/huaguruncho-chico-2011-expedition.html [Accessed May 2012].

Rab (2012). http://rab.uk.com/about-us/heritage.html [Accessed on May 2012].

Shell (2012) http://www.shell.com/home/content/motorsport/ferrari/formula-one-2012 [Accessed 21 June 2012].

Sinclair J.M. *et al* (1984) *English Dictionary*, Collins.

QUICK QUIZ

1 Define a product in less than 12 words.

2 Draw the PLC.

3 List the elements of NPD process.

4 Describe a brand.

5 Give two reasons why Michelin would sponsor motor sports.

6 Within the PLC, name the six major stages.

ACTIVITY DEBRIEFS

It is the intention with the majority of these activities to facilitate thoughts and ideas on how you might best fit the marketing theory into the real world, your world. We are all affected by marketing, at home, at work or in the wider environment so it is important you have the opportunity to relate the theory within the chapter to your own experiences.

Activity 5.1

This depends on your own research. But consider the following: a supermarket, for example, could include the offer of fresh and frozen food for sale; Oxfam could be the thought that you have helped someone who is suffering in a third world country; and for SeeAbility, a charity that supports individuals with visual impairment and complex needs, the feel-good factor, when you give and SeeAbility use your donation.

Activity 5.2

HJ Heinz

1 Why would Heinz drop its pet foods range, when the products were still making money for the firm? The pet foods range may have been making money, but since the range would require a completely separate marketing programme, it seems likely that resources would have been better directed towards new products in the food for humans range. There would undoubtedly be marketing synergies and economies of scale which would not exist in the pet food market. It is also possible that the pet food range was too small a part of an essentially stable, even stagnating market: as 'Dog' products, the pet food range might have been too unattractive to remain in the portfolio.

2 What is the importance of packaging to Heinz? Packaging enables Heinz to show a corporate image through the keystone design and also provides possibilities for making the product more attractive, as with the turquoise colour of the baked beans can and the squeezable ketchup bottle. In common with other food companies, Heinz is required to provide nutritional information on the packaging, and can use the packaging to promote other products.

3 How has the Heinz brand developed across the range? The original 57 Varieties slogan and the keystone link the brand, but brand managers have been able to operate within this framework to develop individual images for products. The brands therefore reinforce each other, while retaining their individual personalities. This process could be developed further.

4 What other changes might Heinz introduce to co-ordinate the branding better? Heinz could co-ordinate the colour of its brands and could extend the 57 Varieties idea further. Establishing an overall Heinz brand personality would help: promoting the entire group of brands as one entity, carrying out cross-promotions in which one product is used as a promotional tool for others, and perhaps promoting the traditional values of the company would also help in establishing the firm's brand identity. This may require a shift in the corporate culture and systems, since each sub-brand apparently operates as an independent entity.

5 Why might the company subdivide its brands into eight categories? Categorising the products into branding groups makes it easier to administer and control the marketing activities and also enables Heinz to produce a more coherent and co-ordinated campaign within each category. Dividing the overall range of 6,000 varieties enables brand managers to build up expertise in specific markets (eg baby foods require special marketing techniques, and seafood requires special purchasing and packaging systems) and gives the company the opportunity to establish itself as an expert in specific areas, rather than a generalist food marketing company.

Activity 5.3

You could just look around your home and see how products have changed; good example would be computers, large desk tops compared to today's smart phones, how they have changed in terms of size, access, power and shape.

Activity 5.4

Smith and Nephew

1 Why would Smith and Nephew sell off its consumer products divisions? Smith and Nephew clearly decided that the ethical medical market (sales to medical professionals and hospitals) was more lucrative and less trouble than selling in consumer markets. The markets are bigger and require (in most cases) much less marketing expenditure. Also, in such a field as medicine, companies need to show themselves as specialists rather than generalists – dealing with professional medical people is a skilled and delicate matter.

2 Why does the company spend such a large portion of its turnover on research? Medical science moves forward very quickly, and other firms in the supply side of the industry spend similar amounts on R&D. If Smith and Nephew fail to match this expenditure, they will be left (eventually) with an obsolete product line: product life cycles are short, in other words.

3 What stage of the PLC was Band-Aid in during 1924? Band Aid was in the introduction stage in 1924: it was almost certainly not yet a truly profitable line. At this point, relatively few people would know the product or be aware of its advantages, and the company would probably be spending a relatively large proportion of the marketing budget on trying to establish the product in its market.

4 What stage of the PLC was Elastoplast in when Smith and Nephew sold it? Elastoplast would be in the maturity stage, since there is still demand for the product but it is facing strong competition from cheap imitators. Essentially, it is currently stable, well known and requiring relatively low marketing expenditure to retain its market share. It is not yet in the decline phase, since there is nothing available to replace it apart from very similar 'me-too' products available from close competitors.

5 To what extent are Smith and Nephew's products customer-specified? Most of Smith and Nephew's products for professionals are customer-specified. The health care professionals need to be involved in identifying needs for new products, in all the fields in which the company operates: consultation with health professionals is essential. Even when the company develops new products, input from healthcare professionals is crucial.

Activity 5.5

This depends on your own research. As an example, you could also look at global brands like Adidas and see their Samba trainer is now the cash cow and Adi Rise Hi Top is the star, Yatra is the dog and question mark would be Taekwondo.

Activity 5.6

Gillette

1 How did Gillette develop his original idea for a disposable razor blade? Gillette began by noticing a need, then went through the development process of finding a technique for manufacturing the blades. Business analysis showed that he could not manufacture the blades cheaply enough without very large-scale production, so market testing demonstrated that giving the razors away would generate large enough sales of blades to make the project viable.

2 Why does the company innovate so much? Many of Gillette's products can be easily copied by competitors, so developing new ones is a good way to keep ahead of the competition. Products quickly become obsolete as competitors enter, and for some products (batteries, etc) technological change means rapid obsolescence. Few, if any, of Gillette's products can be protected effectively by patents.

3 How does Gillette handle the problem of new products cannibalising sales of existing products? Gillette is not unhappy about new products taking over sales of existing products, but the company sells existing products at lower prices and encourages consumers to 'trade up' to the new ones. Keeping obsolescent products in the range for as long as possible allows the company to harvest from its Dogs and Dodos, and also shuts out competitors effectively.

4 What was the relationship between marketing and production in the case of the original blades? In the original case, marketing drove production. Especially in the area of pricing, Gillette worked with the market: production would never have reached an economic level without his innovative approach. In fact, Gillette need never have manufactured anything – the whole of production could have been subcontracted.

5 How might trading up work in global markets? In a global market, obsolescent products can be re-launched in less developed markets, with the more up-to-date products following on later so that people can then trade up. This allows the company to obtain a maximum return on its development costs, while opening up new markets for the later products.

Activity 5.7

This depends on your own research.

Activity 5.8

1 How might Rab seek to develop its target market? Extending the target market will allow Rab to gain more sales revenue and therefore enable it to develop new and innovative products for the future mountaineer. To an extent, the segmentation problem is self-correcting since people are able to search the retailers and online to obtain this technical clothing even when they are not looking to climb a mountain.

2 What might be the appeal of Rab clothing to the average person? Rab has an interesting proposition to offer the market, technical clothing to keep you warm. However that is something everyone wishes to achieve when they live in colder climates, so customers will search out opportunities to find products which satisfy that need.

3 What factors enable Rab to have continued success? Continuous development of technical clothing that is tried and tested in the extremes of climate at the tops of high mountains. When it arrives on the 'high street' it will outperform the requirements of most customers. The specialist user will gain with the development of new and exciting products based on the revenue provided from all markets.

4 Why would someone buy a Vapour-Rise light weight Pertex coat? They wish to keep warm in the cold. This is a core product, but with the added advantage that the product has performed that task well in the extreme climates of high mountains. This will give the customer the confidence that the product has the ability to perform at an expected and augmented level as well.

Activity 5.9

This depends on your own research. But consider the following: turning your sink into a water fountain allows customers to drink from their bathroom or kitchen tap in a similar way to a water fountain in a workplace or park.

QUICK QUIZ ANSWERS

1 The thing that satisfies customers' needs with a bundle of benefits.

2

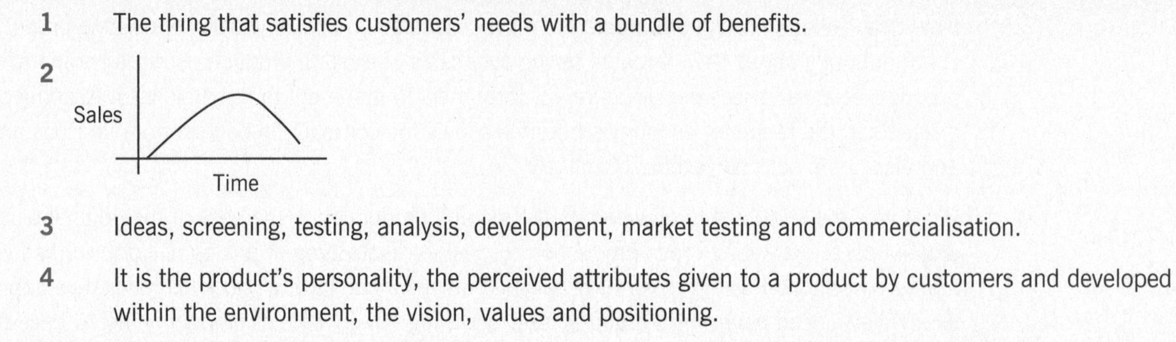

3 Ideas, screening, testing, analysis, development, market testing and commercialisation.

4 It is the product's personality, the perceived attributes given to a product by customers and developed within the environment, the vision, values and positioning.

5 Product development, increased brand awareness, brand development – personality.

6 Development, introduction, growth, maturity, decline and obsolescence.

CHAPTER 6

The marketing mix – price

Introduction

In this chapter we look to develop coverage of the marketing mix by introducing the basic concepts of pricing strategies and decisions. We will look at many different pricing strategies and how they fit into the marketing mix and work with the other elements to ensure the right price for both organisation and customer. This links to the understanding of value. We will discuss different price methods to achieve various results.

The role of price is important both internally within the organisation and, of course, it can be affected by external factors. These various factors will influence pricing policies that may be adopted by an organisation over time.

After working through this section, and carrying out the associated reading, you should be able to:

- Explain the effect of price on the other elements of the marketing mix.
- Describe the different pricing methods.

Topic list

Syllabus references

3.5	Explain the importance of price as an element of the marketing mix: ▪ Brings together the marketing mix elements to fulfil customer needs ▪ Income, revenue and profit generation ▪ Contributing to the organisation's business and financial objectives ▪ Limitations of price as a competitive tool
3.6	Identify and illustrate a range of different pricing approaches that are adopted by organisations as effective means of competition: ▪ Absorption costing ▪ Cost base and marginal costing ▪ Cost plus ▪ Price skimming ▪ Penetration pricing ▪ Loss-leader ▪ Promotional pricing

1 The importance of price

> **Key term**
>
> **Price**: In short, willingness to pay equals willingness to sell for.

Price can be defined as: the price point at which the customer is willing to pay to obtain the product and the price at which the seller is willing to sell the product to the customer. In short, willingness to pay equals willingness to sell for. It is a simple exchange process, but is fundamentally important for both the organisations and individuals involved as it links to perception of value, income, profit and many more aspects of the relationship between customer and organisation. From the days of barter to today's complete network of payment method, price is the value given to both sides of the exchange. Price can also been seen as a measurement of the value offered by the buyer to the seller in the exchange process.

Price is often regarded as one of the least interesting aspects of marketing, but in fact it is crucially important to the firm to set the right price for a product. This is for the following reasons:

- **Price brings together the other elements of the marketing mix and affects each one of them**. For example, price is often used by consumers to judge the likely quality of the product (a product function), and price can also be used as a short-term incentive to buy (a promotion function). Price can also be used to encourage people to buy online (a process function).
- **Price determines the firm's income and profits for each product and each market**. A relatively small increase in price can lead to a very large increase in profits, unless of course the higher price means customers buy competing products instead. It is therefore important to set the price at a level at which the appropriate number of customers will purchase the product. This should be at a level that achieves the required amount of income over costs and which provides the desired profit for the stakeholders involved.
- **Price contributes to the firm's business and financial objectives**. Pitching a low price will probably increase unit sales (at the cost of losing profit), so price can be used to control demand, perhaps in order to maintain efficient use of production capacity. This is particularly important in service industries, where the product cannot be stockpiled – this is why many restaurants offer early-evening discounts or weekday discounts to use capacity at less popular times. Controlling demand in this way is sometimes called loading: the same result can be achieved by increasing customer value, perhaps by offering a free aperitif to early diners. There is a direct link, therefore, between the price, the level of sales and the objectives of the business, in terms of profit.
- **Price can operate as a competitive tool** – with care. Competing by reducing prices can lead to retaliation by competitors, and a price war will always favour the firm with the most cash resources.

Because price has an immediate effect on the **value proposition**, it can be used to boost sales temporarily (eg a sales promotion which offers a discount). The drawback with this is that cutting the price has a dramatic effect on profits – if, for example, the company has a 20% profit margin, a cut of 10% off the price to the customer (which is a relatively small discount in some markets) results in halving the supplier's profit margin. In most cases, competing on price is just a quick way to lose money. On the other hand, raising the price by 10% (a figure which may go unnoticed by buyers in some markets) increases profits by 50%.

Price is an important surrogate for **judging quality**. People tend to assume that the higher priced product is better quality, and if the price/quality ratio is right, higher priced products actually represent better value for money since they offer more benefits: people often think that paying extra is worthwhile in order to obtain a better product. Of course, the product has to meet the customers' expectations, or no repeat purchases will result.

Exam tip

In most cases, examiners will regard competing on price as being a poor strategy. Often you will be asked to offer suggestions for launching a new product: students frequently recommend cutting prices below that of existing competitors, which of course means cutting profits and reducing the company's ability to invest meaningfully in the product's development and promotion.

Price needs to be pitched at the level consumers believe represents fair value for money – which does not mean cheap!

ACTIVITY 6.1

Imagine you have been in a lifeboat at sea for ten days; how much would you be willing to pay for a bottle of fresh water. Now think about drinking water at home all day whenever you wish. Is your willingness to pay different in the two differing environments?

Relatively few people consistently buy the cheapest products. People only do this if the reasons for buying a more expensive product are not immediately apparent, in other words if advertising or point-of-sale materials have been inadequate to explain why one product is superior to another. If this were not so, the most popular cars on the road would be cheap Eastern European models or basic cars such as the Fiat Seicento. In fact, the most popular car in Europe in 2006 was the Opel Astra, selling almost half a million vehicles: the tenth most popular was the BMW 3 series, which is of course a premium-priced car. Since the BMW out-sold many cheaper, more basic vehicles such as the Ford Mondeo and the Renault Megane, it is obvious that a large number of people are prepared to pay more for a better product and consider the BMW to be better value for money than the Ford or the Renault.

THE REAL WORLD

The international software market

Computer software is an unusual product. It is entirely intangible, and the costs of supplying it can also be negligible – it is the cost of writing it in the first place which is the main expense. Once the software exists, the costs of putting it onto CDs and packaging it are tiny in comparison. Still cheaper is distribution over the internet – which is why there is so much free software available online.

Software is also easily copied by pirates, which makes life difficult for major software companies, and also each company seeks to make its own software the industry standard, so that they can sell upgrades and add-ons. The switching costs for someone who has adopted a particular company's software can be high, so there is a considerable advantage in being the first software a customer commits to.

The situation is further complicated by international marketing. Obviously, the software company needs to make an overall profit and therefore generate a substantial turnover from worldwide sales of the software, but on the other hand customers in the wealthy countries of Western Europe, the United States and Australia can afford to pay much more than customers in the developing world such as India, parts of Asia and Africa. At the same time, computers are a global phenomenon, so it pays for companies to ensure that each country uses the same systems. In other words, it is worthwhile to subsidise poorer countries, because it helps adoptions in wealthier countries.

This creates a nightmarish problem for software marketers. Setting a price which people will pay is one thing, but ensuring that people in the wealthier countries do not feel that they are being cheated is another. For major players such as Sun Microsystems and Microsoft, the stakes are high – customers in the developing world are numbered in the billions, and in the software industry plans for world domination are constantly on the agenda. Companies that do not dominate will go to the wall – there is no room for second-best. Microsoft always operated on a one-price basis – everybody paid the same, whatever country they were in. This ensured that customers in the developed world did not feel cheated and also prevented software from being bought in one country for use in another. However, as the 21st century began, it became obvious that this position would not be tenable in the long run. Something would have to change in Microsoft's pricing!

Companies in the software business have been forced to use differential pricing (using a different price in each market for the same product) in developing countries, simply because a price tag of $90 seems very expensive in countries where most people only earn an average of $2 a day. Even though people who can afford a computer are in much higher income brackets, the temptation to buy pirated software is high.

Microsoft's answer to this was to introduce cut-down versions of Windows XP specifically adapted for the developing world. In December 2004, the company began offering versions of XP in the local language, with some features removed, in India, Russia, Malaysia and Indonesia. The product had already been piloted in Thailand and had been greeted with great enthusiasm. Microsoft's Kenneth Lundin said that the move was intended to give more people access to software and also reduce the incidence of pirating of software. Because the cut-down XP systems are only available in the local language, grey-market copies were unlikely to be shipped out to the wealthier Western markets, and also the software was only being made available to computer manufacturers – not to the general public. This means that the software either comes ready-installed on the computer or is protected so that it can only be installed once. Microsoft has agreed this as part of a deal with the Malaysian Government, intended to increase the use of computers in the country from its current 15% of the population to 35%. The company is understandably coy about exactly how much it is charging for the software, but since the simplified computers sell for around £350, the software has to be a lot cheaper than the £100-plus price tag of the UK version.

At the same time, Sun Microsystems is entering the business sector with a version of its Java software. Sun is using a unique pricing system, based on the number of people in the country and the country's state of development as verified by the United Nations. John Loiacano, executive vice-president of software at Sun, said: 'With our new per-citizen pricing model, governments of developing nations can now reallocate punitive software licensing fees to critical tasks such as healthcare and education. And the expanded platform support allows these nations to deliver network services to citizens and customers on the architecture of their choice.'

Both companies are suggesting that their actions are at least partly philanthropic: Microsoft talk about extending the benefits of computer ownership to the poorer nations, and Loiacano of Sun talks about allowing countries to spend their money on hospitals and schools rather than on education. Seeking the moral high ground is, of course, fine and what the company spokesmen say is

quite true – but the fact remains that both companies have now won a captive market for their software, probably for the next 20 or 30 years at least. In Malaysia alone, Microsoft looks set to pick up around 3 million new customers – and Malaysia has a population of only 26 million.

ACTIVITY 6.2

1. What is the role of consumer characteristics in software price setting?
2. Why should companies not charge one price for everyone, regardless of location?
3. Why might the product not represent the same value for money in each of its markets?
4. The market is huge, so why is there not room for many players to compete?
5. How might a new software supplier (eg an Indian or Chinese supplier) price its products effectively in the world market?

THE REAL WORLD

Lucie's Farm

Farmers in the United Kingdom often have a hard time. They are price takers, not price makers, because the market decides the prices (on the basis of supply and demand), and no one farmer is large enough to affect demand or supply – and since farmers are dependent on the weather so much, the supply is largely determined by the British climate, which is uncertain at best (and certainly bad at worst).

Escaping from the tedious cycle of failed crops, uncertain European Union subsidies, and ever-rising costs and paperwork has proved difficult or even impossible for most farmers. Some, however, like Craig and Marjorie Walsh, have found a way to break out of the ever-decreasing circle.

In 1985, the couple saw the movie Rob Roy and were so impressed with the Highland cattle in the film they decided to breed them. They are now the leading Highland Cattle breeders outside Scotland and are happy to sell the animals for meat, or for breeding or (perhaps spectacularly) as 'lawn ornaments' for wealthy people with large gardens. What has helped Craig and Marjorie escape the price-taker trap is the fact that they produce beef to a very high standard. Their beef is aged for 21 days after slaughter – about 3–4 times as long as the average pre-packed supermarket steak – and is organically reared. The flavour and tenderness of their beef is already legendary, but the couple recently went a stage further and began producing Kobe-style beef.

Kobe beef originates in Japan and is produced from cattle which are treated better than royalty. The cattle drink beer from the local microbrewery, eat grain and are regularly massaged with sake to make the beef tender. The end result is an incredibly tender, delicious meat – which of course sells for a premium price! Craig and Marjorie's farm, Lucie's Farm in Worcestershire, is a Mecca for restaurateurs and foodies prepared to pay around £60 for enough meat for four people (even four hamburger patties comes out to around £12).

In an affluent society, there will always be a market for the 'special treat', and even for luxurious foods on a daily basis. Lucie's Farm, by adding value to the product, has tapped into that market extremely successfully.

Taking control of pricing, as in the case of Lucie's Farm, is an important factor in competition. Competing on price (ie trying to be the cheapest in the market) is unlikely to be as effective as competing on value for money, since it is very simple for competitors to retaliate by cutting their own prices. In practice there will always be a competitor who is able to cut prices to the bone – even to the point where they are losing money – if they are desperate to retain market share.

Adding to the customer value (what the customer gets in exchange for the price paid) is a much safer alternative, provided the value added is greater for the consumer than the price increase entailed, and the cost of adding the value is less than the premium charged. If this is the case, both sales and profits will increase.

Exam tip

It is worth bearing in mind that the price people are prepared to pay for a product bears no relationship whatsoever to the cost of making the product. Ultimately it is the price people are prepared to pay which will determine what can be charged.

You can probably think of many examples of this – the price of T-shirts which cost pennies to make is sometimes as high as £10. Having some examples in mind is useful in exams, but it is even more useful to your career, as you will often find yourself in the position of defending customer-based pricing in the face of engineers and accountants who are more likely to favour cost-based pricing.

2 Pricing methods

You will be expected to **understand different methods of pricing** and be able to apply them: you may well be asked to compare the **advantages and disadvantages** of each method, and to make recommendations as to which approach to pricing is most appropriate in any given set of circumstances. In the 'real world', you will need to understand pricing methods in order to argue your case with colleagues, many of whom will have been taught pricing approaches which are not customer orientated.

THE REAL WORLD

Price comparisons

There are many and varied ways to price any product or service and every organisation has a differing set of resources they must cost into their price to ensure they achieve the organisational objectives. Insurance, utility suppliers and holidays are just a few products for which a whole range of comparison websites have been developed where you can compare the price differing organisations offer, before you decide what you are willing to pay.

Two examples would be Confused.com (the first price comparison website in the UK which was launched in 2002) and Gocompare.com (which launched in November 2006 and was the first site to look at product features as well as just listing prices). Confused.com and Gocompare.com both offer a comprehensive insurance comparison services in the UK, committed to finding you the right product at the best price, and dedicated to saving you time and money. They look at a wide range of insurance products which include car insurance; home insurance; holidays and travel insurance; pet insurance; caravan insurance; gas, electricity and other utilities for your home; and money products such as credit cards, savings and life insurance.

Both companies use the same process to get paid, by charging the service provider or partner company a small fee every time customers buy through one of their websites. So, in simple terms, it is free at the point of delivery, it costs the customer nothing extra, they will pay the same prices even if they were to go direct to the insurance company.

There are also benefits in terms of time and effort to the customer, as once they have input their details these are held on the system and therefore they do not have to go through the whole process again when looking for cheaper insurance next time.

They have both become trusted household names and their customers can be confident that they will find the quotes that are offered are not just estimates of price, but the price seen on the screen will be the price paid. With the backing of much larger insurance companies such as Admiral and Esure Services Limited both organisations have developed into hugely successful companies and maintain their profits alongside offering a service of price comparison within the rules and regulations of such organisations as the British Insurance Brokers Association and Information Commissioner's Office, which have the responsibility of upholding the regulations contained within the Data Protection Act 1998.

> **Exam tip**
>
> It is worthwhile to practise seeing problems from the other person's viewpoint. For example, in your own workplace try considering what an engineer or an accountant would think of your pricing policy. You can apply this across the spectrum – what effect will your marketing communications have on your colleagues? How would an NPD suggestion come across to an engineer or a designer?
>
> The same, of course, applies in service industries: try suggesting a new menu item to a chef, for example! Yet if we are to achieve anything as marketers, we have to understand other people – that is what marketing is all about.

The following are the categories of method you will need to understand:

- **Absorption costing**. This method prices according to a formula which includes all the costs of producing the product, including an allowance for overheads. It takes no account at all of what customers are prepared to pay, so it is not a market-orientated approach.
- **Cost base and marginal costing**. These again start from the costs the firm incurs, but this time the price is set at the point where producing one more unit of production would not be profitable. In practice, this is extremely difficult to calculate and again takes no account whatsoever of customers.

> **Key term**
>
> **Cost-plus**: the method of setting a price based on production costs plus profit.

- **Cost plus pricing**. This is the method most accountants and engineers are taught. It involves calculating the costs of production for a given production run, then adding on a fixed percentage for the profit. It is not market orientated, since it takes no account of competitors or of what customers might be prepared to pay.
- **Demand pricing**. This method is customer orientated, because prices are set at a level which will ensure that demand for the product is at a point which will meet corporate objectives. For example, a company may be able to produce economically at a particular level, so the price will be set to ensure that demand reaches that level, no more and no less. Alternatively, demand pricing can be used to determine the point at which profit will be maximised, that is, the point at which a further increase in price will reduce the production run past the most economical point, or a reduction in price will simply reduce profit without materially affecting sales.

> **Key term**
>
> **Penetrating pricing**: the pricing of a product below the competition in order to gain market share.

- **Penetration pricing**. Here the company sets prices low in order to capture a large part of the market before competitors can respond. This is a dangerous policy unless the company has very large resources: the risk of starting a damaging price war is high, and of course profits will be minimal or even negative, that is, a loss will be incurred. In some contexts, penetration pricing is illegal, because it represents unfair competition; in international markets, it is known as dumping or predatory pricing.

> **Key term**
>
> **Price skimming**: takes advantage of a new product's ability to maintain higher prices. The price is then reduced over time.

- **Skimming**. The company sets the price high initially so as to 'skim' the consumers who are prepared to pay a premium to be the first to own a new product. The price is then gradually reduced so as to 'skim' consumers who are prepared to pay a lesser price and so forth. This method is commonly used in consumer electronics markets, where the company has a technical lead which can be maintained long enough to shut out competitors. Unfortunately, most consumers know enough about marketing to realise that the price will fall if they are prepared to wait, so they often delay purchase.
- **Loss leader**. Some retailers will offer some basic commodities at a price which will actually lose money in order to lure customers into the store. Inevitably people will buy other goods while in the store as well as the loss leader, and the store makes its money on these other purchases. This principle has been carried over into other marketing situations – for example, companies manufacturing printers for home

computers sell the printers for less than the price of replacement ink cartridges and make their profit on the ink.

▶ **Key term**

Promotional pricing: price based around a promotion in the short-term.

- **Promotional pricing**. In order to even out demand or bring sales forward for other reasons, firms often offer extra discounts or 'sale prices'. Because such promotions cut profits, it may be cheaper to offer some other kind of promotion, but promotional pricing does have the advantage of being quick to put in place, and it is also very effective very quickly.
- **Odd-even pricing**. This is the practice of ending the price with 99p or 95c. Some studies have shown that this adds 8% to sales volumes, while other studies are less conclusive: certainly, it is less effective in some markets. An extension of this type of pricing is found in China, where some numbers are regarded as lucky: collectively, pricing which creates perceptions of this type is called psychological pricing.

▶ **Exam tip**

You are likely to be asked about the pricing of new products. If so, you should bear in mind that penetration pricing is extremely risky: it will almost always trigger a competitive response, and therefore a price war. Price wars are extremely damaging to profit margins, and sometimes companies end up bankrupt as the firm with the greatest level of reserves can undercut for the longest period of time. In some circumstances, penetration pricing may be illegal, if it is seen as unfair competition.

Many students imagine that cutting prices is the best way to compete. In most cases, it is probably the worst way to compete: it is certainly avoided by the vast majority of companies, because it cuts profits and it signals poor quality to the consumers. Incidentally, there is a general point here: whatever recommendations you make, you will need to consider competitive response. Competitors will not stand by and let you eat their lunch!

THE REAL WORLD

Internet auctions

The internet has opened up many opportunities for increasing consumer power, and nowhere has this been more apparent than in the proliferation of internet auction sites. Sellers are able to post goods for sale on sites such as eBay or eBid, with or without a reserve price, and buyers are able to place their bids from (theoretically) anywhere in the world. The price rises as more people bid, until there is only one buyer left, who then buys the product at the final bid price. Buyers can pay by credit card through an escrow company (which holds the funds until the goods are delivered) or can make arrangements directly with the seller for payment.

In recent years, the process has moved a step further with the advent of reverse auctions. Firms such as Letsbuyit.com bring buyers together to bid for products. The philosophy is simple: rather than bidding against other purchasers, and forcing the price up, the reverse auction arranges for buyer to join together and force the price down. For example, a manufacturer may offer an LCD TV for £800. If, however, 100 people are prepared to place a single order, the price might drop to £600. If 200 people are prepared to buy, the price might drop to £500. The price paid to the supplier will be dictated by the number of buyers, so Letsbuyit.com begins by negotiating a series of steps at which the price will fall. The prices are posted on the website for a set period, but once the product is sold out it will not be available to later bidders. If the number of people wishing to buy the product does not meet a pre-set minimum, the purchase does not go ahead, and the bidders pay nothing. Those who bid therefore run the risk of getting nothing: on the other hand, if the deal goes through, they will undoubtedly walk away with a real bargain.

The implications of this for traditional High Street retailers are potentially extremely damaging. Although they might argue that consumers will still prefer to come to a store where they are able to examine the products, get advice from the staff and even try out products, there is obviously nothing to stop consumers doing this and then making the actual purchase via a reverse auction. The implications for manufacturers are equally far reaching: although the power of retailers will be curtailed, which for many manufacturers would be a godsend, the power of consumers is likely to increase dramatically.

On the one hand, reverse auctions offer manufacturers a kind of instant marketing research; on the other hand, the process may mean the end of price skimming, psychological pricing and all the other tried-and-tested techniques for maximising the profitability of innovative products.

In some cases, consumers have gone even further by cutting out the internet service provider altogether. They have taken to send tenders to car dealers and other retailers asking them to bid for supplying the product. On a new-car purchase, an astute logged-on consumer might save hundreds or even thousands of pounds in this way – a saving that more than compensates for a few minutes spent sending out e-mails.

If these consumer-led techniques catch on, the outcomes are by no means entirely bad for manufacturers, but the overall effect is a major change in the way pricing is carried out. Prices are much more directly controlled by the end consumer than ever before – and marketers need to adjust to that fact.

ACTIVITY 6.3

Consider the internet auctions example.

1. How might a manufacturer retain a skimming policy when dealing with a reverse auction?
2. How might a car dealer encourage a prospective customer to increase the tender price?
3. What advantages might there be for manufacturers in participating in reverse auctions?
4. How might a manufacturer calculate the appropriate price bands for a reverse auction?
5. What might retailers do to counteract the effects of reverse auctions?

CHAPTER ROUNDUP

- Price has two major goals: value in the eyes of the customer and the achievement of the organisation's objectives.
- Price enables both the customer and the organisation to be satisfied and to feel they have achieved something, whether that be profit for shareholders or increased charitable donations, for example.
- There are several pricing methods that you need to be aware of including: cost plus pricing, demand pricing, penetration pricing and promotional pricing.

FURTHER READING

Since the marketing mix is such a large part of practical marketing, the reading tends also to be comprehensive. For more detail on the mix elements:

Baker, M. J. *The Marketing Manual.* Butterworth Heinemann. Chapter 7.

Blythe, J. (2009) *Essentials of Marketing.* 4th Edition. Harlow, Prentice Hall. Chapters 1, 6, 7, 8 and 9

Blythe, J. (2008) *Principles and Practice of Marketing.* 2nd Edition. Andover, Lengage. Chapters 1 and 12–22.

Brassington, F. and Pettitt, S. (2006). *Principles of Marketing.* 4th Edition. Harlow, Prentice Hall. Chapters 7–19.

Kotler, P. *et al* (2008) *Principles of Marketing.* 5th Edition. FT Prentice Hall.Chapters 13–22.

Jobber, D. (2009) *Principles and Practice of Marketing.* 6th Edition. Maidenhead, McGraw-Hill Chapters 8–17.

http://www.berr.gov.uk/index.html: The official website of the Department for Business Enterprise and Regulatory Reform. It contains a large number of articles and statistics on innovation, as well as advice for innovative businesses.

www.myoffers.co.uk: This website directs users to many sales promotions, providing a useful set of examples.

http://www.advertisingarchives.co.uk: This site contains advertisements going back over a hundred years.

http://brand.blogs.com/mantra/2005/02/lovehate_brand_.html: This is a chat room for people to post their messages of love or hate about brands. It offers some interesting insights into what goes wrong with brand messages.

http://www.strangenewproducts.com

National broadsheet newspaper

Marketing magazine

Product-based magazine in your organisation's area of specialism

REFERENCES

Booms, B.H. and Bitner, M.J. Marketing strategies and organisation structures for service firms. J.H. Donnelly, W.R. George. (ed.). In: *Marketing of Services.* 1982, Chicago: American Marketing Association 47–52.

Levitt, T. (1986) *The Marketing Imagination*. New York, Free Press.

Sinclair, J.M. *et al* (1984) *English Dictionary*, Collins.

QUICK QUIZ

1. Define a price in less than ten words.
2. Do not cut price, add what?
3. Why is price important?
4. Describe customer value.
5. Give two reasons why BMW out-sell cheaper vehicles in Europe.
6. List four of the differing pricing methods.

ACTIVITY DEBRIEFS

Activity 6.1

Consider what you would be willing to pay for a bottle of water in a desert or lifeboat, a large amount dependent how thirsty you were. Customers' willingness to pay can be directly influenced by their need and/or desire for the product. The higher the desire or need, the higher the price you maybe willing to pay, put simply.

Activity 6.2

The international software market

1. What is the role of consumer characteristics in software price setting? Consumers may want very different things from the software and have very different ideas on what is worth paying for and what is not. In different parts of the world, wealth and price perceptions clearly play a role: what appears cheap in one market appears expensive in another, and people's view of what represents value for money will also vary according to the cost of other products in the market, especially those against which people make comparisons.
2. Why should companies not charge one price for everyone, regardless of location? Perceptions of value for money will differ greatly between wealthy countries and poorer countries, since people are likely to translate prices in terms of how many hours they need to work to buy the item. Charging a lower price in poorer countries is still economically viable for software companies, since the upfront costs of developing the software have been met by consumers in wealthy countries. Charging a lower price simply opens up extra revenue at little cost.
3. Why might the product not represent the same value for money in each of its markets? Value for money is based on what the product will do for the customer. In a wealthy market, the labour savings gained by using computers soon pay for the software, because labour is expensive: in poorer countries the gains are less obvious, since pay is much lower. Software costing £100 represents a day's pay to the average Briton, but perhaps 3 months' earnings to the average Indian. Of course, wealth concentration is higher in India, so the 'average' Indian is unlikely to be in the market for either a computer or the software to run on it.
4. The market is huge, so why is there not room for many players to compete? Because of standardisation and compatibility issues, one standard for the world is likely to emerge. Competition is therefore aimed at dominating the entire market, not just at capturing a section of it: in a sense, there is only one market to go for. Smaller players have very little chance of entering the market, because of the economies of scale involved: the huge upfront costs of developing software can only be amortised over a very large production run, hence the product orientation is commonly seen in the software market.
5. How might a new software supplier (eg an Indian or Chinese supplier) price its products effectively in the world market? New suppliers would probably enter the market competing on price at first, but (given that their products would have to be compatible with other products) an Indian or Chinese supplier would still need to enter the world market on a similar pricing structure as the current major players, since they would find it difficult or impossible to fight a lengthy price war.

Activity 6.3

Internet auctions

1. How might a manufacturer retain a skimming policy when dealing with a reverse auction? Manufacturers can set a series of price levels according to the quantities bought and can set those levels wherever they want: this is, in effect, what skimming does. However, there is no control over when each price applies, only over the number of people needed to trigger the next price reduction. This means that people who would have been prepared to pay a higher price will in fact obtain the product at the lower price, which destroys the point of skimming.

2. How might a car dealer encourage a prospective customer to increase the tender price? Car dealers can offer extras, but in particular a car dealer might be able to offer something which other car dealers are unable or unlikely to match, for example, free delivery to the customer's home or free driving lessons for the customer's older children.

3. What advantages might there be for manufacturers in participating in reverse auctions? From a manufacturer's viewpoint, a reverse auction represents an opportunity to sell a lot of products in one sale, often for more than would be the case if the firm went through wholesalers. However, the extra administrative effort and the possibility of annoying the existing distributors might outweigh the benefits. Clearly, it is in the manufacturer's interests to sell large quantities of product in one hit, but not at the expense of damaging the existing distribution chain, which will undoubtedly represent the bulk of the business.

4. How might a manufacturer calculate the appropriate price bands for a reverse auction? Manufacturers would need to take account of the economies of scale involved in making a bulk sale, the extra administrative burden of dealing with the sales, and the extra risks involved. They would also need to consider delivery costs to a lot of individuals rather than to a single distributor, and the potential costs attached to auctions which fail to reach the minimum number needed to make the sale worthwhile.

5. What might retailers do to counteract the effects of reverse auctions? Retailers probably have little to fear from reverse auctions, as they are time-consuming and potentially unproductive for consumers – the savings may well be outweighed by the hassles. Having said that, retailers should be able to emphasise the greater convenience, the availability of advice and the quality of their after-sales service. Retailers can generally compete well, provided they offer a good enough service to their customers – which is, of course, the basis of marketing.

QUICK QUIZ ANSWERS

1. Willingness to pay equals willingness to sell for.
2. Add value.
3. Contributes to profits and financial success of business, can give perception of quality, competitive tool in the market.
4. It is the understanding that customers get more than just the product or service from the price paid.
5. Customers are willing to pay a higher price for what they see as a higher quality product, therefore better value for money.
6. Absorption costing, cost-based/marginal costing, cost-plus pricing, demand pricing, penetration pricing, skimming, loss leader, promotional pricing and odd-even pricing.

CHAPTER 7

The marketing mix – place

Introduction

Availability is a critical factor in managing the marketing mix. Here in Chapter 7 we will look at the channels of distribution organisations may have in place to enable them to satisfy customers' needs effectively, and, of course, to meet their own requirements for profit or value. You can have the best product in the world but if no one can locate it you will be unsuccessful. There are many factors to consider when selecting an appropriate distribution channel. This may be as simple as how far we have to travel with the product, or the characteristics of the product itself. Distribution and logistics will look at how we get buyers and sellers together, having the correct quantities available, maintaining the price or providing the right level of service.

The choice of distribution channel may depend on how far a manufacturing organisation wishes to carry its product, or where the customers are based. This chapter will explore key issues in channel decisions and supply chain management including the role of distribution in the marketing mix. It will look at various channels of distribution and consider the importance of the technologies that we now have in the digital age.

After working through this section, and carrying out the associated reading, you should be able to:

- Define the different components of distribution channels and show how they work together to create a distribution strategy.
- Explain the factors that influence channel and distribution decisions.

Topic list

Syllabus references

3.7	Define the different channels of distribution, and the roles they play in a co-ordinated marketing mix: ▪ Wholesaling ▪ Retailing ▪ Direct marketing ▪ Internet marketing ▪ Vending ▪ Telephone selling ▪ Franchising ▪ Digital/e-channels
3.8	Explain the factors that influence channel decisions and the selection of alternative distribution channels: ▪ Multiple channels ▪ Location of customers ▪ Compatibility ▪ Nature of the goods/services ▪ Geographic/environmental/terrain ▪ Storage and distribution costs ▪ Import/export costs

1 Different distribution channels

Place is often replaced with **distribution**; it describes the process of making the product or service available to the customer. So in today's market many traditional high street retailers use the internet to also allow their customers to buy online, therefore making the service of retailing available 24 hours a day. Alternatively high priced, exclusive products such as expensive jewellery will only be available from very few global outlets, maintaining their exclusive label with the lack of availability.

> **Key term**
>
> **Place**: an understanding that customers can only buy if the product is available and easily obtained.

Getting the product into the right place, at the right time and in the right condition for customers to buy it is the 'place' element of the marketing mix. Many firms have differentiated themselves entirely on the place element: Avon Cosmetics, for example, broke new ground by selling products door-to-door rather than through department stores and pharmacies. By so doing, the company opened up an entirely new market among women who were housebound for whatever reason.

> **Key term**
>
> **Distribution**: the means by which products and services are moved from producers to consumers.

There are various players in the **distribution process**, as follows:

- **Wholesalers**. These firms carry out a number of useful functions in terms of bulk breaking of large shipments, assorting different types of product into convenient quantities for shipping out, and so forth: they buy goods themselves and sell them on, but not to the final consumers.
- **Retailers**. These intermediaries sell to final consumers. They may or may not operate from a store: mail order and internet retailing are also retailers. Any organisation which sells to end users is a retailer, whatever the medium involved.
- **Agents**. These people do not buy goods themselves, but they do act as go-betweens, selling manufacturers' goods to wholesalers and retailers. Agents can be particularly useful in overseas markets, where they know the local laws and customs and have local knowledge: often an agent can save a small firm from having to set up warehousing and marketing operations overseas.

- **Export houses and import houses.** These firms specialise in buying or selling goods from other countries. They may or may not take possession of the goods – in many cases, goods are shipped directly from the producer to the foreign wholesaler.

Key term

Intermediary: organisations that are part of the distribution channel.

There are several other types of **intermediary**, but the following routes allow the supplier to remove intermediaries from the equation altogether and sell directly to consumers.

- **Direct marketing.** This is a set of techniques by which products are promoted via a medium which allows a direct response from the customer, for example, a press advertisement which contains a coupon, or a mailing which contains a reply-paid order form.
- **Vending machines.** These allow people to purchase directly from the machine, using coins or (in some cases) credit cards. Vending machines need to be filled with product and emptied of cash, of course, and also the site owners will charge a rental, so the overall cost might be higher than using a traditional retail route. What vending machines do best is provide access to places traditional retailers might have trouble reaching – station platforms, office corridors, factory floors and so forth.
- **Telephone selling.** Generally considered to be a part of direct marketing, telephone selling can be inbound (customers call as a result of seeing a marketing communication) or outbound (customers are called by telesales operators). Outbound telesales has proved extremely unpopular with consumers in recent years, and verbal attacks on telesales operators mean that staff turnover is high and stress levels can become excessive. Some firms have relocated their call centres overseas, which has two advantages: first, costs are likely to be lower if the call centre is relocated to a low-wage economy, and second, time-zone differences sometimes mean that a 24-hour service can be maintained without requiring staff to work through the night. Again, overseas call centres have proved unpopular with the public, partly because of concerns about security and partly because of concerns about job losses in the United Kingdom.
- **Franchising.** A business franchisor offers exclusive rights to a franchisee to use the corporate brand name within a specific geographical area or other segment. McDonald's is probably the best-known example of a franchise: such businesses are closely regulated by the franchisor to ensure that the brand values remain intact. There are often detailed contracts which set out instructions on how the franchisee will use the product, what marketing approaches to try, what operating procedures should be used and details about the quality of service provided. In return the franchisee will be offered some payment or profit on the sale of the products. Of course, the franchisor gains market coverage, increased sales, control over the operation, access to information and secure distribution. There are some disadvantages, however, including lack of total control, potential conflict within the franchisee network, and in addition it can be expensive to start as a franchisee.
- **Electronic retailing.** Online retailing is becoming more and more commonplace as consumers become more internet-literate. There are drawbacks: delivery of goods can be problematic, especially to people who are not at home, and mistakes happen when people are using unfamiliar websites.

Because intermediaries usually add value by the various activities they undertake, it is often not beneficial to cut them out of the picture. For example, a cash-and-carry wholesaler adds place value for small retailers or caterers. They are able to obtain most or all of their supplies in one place, which is a considerable saving in time and effort: cutting out the wholesaler would mean that each producer would have to deliver to each retailer, probably in uneconomic quantities, and giving the retailer the problem of dealing with a constant stream of deliveries happening at all times of the day.

The value added by each intermediary will be greater than the profit margin 'charged', otherwise other intermediaries will quickly appear to replace the inefficient one.

▶ **Exam tip**

It is very common for people to talk about 'cutting out the middle man' as a way of reducing the cost of goods. After all, wholesalers and other intermediaries do add on a profit for themselves. However, the efficiency gained by having a single point for shipments, plus help with marketing goods (sometimes into specialist markets) more than compensates for the profit added. Therefore, removing intermediaries (disintermediation) almost always increases costs.

Familiarise yourself with various channels of distribution and consider which would be most suitable for each of several categories of product.

THE REAL WORLD

Cafédirect

This case looks at how organisations choose their distribution channels and what influences these decisions. It will also discuss why retailers are often the last link in the channel from raw material to consumer.

Cafédirect was born from a crisis in 1989, when the international coffee agreement collapsed, which resulted in the fixed price of coffee across the globe being removed. These this fixed global prices had been based on the cost of production. Once removed, intermediaries descended into the market. These intermediaries were able to buy coffee and the businesses and lives of millions of smallholder farmers around the world were threatened as they could only sell their crops to these intermediaries at the lowest prices. In answer to this huge business, economic and human problem, three countries – Peru, Costa Rica and Mexico – packed a container with coffee and shipped it to the UK. On arrival the beans were roasted and then sold via church halls, charity shops and at local events: Cafédirect was born.

This pioneering company then spent three years obtaining its Fairtrade Foundation mark and was one of the first coffee brands to achieve this. In 2012, the business is still innovating and moving beyond sustainability to prove that business can be a power for good by ensuring that its activities have a positive impact on the people, communities, countries and the planet.

Cafédirect is passionate about working with smallholder growers and businesses because they see the benefit in taste. It believes in business being a force for good. So the partnerships of growers and suppliers are at the very heart of the business. Cafédirect will bypass the conventional market, obtaining its coffee, tea and cocoa directly from the growers, building long-term and personal relationships. It has built an ethical business which now is the gold standard and in 2010 it received the Sustainable City Awards (City of London). It is a business that pays growers a fair price for their crop, but it also funds programmes of development.

The Cafédirect range of Fairtrade products has now moved on from just coffee sold in churches and community centres and now has a range of coffees, teas and hot chocolates which are sold via a range of retailers, which include: Waitrose, Sainsburys, Morrisons, Tesco, Asda and Dunnes Stores in Ireland, together with a number of independent stores and of course online at their own Ethical Superstore. They were ranked the number one ethical tea and coffee brand in the Good Shopping Guide 2010 and achieved the top rating in each of the 15 categories.

(Cafédirect, 2012)

ACTIVITY 7.1

Consider the Cafédirect example:

1 Why do you think Cafédirect moved from church halls to supermarket retailers?
2 What factors do you think influence Cafédirect when choosing a retailer?
3 What factors influenced the choice between direct and now indirect?

Exam tip

If you are asked about distribution channels, you will be expected to understand the strengths and weaknesses of different approaches. Short distribution channels give more control to the producer, but are often less efficient and increase costs. Ensure that, if asked a question which involves distribution, you consider both the strategic aspects of channel choice and the role of logistics in getting products to customers.

THE REAL WORLD

Amway: Place/Distribution

This case study looks at the alternative distribution method of a traditional range of products which would normally be sold via a retail outlet, either shop or supermarket. Household cleaning and cosmetics products sold by individuals from their own home, which gives Amway a competitive advantage and unique selling point over its competitors.

In 1959, Rich DeVos and Jay Van Andel founded Amway, operating out of the basements of their homes. The partners were ex-servicemen who believed in the American way – hence the name of the firm. Amway operated then, and operates now, by encouraging people to found their own businesses to sell Amway products. The products range from household cleaning materials through to cosmetics and all are sold by individuals operating from their own homes. Amway products are not available in retail shops and most of the individuals selling them deal only with their friends, work colleagues and families.

The system is relatively straightforward (see below). Amway sells the products to individuals (called Independent Business Owners or IBOs) who then have two responsibilities. First, they sell products on to final consumers and, second, they recruit more people to become IBOs. Recruiting more IBOs means that the recruiter moves up the Amway hierarchy and earns commission based on the new recruit's sales levels. This system, known as multi-level marketing, means that Amway has automatic growth built into it, and so by 1980 the firm's turnover passed the billion-dollar mark – no mean achievement in only 20 years. By 2009 the company had 3.3 million IBOs in 80 countries worldwide, a turnover in excess of 8 million US dollars and with little sign of the growth slowing down. In the same year, their 50-year anniversary, they launched a new business strategy – 'creating change through leadership'.

In February 2012 Alticor Inc. the parent company of Amway UK announced that global sales had exceeded $10.9 billion for 2011. This result represented a 17 percent growth over 2010 and is the sixth consecutive year of growth for the company. More than 3 million people in 80 countries worldwide now sell Amway products in the Amway way: direct selling.

Diagram demonstrating the differing Amway approach to distribution/place

Traditional approach	Amway
Raw materials	Raw materials
Manufacturer	Manufacture and distribution
Retailer	IBO
Customer	Customer

(Amway, 2012)

2 Influences on channels of distribution

Distribution falls into two main areas: **choosing the right channels** and **physical distribution** (or logistics) which is concerned with transporting products to the right locations. Choosing the right channels through which to send goods is a strategic decision based on the choice of target market and the product characteristics, whereas **logistics** is a set of tactical decisions which involve transport decisions, warehouse decisions and financial decisions. Logistics is also based on product characteristics, as well as market infrastructures and market conditions.

When setting up a channel of distribution the supplier/manufacturer should consider a number of different things. These would include: customers; the nature and type of goods and/or service; competition; costs; and supplier and intermediary characteristics. Organisations should also consider the intensity of the availability they require which could be linked to brand values or the overall market. Organisations could consider one of three methods:

- **Intensive**: the product is supplied in as many places as possible to improve sales. A good example is Coca Cola, which is sold in every possible way, from vending machines to high class restaurants and bars.
- **Selective**: the product is supplied to a limited number of outlets which would suggest it is harder to obtain and costs more. If you consider new car sales, you do not want a high number of outlets because the purchase of a new car happens very few times in a customer's life.
- **Exclusive**: the channel of distribution is very limited, enabling the retailer to give their product an air of exclusivity. There may be only one outlet per country, for example.

Figure 7.1 Potential channels of distribution

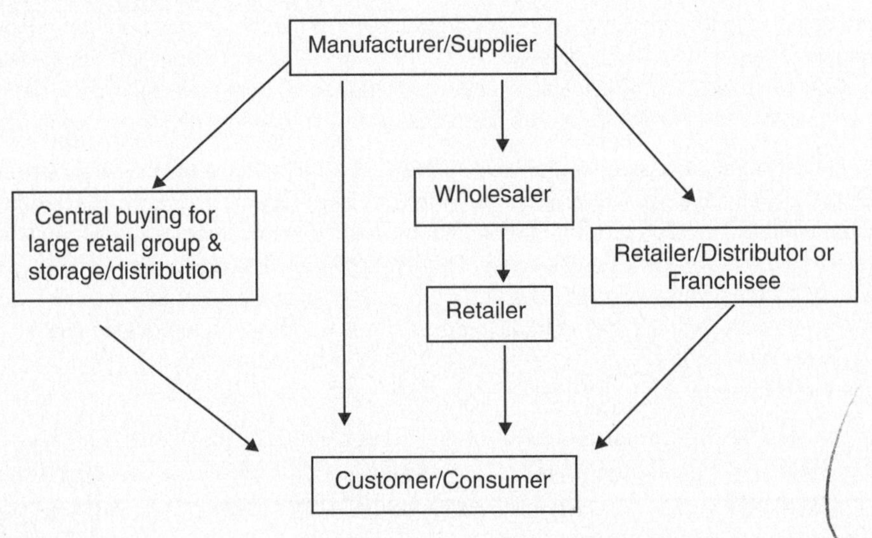

Each stage can increase costs and therefore price, as each intermediary will need to make profit. However it can also assist in breaking bulk, storage, increase the range available, giving market information and developing different markets.

ACTIVITY 7.2

Consider the last item you purchased; now think about how many individual organisations were involved in making that product or service physically available to you.

> **Key term**
>
> **Physical distribution**: how a product is handled and moved about to ensure its availability.

The next case study considers **logistics. Logistical issues** include the following decision areas:

- **The possibility of using multiple channels**, which means a different delivery system for each channel. For example, a food manufacturer might have one system for delivering to caterers (perhaps through a cash and carry warehouse), another for delivering to supermarkets (perhaps direct delivery using the company's own trucks), and still another for independent grocers. Multiple channels need to be handled carefully, since some channel members (eg wholesalers) might feel that they are being bypassed and therefore undermined.

- **Location of customers**. Customers in remote locations will need different physical distribution solutions from those located in urban areas. Obviously, a global market will require special measures.
- **Compatibility**. The selected delivery method must be compatible with the channel, the product, the customers and the supplier. Some customers will need rapid, reliable deliveries (spare parts delivery to car repairers being one example), whereas for other customers rapid delivery is less important than, say, reliable delivery times.
- **Nature of the goods/services**. Perishable goods clearly need to be delivered more quickly (and probably therefore more expensively) than non-perishables. Often air freight is actually cheaper than surface transport for items such as fresh fruit or fish, because there is less wastage.
- **Geography, environment and terrain**. Clearly deliveries into northern Alaska require different techniques from deliveries into Iquitos in Peru: apart from the obvious climatic differences, Iquitos has no road access to the outside world, so everything has to be delivered either by river or by air.
- **Storage and distribution costs**. Warehousing can be an expensive issue, hence the idea of just-in-time purchasing by which components are delivered in small batches, theoretically at the exact time they are needed in the factory, thus avoiding the cost of managing a store. Just-in-time has fallen into disrepute in recent years because it often results in trucks waiting outside the factory gates for the exact moment to deliver, resulting in greater waste on the part of the supplying company.
- **Import/export costs**. Apart from transport costs, there may be customs duties to pay on goods, and there will always be international insurance payments to make.

Key term

Logistics: describes the movement and handling of products. It includes warehousing, materials management, stock levels and information systems.

THE REAL WORLD

Giant Bicycles

In 1972, the Giant Manufacturing Company was first established in Taiwan, producing bicycles for the local market. In fact, the company was not giant at all at that time, but the name proved to be a prophetic one because within eight years Giant was the largest bicycle company in Taiwan and was looking to expand internationally.

An obvious overseas market for Giant was the Netherlands, where everybody owns at least one bicycle and the entire country is networked by bicycle tracks. In 1986, Giant opened its first overseas sales office in Holland: in the following year, the company opened up in the United Kingdom and the United States, and by 1991 had offices in six overseas countries, including Japan and Australia. Its first overseas factory was opened in the Netherlands in 1996.

Giant has had notable successes on the racing circuit and has its own race team: the team won the team prize in the Tour de France and the World Cup, and the company expects to build on this success in the future. The rapid expansion of the company has not been without its problems, however: despite a huge investment in IT, and a commitment to 'the local touch', the company still faced an enormous problem in terms of logistics.

Apart from having to consider local needs and tastes (eg Dutch cyclists predominantly use their bikes to commute to and from work, whereas Americans use their bikes for leisure and exercise), the company has been faced with the problem of shipping bikes worldwide from only three factories (Taiwan, China and the Netherlands). Because of the wide range of characteristics of cyclists (Dutch people are the tallest in the world: Japanese people are among the shortest), the company not only needs to produce a wide range of bikes, but also needs to ensure that stocks of bikes in the various retailers throughout the world can meet the demand. Giant makes over 3 million bicycles a year, but may need to deliver only one or two to a specific small retailer, perhaps in a remote area.

For Giant, the problem is complex. Worldwide distribution is difficult to arrange at the best of times, but given the huge variation in needs of customers, and the wide range of retail outlets which must be supplied, the company had a major logistics problem. Giant bikes are available on every continent, through over 10,000 retail outlets.

Giant therefore contacted Wincanton Group, a major European logistics company. Wincanton offers a full logistics service, including warehousing, intermodal transport (transport which involves different types of vehicle), customs clearance, document and records management, store services and even aircraft refuelling. Wincanton operates a fleet of vehicles, including lorries, barges and trains, and the company even manages sea ports and inland ports for barge transportation.

Wincanton's roots lie in the United Kingdom (it was originally a subsidiary of the dairy company that later became Cow and Gate), but its operations now cover almost the whole of Europe. The company handles logistics for major firms such as BMW, Tesco, Dow Chemicals, Electrolux and Hewlett–Packard, so shipping and storing bicycles presented no major problems.

Wincanton's success is due in no small measure to the company's innovative use of IT. Since Giant Bicycles also has a strong IT base, the companies were able to interface their systems and exchange data directly, greatly improving the efficiency of the overall system.

Giant Bicycles Ltd is moving into the 21st century with more new products – an electrically assisted bicycle was introduced in 1999, followed by a range of models which are available worldwide. The company's innovative Maestro suspension system has proved to be hugely popular, and the company also makes folding bicycles. However, no matter how many new models the company produces, and no matter how many markets it targets, Wincanton is confident in being able to provide the necessary logistical support.

ACTIVITY 7.3

1. What are the advantages of using a firm like Wincanton?
2. How might Giant Bicycles enter markets where Wincanton is not represented?
3. What are the main problems Giant faces in terms of logistics?
4. What challenges does Wincanton face in the 21st century?
5. What type of information might the companies exchange via their mutual IT systems?

CHAPTER ROUNDUP

- 'Distribution', 'place' or 'logistics' are about making a product available to the customer.
- There are many different ways to get your product from maker to buyer.
- There is a vast array of different intermediaries involved and the organisation must choose the best way to achieve its objectives.
- Today's environment allows marketers to use new technology to connect with their customers and use new distribution methods to make products available.

FURTHER READING

Since the marketing mix is such a large part of practical marketing, the reading tends also to be comprehensive. For more detail on the mix elements:

Baker, M. J. *The Marketing Manual*, Butterworth Heinemann. Chapter 7.

Blythe, J. (2009), *Essentials of Marketing.* 4th Edition. Harlow, Prentice Hall. Chapters 1, 6, 7, 8 and 9.

Blythe, J. (2008), *Principles and Practice of Marketing.* 2nd Edition. Andover, Lengage. Chapters 1 and 12–22.

Brassington, F. and Pettitt, S. (2006). *Principles of Marketing.* 4th Edition. Harlow, Prentice Hall. Chapters 7–19.

Kotler, P. *et al* (2008) *Principles of Marketing.* 5th Edition. FT Prentice Hall.Chapters 13–22.

Jobber, D. (2009) *Principles and Practice of Marketing.* 6th Edition. Maidenhead, McGraw-Hill Chapters 8–17.

http://www.berr.gov.uk/index.html: The official website of the Department for Business Enterprise and Regulatory Reform. It contains a large number of articles and statistics on innovation, as well as advice for innovative businesses.

http://www.myoffers.co.uk: This website directs users to many sales promotions, providing a useful set of examples.

http://www.advertisingarchives.co.uk: This site contains advertisements going back over a hundred years.

http://brand.blogs.com/mantra/2005/02/lovehate_brand_.html: This is a chat room for people to post their messages of love or hate about brands. It offers some interesting insights into what goes wrong with brand messages.

http://www.strangenewproducts.com

National broadsheet newspaper

Marketing magazine

Product-based magazine in your organisation's area of specialism

REFERENCES

Amway (2012) Amway Parent Surpasses USD $10.9 Billion in Sales. http://globalnews.amway.com/index.php?s=2933&item=122414 [Accessed June 2012].

Booms, B.H. Bitner, M.J. Marketing strategies and organisation structures for service firms. J.H. Donnelly, W.R. George. (ed.). In: *Marketing of Services.* 1982, (Chicago: American Marketing Association 47–52.

Cafédirect (2012) http://www.cafedirect.co.uk/shop/ [Accessed June 2012].

Cafédirect (2012) http://www.cafedirect.co.uk/wp-content/uploads/downloads/2011/05/Strategy-DIAGRAM_based-on-2009-AR_for-download.jpg [Accessed June 2012].

Ethical Superstore (2012) http://www.ethicalsuperstore.com/cafedirect [Accessed June 2012].

Levitt, T. (1986) *The Marketing Imagination*. New York, Free Press.

QUICK QUIZ

1. Define *place* in less than 12 words.
2. Who are the major players in the distribution process?
3. Name the direct methods.
4. List three factors that may affect the distribution of ice cream.
5. List a transitional 'place' for an tomato.
6. Describe *logistics*.

ACTIVITY DEBRIEFS

Activity 7.1

1. Why do you think Cafédirect moved from church halls to supermarket retailers? You would need to consider various aspects of Cafédirect strategy and its policies about free trade and environmental issues. The company's retailers would need to have similar views on these types of issues. The intermediary/retailer would also look to take their profit, which in this case could not affect the price received by the growers. The infrastructure would need to be improved to ensure these retailers had stock. Finally, the retailer would need to follow Cafédirect in terms of its marketing and promotional activities.
2. What factors do you think influence Cafédirect when choosing a retailer? It would be looking for a retailer who offered the same type of fair trade and ethical trading opportunities. It would need a retailer who offered access to the right type of customer and was willing to pay more for a product with such a level of environmental and ethical standards. A retailer who had access to a larger market to increase sales both internal and external.
3. What factors influenced the choice between direct and now indirect? Access to a larger market of coffee and tea drinkers. The ability to increase sales overall as the retail stores have wider coverage. The ability

to market and promote the ethical and environmental issues which are at the heart of Cafédirect to a much wider target audience.

Activity 7.2

This could be as simple as a cup of coffee, where the coffee bean grower would sell to a wholesaler and/or an agent in the country of origin. They would then sell through an export agent to a distribution service who would transport the beans to a roasting house who could then sell to a packaging company, who would then transport the bean to a distribution centre to enable the breaking of bulk before it reaches your local coffee shop who grind and add water for you. A huge number of individual companies and organisations are needed to get the coffee bean from plant to cup.

Activity 7.3

Giant bicycles

1 What are the advantages of using a firm like Wincanton? Wincanton supplies specialist services and is already familiar with distribution in most or all of Giant's markets overseas. Wincanton can also operates more efficiently when delivering to small outlets, since it would be able to fill a truck or container with goods bound for nearby destinations.

2 How might Giant Bicycles enter markets where Wincanton is not represented? Giant might look for a local distributor or agent, or might operate through wholesalers in the area. It may be possible for them to find another logistics firm able to fill the gaps in Wincanton's coverage.

3 What are the main problems Giant faces in terms of logistics? The main problems are the global nature of the business, the differing sizes of retail outlets, the location of outlets in terms of national transportation infrastructure and (occasionally) the small delivery quantities.

4 What challenges does Wincanton face in the 21st century? Wincanton is facing problems from global competition and from the rapid growth in alternative distribution systems. A growing expectation for just-in-time delivery, and an impatience with failed deliveries, will also impact on the firm. Increased customer expectations, particularly regarding delivery reliability and order tracking, may also affect Wincanton's operations.

5 What type of information might the companies exchange via their mutual IT systems? The main type of information will be order tracking, since customers will contact Giant with the query but Giant may not have the information. Sales forecasts would be useful for Wincanton to have, since these will help with their own forward planning, and obviously ordering information will be important.

QUICK QUIZ ANSWERS

1 How the product or service is made available to customers.

2 Wholesalers, retailers, agents, export/import houses, manufacturers, raw material providers.

3 Direct marketing, vending machines, telephone selling, franchising, online.

4 Intermediaries such as wholesalers, retailers, transport/distribution organisations must have facilities to keep frozen; centres of population; and climate.

5 Farmer/grower, specialist chilled transport company, wholesaler, fruit and vegetable retailer/supermarket, customer.

6 Physical distribution or transporting products to correct location.

The Chartered
Institute of Marketing

CHAPTER 8

The marketing mix – promotion

Introduction

This chapter looks at the last of the 4Ps – promotion. The word promotion implies that the seller is doing all the talking, however in marketing-orientated organisations this is all about two way communication, whereby the buyer responds to the seller's communication because there is a 'call to action'. So we can see that the term 'marketing communications' has become popular, which is used in the syllabus and the examination.

It could be suggested that without promotion the other 3Ps are useless. You could have a great product at an excellent price in the right distribution channel, but without promotion no one will ever know it is there and therefore it will fail. It is all to do with the combination of all the elements because if one of the 4Ps is not right then everything will fail – price speaks volumes and the choice of distribution outlet says something about the product.

Within this chapter we will look at the types of tools you can employ, the media that could be used and how the audience will be important in the process. There have been huge changes in the way we communicate in the last few years, and new technologies and communication models have meant marketing communication needs to adapt and change to use new methods like the internet, email, Twitter and Facebook. So we will look at how we can harness these new and existing communication systems to put the right product in the right place at the right price.

After working through this section, and carrying out the associated reading, you should be able to:

- Evaluate the range of marketing communication tools and consider their usefulness in different circumstances.
- Evaluate the range of communications media and consider their impact in different circumstances.

Topic list

Promotion	1
Media decisions	2
Measuring the success of promotions	3

Syllabus references

3.9	Evaluate a range of marketing communications tools that comprise the marketing communications mix and consider their impact in different contexts: ■ Direct Response Advertising ■ Personal selling ■ Sponsorship ■ Public relations ■ Direct marketing ■ Sales promotions ■ Digital technologies ■ Website
3.10	Evaluate the range of marketing communications media and consider their impact in different contexts: ■ TV ■ Cinema ■ Bill boards ■ Press ■ Magazine ■ Web-advertising ■ Sales promotions

1 Promotion

> **Key term**
>
> **Promotion**: can also be called 'promotional mix' and consists of many different communication methods to tell potential customers about the products on offer, where to find them and at what price.

Promotion is **how we tell the customers**, consumers, distributors, trade intermediaries, retailers and potential customers about the product or service we have developed to satisfy their needs and wants. Most importantly, to tell them **where it is available**, **what it can do for them** and **how much it might cost**, so information about the other **3Ps** of the marketing mix. Non-marketers tend to think of promotion as being the whole of marketing, and it is certainly the most visible area that marketers manage. Promotion encompasses all forms of marketing communication, so many marketing academics and managers use the term 'marketing communications' to cover promotion in general.

Promotion has its own system of subdivision, **the promotional mix**. In its most basic form, it consists of the following five elements:

1.1 Advertising

> **Key term**
>
> **Advertising**: Advertising is 'any paid form of non-personal presentation and promotion of ideas, goods or services by an identifiable sponsor'. (American Marketing Association).

This is the paid insertion of a message in a medium. There is therefore no such thing as free advertising: promotion which is 'free' might be classified as public relations or word of mouth, but it is not advertising. Although advertising is often thought of as the main element in marketing communication, it is actually only the most visible element: the other elements can be equally, or more, important and may even absorb more of the firm's resources. Advertising has the advantage that the marketers can control the content and to some extent the audience by choosing the most appropriate medium. The biggest drawback of advertising is that people find it relatively easy to avoid – they skip past the pages the advertising is on or change channels while the TV commercials are on. Advertising also suffers from a lack of credibility: people are aware that the advertiser has an agenda to follow and usually assume that the advertiser's needs will come ahead of the consumer's needs.

1.2 Public relations

> ▸ **Key term**
>
> **Public relations**: a planned and sustained set of communications established to gain and maintain goodwill and understanding between the organisation and its markets.

This is all the activities that create a positive image of the company and its brands – press releases, sponsorship, event management and so forth. Public relations is about creating an impression of a company that is good to do business with, but it does not directly bring in sales. Companies with a good PR record have little trouble in selling their goods, however; for example, imagine the difference between an IBM salesperson arriving at a new prospect's offices and a salesperson from some unknown computer company arriving at the same time. The IBM salesperson would almost certainly have a much more positive reception and would be taken seriously immediately, whereas the unknown salesperson would have to begin by establishing some credibility before even being allowed to discuss products. Public relations has a major advantage over advertising in that it is much more credible – a press release is read as news, sponsorship builds on the reputation of the sponsored person or event, and so forth.

1.3 Personal selling

> ▸ **Key term**
>
> **Personal selling**: the presentation of information about a product given directly by an individual representing the provider of the product.

Probably the most powerful marketing tool, a salesperson calling on prospective customers to present the firm's products is also probably the most expensive tool, at least in terms of number of contacts made, but it has the major advantage that a salesperson can identify specific needs of a customer and propose suitable solutions from among the company's range of products. Top-class salespeople will often propose solutions from elsewhere as well, if the company's product range is insufficient. The important point to note about personal selling is that it is not about persuading people to buy things – it is about identifying and solving customer problems.

1.4 Sales promotion

This includes money-off discounts, buy-one-get-one-free offers, extra fill of the pack and in fact anything intended to give a short-term boost to sales. In most cases, the switch from one brand to another caused by a sales promotion is only temporary: typically, people either switch back to their usual brand, or (in the case of bargain-hunters) switch to whichever brand is on offer this week. Sales promotions rarely increase sales overall – they are good for bringing sales forward (because people stock up) and are good for shutting out competition (sometimes this is a good thing to do at traditionally busy times, such as Christmas, because it damages competitors' sales at a time when they were expecting a high revenue stream).

> ▸ **Key term**
>
> **Sales promotion**: a range of techniques designed to add value and achieve specific sales or marketing objectives.

Sales promotions can also be used in the business to business (B2B) sector to increase sales or shut out competition. Very similar methods are used but of course the quantities are much larger and the intermediary has the option of passing on the discount to the final consumer or retaining all the advantage themselves.

1.5 Direct marketing

Develops a direct relationship with the customer and has been much improved since the development of mobile and computer based communication and data capture tools such as CRM, SMS, call centres, mail order, loyalty cards, Twitter, YouTube and Facebook. It can be defined as 'The planned recording, analysis and tracking of customer behaviour to develop relational marketing strategies' (Machattie, 2010). The important elements of successful direct marketing include interaction between customer and organisation that can be tracked, recorded and analysed. This helps to ensure the interaction continues and the responses are correct for the customers' needs. Direct marketing is about a one on one relationship. For example, online retailer Amazon knows what its customers have searched for and therefore is able to offer them similar products (or opportunities to view products) that would be complementary to their purchase.

THE REAL WORLD

Promotion

This case looks at how stories can build a brand, an image or personality of a product over time and therefore link into any of the differing promotional tools to give the customer one or two simple messages: what can I do for you, where can I get it and how much will it cost me?

To quote Sir John Hegarty, founding partner and Worldwide Creative Director of Bartle Bogle Hegarty (BBH), "Story telling is probably the most powerful form of communication we have at our disposal. It has been incorporated by virtually every civilisation into their culture. It is the simplest, most memorable device we have for engaging, learning, entertaining and persuading. It's not surprising then, that so many great advertising campaigns are based around this simple devise."

So what better to communicate your products and services than a family. For the best part of six years the public has followed the ups and downs of the couple – as well as Jane's children from a previous relationship – including moving house, breaking up, getting pregnant and preparing for a wedding. All these family stories have been shown with 40 TV adverts along with bill boards, website and other press coverage.

The BT existing and potential customers were first introduced to the Family back in 2005 with Kris Marshall appearing opposite former Spooks actress Esther Hall, who plays his on-off partner, Jane. The Family are now looking to take a different direction as the children grow and mature, leaving the family home and looking for products and services of their own, evolving with new stories into 2012 and will include both familiar and new faces.

As the storylines have evolved and the Family became increasingly well-known, BT has developed the stories in a much more collaborative way, asking members of the public what they think and increasing the differing communication methods to include social media. For example when BT asked the public to decide on an outcome of the cliffhanger storyline, more than 1.6m votes were cast on Facebook, and the decision was made for Jane to become pregnant. They also made decisions about the wedding dress, car and first dance and this was then linked into the Britain's Got Talent TV show in mid-2011.

The introduction of new characters at the beginning of 2012 will examine the laughs, trials and tribulations of sharing a flat. This story has been based on sound research that shows that at least two in five people have lived in a flat or house share, and have done so with someone that they would happily never see again, so once again adding to the story. Hopefully the stories will not have to show any annoying flat sharing habits on screen, which includes stealing food, playing loud music at unsociable hours and not letting anyone else have the TV remote!

This case study demonstrates the value of telling a story in the marketing communications and/or promotional activities undertaken by organisations when promoting their products.

(Hegarty, 2011 and Sweney, 2010)

In fact, you can see our list is far from comprehensive: in recent years, direct marketing has been added by many commentators, but there are still many more promotion tools in the locker. Some of these are as follows:

- **Ambient advertising**. This is advertising which becomes part of the physical environment – messages on stair risers and petrol pump nozzles, art installations in city centres and so forth. Ambient advertising often cuts through advertising clutter (the effect of having so much advertising targeted at people that they simply ignore all of it). It also often has novelty value, so that people remember it and sometimes even tell their friends about it.
- **Websites**. An internet website can be interactive (almost all UK and American sites are interactive, but there are still some which are static, mainly in Eastern and Southern Europe). Websites offer an entirely different communications medium from any other, because they establish an automated dialogue with the customer. They therefore give the consumer a degree of control over the dialogue, whereas in most

cases promotions are either one-way monologues, in which the consumer has only a passive role, or managed by salespeople rather than by the customers.

- **Word of mouth**. This is probably the most powerful promotional medium available, since it is the most likely to be believed and acted upon. Word of mouth is informal communication between friends and family members: people like to talk about products they have bought and companies they have dealt with, so marketers try to ensure that word of mouth is positive rather than negative. This is, of course, out of a marketer's control, but it is possible to influence it considerably and encourage it. For example, positive word of mouth is generated by bring-a-friend schemes, whereby someone who brings a friend along or encourages a friend to buy is rewarded in some way. In fact, these schemes work even better if the friend is the one who gets the reward – it is a chance for the customer to do a favour for a friend and is more likely to result in repeat business as the friend is the one who feels grateful.
- **Word of mouse**. This is the online version of word of mouth and is also called viral marketing. Marketers put games or jokes online, with a hyperlink to send the URL to a friend. If the game is enough fun, or the joke is good (some companies use spoof advertisements for this), people will involve their friends in the joke or game. Sites such as Facebook, YouTube and Twitter have become home to many commercial organisations, however the benefit of following a soap powder, for example, on Twitter must be questioned. Clearly, if a posting on YouTube is a well-made spoof advertisement, the moderators allow it to remain. Viral marketing should be distinguished from spam: spam involves sending an advertising message to everyone in the individual's address book, so that the message is sent (eventually) to an audience numbered in the millions.
- **Product placement**. This means supplying products to film and TV companies to be used in the shows. At one time, producers were happy simply to be given the products to use as props, rather than have to go out and buy them, but the advantages of having a product appear and re-appear in a film, perhaps for many years as it is shown on TV, became so obvious that film companies now charge substantial fees for including branded products. In some cases, product placement deals are enough to fund a film entirely, and firms such as Coca Cola use product placement very extensively indeed.

▸ Exam tip

If you are asked to make recommendations about a communications campaign, you should consider carefully the needs and likely behaviour of the target audience. For example, some products are better suited to mass advertising than are others, and some people are more likely to take an interest in advertising than are others. Professional people such as doctors or lawyers will be interested in anything which relates to their profession – doctors want to find out about new medicines, and lawyers want to find out about changes in the law or the regulation of the profession. This means that they will read their respective trade journals and will probably read the advertisements.

On the other hand, instant coffee (which is a mass-market item) should be advertised in a mass medium, using an advertisement which cuts through the clutter. It is quite certainly the case that mass advertising will cost a great deal more than tightly targeted advertising, so it is essential that you do not recommend such a course unless you know there is a mass audience.

The promotional mix is similar to the marketing mix in that one element cannot substitute for another, and each element acts on the others to create an overall effect. In recent years, the concept of **integrated marketing communications** has dominated academic thinking: the idea that all the messages emanating from the company should be essentially the same, no matter which route is chosen, is intended to ensure that there is no conflict between different messages or media. In practice, integration is hard to achieve because of the wide variety of possible messages and, of course, the wide variety of media involved: for example, sales people are likely to tell customers whatever they need to know in order to make a purchase decision rather than simply repeat the corporate story verbatim. Likewise, a message placed on the internet has a different appeal and creates different perceptions from the same message placed in a specialist magazine or on a billboard.

ACTIVITY 8.1

Consider the last time you bought something from a salesperson (perhaps a shop assistant). To what extent did the salesperson discuss your personal needs? Were you asked about the uses you have for the product? Were you asked about how much you were expecting to spend? Did the salesperson seem interested in you?

If so, how did that make you feel? Would you be more or less likely to buy from someone who shows a genuine interest in your needs? Or would you prefer someone who just talks about the product?

THE REAL WORLD

The Mini Cooper

In the late 1950s, a designer by the name of Alec Issigonis was commissioned to design a completely new car. At the time, there was a world oil shortage due to the Suez crisis, so the new car had to be small, cheap to buy and run, but roomy: it should also break the mould of previous car design. Issigonis came up with a revolutionary design – the Mini.

The Mini was one of the first production cars to have front-wheel drive and the first to have the engine mounted transversely rather than in a fore-and-aft configuration. This made the engine compartment rather tightly packed, but gave more room for the passengers – and the lack of a transmission hump gave more space in the passenger compartment. Issigonis even gave the car tiny 10-inch-diameter wheels, so as to reduce the space taken up by wheel arches. The car was finally launched in August 1959, to a rapturous reception by the motoring press – the car was so revolutionary that people were hard-pressed to find anything ordinary in it.

During the 1960s, the car became a British icon. Despite some early teething troubles (the car leaked copiously whenever it rained and had an extremely lumpy gear change, for example), further versions were designed and snapped up by an eager public. Van versions, estate cars, convertibles and even the (supposedly) off-road Mini Moke were marketed. Issigonis said later, 'We made a car that was so unusual that it automatically became a status symbol.' Minis were seen everywhere and were owned by rich and poor, old and young: the car even featured prominently in the film, 'The Italian Job', starring Michael Caine and Noel Cowerd. Alec Issigonis was knighted by the Queen for his services to industry – a rare event for a humble industrial designer.

During the 1970s and 1980s, the car's fortunes slumped. Other small cars had entered the market, and poor quality of manufacture, frequent strikes at the factory and heavy competition from better-engineered Japanese cars caused sales to dwindle. Altogether, 5.5 million Minis were manufactured: many of them are still running, and in fact every part of the original Mini is still being manufactured somewhere to serve the army of Mini enthusiasts who keep these cars on the road.

Issigonis is quoted as saying, 'When I design my cars, they are styled so that they couldn't be obsolescent.' This has proved to be a telling statement. After BMW took over the Rover car company, it acquired the rights to the Mini design and decided that the car was due for a revival – updated, to a modern specification, with the 21st century safety features, but recognisably the Mini. For BMW, the problem shifted: they had to figure out the best way to cash in on the Mini's iconic status!

At first, the Mini Cooper was launched in the United Kingdom, to great critical acclaim. The car was no longer the cheap runabout of the 1960s – but the baby boomers who had owned the originals were now in a position to pay the price to own a design classic. In addition, a new generation of Mini fans had been born.

For Rover, the key market to get into was the United States. With almost as many cars as people, the United States is the biggest car market in the world, and Rover intended to make inroads into it. The firm therefore hired US advertising agency Crispin Porter and Bogusky to run a $20 million campaign, with 25% of the spend going into print media. The objective of the campaign was to launch Mini into the United States by promoting it as an alternative culture called 'motoring' (as opposed to 'driving'). The British terminology helped to drive the campaign into becoming one of the most successful ever: the campaign won awards from Adweek and MPA Kelly, but more importantly it created such a demand for the car that long waiting lists appeared at dealers throughout the United States. The car itself won awards from consumer organisations, car journals and even the Kelley Blue Book (the car dealers' guide to used-car values). In 2003, the car had a further boost in its fortunes when 'The Italian Job' was re-made using Mini Coopers as the getaway cars.

Mini even has its own website (common for a car manufacturer – unusual for a car) on which the themes of motoring, fuel economy and quirky originality are combined. The site is extremely interactive (it even tells users to get out in the sunshine more

if they remain logged on for too long), and the site encourages visitors to 'e-mail a friend'. The website links to websites in other countries, each of which has a local character, but also conveys an air of Britishness. Each site includes an area where owners can join a Mini-owners club and can receive newsletters and special offers.

The overall aim is to recreate the sense of fun and uniqueness that characterised the first Mini, in the 1960s – and so far this seems to be paying off handsomely.

(BMWAG, 2012)

The Mini Cooper story shows us how a firm can integrate several communications media to generate a strong brand personality (or perhaps emphasise an existing brand personality). The agency, Crispin Porter and Bogusky, used the 'British' tag to create a novel and eye-catching campaign. Placing the product in 'The Italian Job' reinforced the brand values to the baby boomers who were the key target audience and also made great use of the internet, playing to the strengths of the medium as well as conveying the message.

▸ Exam tip

The promotional mix concept was first outlined in the late 1960s. There are many more tools available to marketers now, although the principle that the tools need to be combined in the right proportions remains. A full account of all the available tools is beyond the scope of this study guide, so you should read around your textbooks and other sources and familiarise yourself with the various tools.

You might also try observing marketing messages around you and categorising each one according to your list of tools – this will help you remember what they are and also give you some ideas, examples and templates to use in the examination.

THE REAL WORLD

Scotiabank

The Canadian banking system has, for many years, been an oligopoly – the major banks have controlled the market, and although regulation has been fairly tight, they have been able to set their own fees and service levels without too much risk of serious competition. As in most oligopolistic markets, however, the customer is the one who ends up losing out.

By the early part of the 21st century, banks in Canada had moved from being trusted custodians of the national finances to being regarded as a necessary evil, monolithic enterprises with little regard for the customer's needs or well-being. Brand image advertising had made promises which never materialised, and banks were not differentiating themselves – banking had become a commodity, and a disliked and mistrusted one at that.

Within this overall structure, Scotiabank decided to break the mould. The bank was at the time Canada's fourth largest – a position it had held since 1919 – and perhaps because of its relatively small size, it was regarded as a friendly, folksy bank. Its East Coast roots helped – Nova Scotia is often regarded as something of a rural backwater in Canada, and Scotiabank was thought of as being somewhat unsophisticated, to put it kindly. This was no bad thing, given the developing climate of mistrust of banks.

The bank saw an opportunity to focus on four areas where management thought the bank could increase its market share:

- **Home lending**. Scotiabank was losing market share, although mortgages were still big business for them: changes in the power of branch personnel to negotiate interest rates with customers were causing the bank to lose share.
- **Online activation**. Scotiabank was falling behind other banks in online banking, a potentially serious failing since online banking cuts costs for banks as well as increasing customer service.
- **Small business**. This represented a gap in the market, since none of the major banks had established itself as having capabilities in the small business loan market.
- **Investment**. Research showed that few customers were prepared to consider Scotiabank for their investment needs, and although this was not yet causing the bank any problems, it was clearly a ticking timebomb.

The bank had recently adopted a new core purpose, as follows:

'To be the best at helping customers to be financially better off by finding relevant solutions to meet their unique needs.'

The bank recognised that each of the markets it was aiming for had its own unique problems – but how were they to convey these effectively in an advertising campaign?

Scotiabank began by considering the unique aspects of each of the markets they wanted to enter. For home lending, they realised that buying the home was only the start of the financial problems – new homeowners need money for curtains, furnishings, legal fees, removal expenses and so forth, and may well have spent every last penny on the down-payment. The bank therefore introduced cash-back mortgages. For online activation, the bank decided that customers needed a lot of help in learning how the systems could help them manage their cash better, without making trips to the bank to check on bank balances. For small businesses, the bank understood that business people are far too used to being rejected by banks. For investment, the problem for customers is not so much about understanding the worth of using their tax breaks to invest, but actually finding the money to invest.

In Scotiabank's research, one word kept coming up: respect. So the bank developed its creative platform on three principles: reflect the truth of customers' lives, be relevant to getting ahead financially (by offering a tangible Scotiabank solution), and reflect the customer's perspective, not the bank's.

The ensuing campaign used a problem–solution format. Each advertisement began by showing a common everyday financial problem, followed by the Scotiabank solution to that problem. The same format was used for television, print and radio advertising – for example, a businessman was shown leaving another bank, having been rejected for the umpteenth time and being offered a deal with Scotiabank through their ScotiaOne business loan package. ScotiaOne offers a single package for the small business, covering both personal and business banking, and also offers business advice.

The results? Over a two-year period, Scotiabank increased its mortgage business by 13% ahead of the projected figures, it went from nowhere to being the industry leader in online banking in a period of only three months, it increased the number of credits in small business by 52% and experienced a 61% increase in dollar credits in small business, and it overachieved by 23% in recruiting new clients and overachieved by 11% in the investment business.

More importantly, compared with its rivals, it achieved the largest percentage awareness improvement of any Canadian bank, despite spending less than any of its competitors – another remarkable achievement, and one which can only have come about as a result of the advertising. In a market with very little differentiation, Scotiabank appears to have tapped into a real customer need - the need to be recognised as real people, not simply as account numbers.

ACTIVITY 8.2

Consider the Scotiabank example.

1. How did Scotiabank translate its vision statement into an advertising campaign?
2. What sales promotion techniques did Scotiabank use?
3. How did the three principles translate into an integrated communications campaign?
4. What difficulties might there have been in offering a single, integrated message to such a wide range of potential customers?

Whether or not the marketing communications are integrated, it is certainly the case that each promotional tool will only work in specific circumstances, and yet each tool has an impact on the others. The co-ordinating mechanism must always be the **brand image** – what is the personality of the brand, and where do we want the brand to be positioned in the customers' minds? This is long-term, strategic thinking: we are trying to develop competitive advantage for the brand by careful use of communication.

For example, a money-off sales promotion might increase sales in the short term, but might damage the brand image by making it seem cheap and downmarket. In some cases, manufacturers have asked stores not to promote their brands in this way, for fear of doing damage to a brand which has been carefully positioned against its competitors as an upmarket brand. Equally, an advertisement might have an effect on a PR campaign (or vice versa – since both might appear in the same medium at the same time).

▸ Exam tip

The promotional mix actually contains more than the four basic items – you will gain marks if you can 'think outside the box' and consider promotional methods which are unusual. You will also need to consider aspects such as the appropriate medium for your message: there is more on this later. You should, of course, link any recommendations to measurable objectives.

Keep in mind that, even though each element is taught as if it were a separate issue, you will be expected to consider all the elements as a whole (just as you did with the marketing mix as a whole). You will also need to distinguish carefully between the elements, in other words do not confuse advertising with PR (if you talk about 'free advertising', you mean PR or something else – advertising, by definition, is not free). Terminology is important in this, as in every other, profession: you need to be precise if colleagues (and examiners) are to understand precisely what you mean.

THE REAL WORLD

Viral marketing

Viral marketing has become one of the buzzwords of 21st-century marketing. To many people, it sounds vaguely distasteful – connotations of virulent disease spring readily to mind, and it almost sounds like the worst kind of manipulation. In reality, it is simply a term for electronic word-of-mouth promotion.

Although viral marketing is not dependent on the internet, it has become strongly linked with internet marketing because e-mail is an extremely easy way to propagate messages. Offline, viral marketing is referred to as 'word of mouth', 'creating a buzz' or 'network marketing', but it is in fact the same thing – it is any strategy that encourages individuals to pass on a marketing message to others, creating an exponential growth in the message's exposure and influence. These messages are powerful, because they are credible: word from a friend is much more acceptable than word from a manufacturer.

The classic example of a successful viral strategy is MSN's Hotmail free e-mail service. Hotmail was one of the first free e-mail services on the internet, and it owed its rapid growth to a very straightforward viral technique: firstly, the company gave away free e-mail addresses. Then, at the bottom of each message sent out by its users, it added the tag 'Get your private, free e-mail at http://www.hotmail.com'. This message was thus sent out to thousands more people, some of whom signed up for the service, and thus added to the number of people who propagated the name further.

Obviously, giving things away is not, in itself, a way to make money. However, Hotmail now has a large number of subscribers, each of whom is a target for buying other products from MSN. Every Hotmail subscriber sees several advertisements each time he or she logs on to send or receive messages, but this is a small price to pay for a free service.

To be effective, a viral strategy needs the following characteristics (Wilson, 2000):

1. There should be a free gift attached.
2. The transfer to others should be effortless.
3. It should scale easily from very small to very large, in other words the system needs the capacity to start small, but handle very large numbers of people fairly quickly, otherwise it will drown in its own success.
4. It should exploit common motivators and behaviours.
5. It should utilise existing communications networks.
6. It should take advantage of others' resources.

The Hotmail example fulfils all of these criteria, as does Adobe Acrobat. The Adobe Acrobat Reader is free software: anybody who receives a PDF file from an Adobe subscriber can download Reader so as to be able to read the file. This has meant that Adobe Acrobat has become the leading software for creating and sending PDF files – which means that everyone who buys Reader is potentially a customer for Acrobat since they are able to see the quality of the documents that it produces. Acrobat, of course, is emphatically not free software. Annual turnover at Adobe is $1.2 billion, and the company has 3,700 employees worldwide – so viral marketing must have something going for it.

Viruses used in viral marketing are not the same as the malicious viruses which occasionally infect innocent computers. The essence of viral marketing is that the sender knowingly transmits the marketing message. In some cases, such as Hotmail, the sender transmits the message automatically every time he or she uses the service. In other cases, websites have a link (labelled

'Send this to a friend' or something similar) which encourages the individual to forward the entire website to a friend who might be interested. In order for this to happen, the website must contain something of interest – a free computer game, a free IQ test, some free software and so forth.

In some cases, viral marketing can use messages and imagery which would otherwise not be allowed in mass media – for example, the viral campaign for Trojan condoms developed by The Viral Factory uses some risqué images to get the message across. These images are likely to be passed on: other campaigns by the same agency are less risqué, but are equally engaging. In each case, they appeal to a particular target market, which is likely to pass them on to people with a similar sense of humour and similar interests.

Viral marketing also takes root in word-of-mouth campaigns. Word of mouth can be generated by allowing customers and others to take guided tours of facilities. A prime example of this is Cadbury World, a theme park outside Birmingham which is dedicated to the history of chocolate. Families and school parties are shown how chocolate is made and how the ancient Aztecs used chocolate, and even shown around a museum of chocolate-related artefacts. There are many other ways to generate word of mouth: the main element in generating word of mouth is to provide customers with something interesting to pass on to their friends.

The bottom line in viral marketing is credibility. People trust their friends far more than they trust a company – and they will listen to their friends far more than they will listen to an advertisement.

ACTIVITY 8.3

Consider the viral marketing example.

1. Advertising is heavily regulated: it must, by and large, be truthful. No such regulations exist on contacts between friends, so why is viral marketing more credible than advertising?
2. How might the power of word of mouth be transferred to advertising?
3. What type of organisation might benefit most from viral marketing on the internet?
4. What other advertising media might be useful in driving customers to the website?

2 Media decisions

Choice of **medium** is as important as choice of tool, because the medium becomes part of the message. An advertisement placed in a cheap tabloid newspaper does not have the same message as the same advertisement placed in an upmarket broadsheet, and even TV advertising conveys different impressions according to the type of programme it is linked to.

Media can be assessed in several ways: the most basic is the cost per thousand, which means the amount it costs to reach a thousand people. This is not, in itself, sufficient: what is equally important is to ensure that the right people are targeted. Putting a message into the wrong medium simply means it will be ignored, because it will be going out to people who have no interest in the product: a popular newspaper might have a high readership and an attractive cost per thousand, but advertising a new material for tooth whitening here, for example, would be futile. The same material would be better publicised in the dental trade press or health and beauty magazines, as readers of these publications are more likely to be interested in the product.

The intention of most marketing communications and promotion is to solicit a reaction from the potential customer base and/or target audience. This reaction could be anything from a simple purchase to a more complex set of activities which may involve the start of a long and fruitful relationship. Whatever the required outcome or reaction it requires a 'call to action' to be included in the communication. 'Visit our website today to claim your discount voucher', 'In store today while stocks last' or 'Telephone 00 0990 9911 to get your free quotation now' are all types of call to action. There are countless others.

Exam tip

If you are asked to develop a promotional campaign, you must start by considering your customer base and aim it at them. Do not use television unless the product is really one which most people would want to buy: you will be wasting most of your budget. The more closely you target what you do, the more efficient use you will make of the budget.

For example, in one exam students suggested using TV to advertise prescription drugs to doctors. This is incredibly wasteful – the number of doctors who would see the advertisements would be very small as a proportion of the viewers, so the bulk of the cost would be wasted. In some countries, of course, such advertising would be illegal anyway.

Again, in any question of marketing – start with the customer!

The main media are as follows:

- **Television**. This medium requires the biggest budgets, but it also reaches the largest audiences. Until recently, targeting has been difficult because there were few commercial stations in the United Kingdom, but the advent of cable and satellite channels has provided at least some opportunity to target specialist audiences. Television advertising is costly but can have a low cost per thousand because of the very large viewing figures for some shows. It is most suitable for products with a very wide range of potential customers, for example, instant coffee or cleaning products.
- **Cinema**. This is often a neglected medium, but since cinema tends to reach a young audience, it can be very powerful, especially as it is difficult for the audience to avoid the advertising. Cinema audiences also tend to be wealthier and better educated than the average, so they represent a particularly desirable target audience for many products. The biggest advantage of advertising in cinemas, though, is that the audience are unlikely to ignore the advertisement. They are unable to switch channels as they would with TV, and they cannot get up and walk out while the advertisements are showing.
- **Billboards**. These are useful for localised campaigns, but are vulnerable to vandalism. Billboards are especially useful for retailers because locations close to the stores can be booked: billboard advertising can also be changed relatively quickly, since all that is needed is a new print of the poster and someone with a pot of paste and a ladder. For this reason, billboards tend to be used a lot during election campaigns.
- **Press**. This subdivides into mass media such as newspapers and popular magazines, and targeted media such as specialist hobby or trade magazines. Advertising in specialist hobby magazines is powerful because people are inclined to read the advertising: for example, someone who is a keen angler is likely to enjoy reading about new fishing lures in an angling magazine. Also, magazines are often kept for long periods (unlike newspapers).
- **Web advertising**. Pop-ups and banners can be powerful, but they can also be irritating for the audience. They do have the advantage of allowing interested consumers to respond immediately by being directed to an appropriate website. Weblinks are likely to be more effective, however, since many pop-ups will be blocked by the individual's firewall.
- **Radio**. This is often neglected as a medium, although it is cheap, flexible and difficult for the audience to avoid. It is often used as a reminder medium for TV advertising. People often listen to commercial radio while doing other things, such as driving, housework, decorating and so forth, so they are often receptive to the advertising.

Exam tip

You will be expected to understand the relationship between the promotional mix tools and the media through which they operate, so it is a good idea to consider how various brand managers use the media to convey the different tools. Try looking at how a product's features and benefits are conveyed in a magazine as opposed to the TV, for example. Consider ways in which the medium affects the message.

THE REAL WORLD

Full Stop

This case study examines an integrated campaign for a charitable organisation (ie not-for-profit). The campaign used a wide range of media to convey messages to several different groups, each with a different angle on the same basic problem and each with different needs.

In 2001, research conducted on behalf of the National Society for the Prevention of Cruelty to Children (NSPCC) showed that one in three people in Britain would not act to prevent a case of child abuse if they knew it was happening. The reason? They would not know what to do.

The NSPCC is over 100 years old. During that time, the charity has set out to protect children from all forms of abuse wherever and whenever it occurs – but without public support, they would have had no way of knowing that a particular child was suffering. The NSPCC relies on people calling in and reporting suspected cases – neighbours, teachers, parents of school friends and so forth. Since the charity was founded, other organisations have taken some of the burden of the work, however. Local authorities have Children's Services departments which investigate child abuse, the police have wide powers to act in child abuse cases, and other charities such as Action for Children and Childline (the emergency number which children can ring) have also contributed.

However, after discovering that many people would not know what to do if they knew a child was being abused, the NSPCC decided to run a major integrated marketing campaign aimed at stopping child abuse altogether. The campaign, called Full Stop, aimed to inform the general public about what to look for, and provided a telephone number (0808 800 5000) which people could call to report abuse.

The campaign included a series of TV advertisements using the Full Stop strapline, a billboard campaign featuring well-known personalities from the entertainment world, sport and politics, a radio campaign, a newspaper campaign and a website. Sponsored by Microsoft, the NSPCC campaign had four aims: first, to encourage people to report cases of child abuse; second, to encourage parents who might abuse their children to seek help when they feel that the stress is getting too great; third, to encourage children to talk about abusive situations in which they find themselves; and fourth, to raise funds for the charity. These aims were addressed at different times and using different advertisements, but the basic Full Stop message linked them all together. The campaign was backed up by a leafleting campaign and by a series of videos aimed at children and adolescents. Booklets distributed to schools, and an impressive website, have also dramatically increased the number of children who have come forward to report abuse.

One of the main outcomes of the campaign has been a huge increase in lobbying activities. Since the Full Stop campaign started, 140,000 people have come forward to help in the campaign; there is now a Children's Commissioner for Wales; 300 members of Parliament have signed the NSPCC Pledge on cruelty to children; and public awareness about child abuse has never been higher.

The NSPCC is realistic enough to know that child abuse will probably always happen. The fact that it could be prevented entirely if everyone worked together is undeniable, though, and the charity continues to work towards this ideal. Effective communication is a key plank in the platform for success.

ACTIVITY 8.4

Consider the Full Stop example.

1. What are the main communication factors which would prevent the NSPCC reaching its goal?
2. How might the NSPCC be more proactive in contacting potential abusers?
3. What other communications media might the NSPCC use?
4. What are the main problems for the NSPCC in producing an integrated campaign?
5. How might the NSPCC improve the integration of its campaign?

ACTIVITY 8.5

Analyse a newspaper in terms of its ratio of advertising to editorial content. You should find that the newspaper is around 40% advertising to 60% editorial. If you have access to a free newspaper in your area, try analysing the ratio for the free newspaper. Normally this would be about 80% advertising to 20% editorial.

How much of the newspaper is devoted to classified advertising (advertising grouped into specific categories such as houses for sale, cars for sale and second-hand goods) and how much is display advertising (advertisements for shops, branded goods, etc.)? Why do people buy newspapers – is it for the news stories, or for the classified advertising? Why do people avoid the display advertising, yet read the classifieds?

3 Measuring the success of promotions

Although an in-depth study of market research is outside the scope of the Marketing Essentials unit, it is useful to have some understanding of how **promotional campaigns** can be assessed.

Many non-marketers believe that the success of a promotional campaign can be measured in terms of sales, but in fact this is not true. For one thing, some tools such as public relations are not aimed at generating sales, but rather at generating goodwill and loyalty. For another thing, sales may be affected by many other factors such as competitive activity, government initiatives or the general economic climate. Today often you will also see organisations develop a whole set of 'Key Performance Indicators' (KPIs) around the success of a campaign. For example, in a new NHS campaign one KPI could be increased public awareness of the health risks of smoking.

For these reasons, it is more effective to measure communications effectiveness in terms of communications outcomes such as brand awareness, positioning of the brand relative to competitors, knowledge of distribution and increased tendency to loyalty. This view of communications was crystallised as the DAGMAR (Defining Advertising Goals, Measuring Advertising Results) model in the 1960s. The model implies that concrete, measurable communications objectives should be set for all advertising and the outcomes measured against these objectives. For example, an objective might be to raise brand awareness by 20% within six months: this objective is concrete and measurable, and is certainly a communications objective rather than a sales objective.

There are various techniques available for researching these issues, as follows:

- **Questionnaire-type surveys**. These are usually problematical due to the difficulty of designing questionnaires which address the issues accurately and do not lead the respondents towards specific answers. However, they can be useful in assessing brand awareness. Brand awareness can be assessed either by using a prompted recall test (in which a list of brands is provided and the respondent is asked to state which ones he or she recognises) or by an unprompted test (in which people are asked which brands in the product category they can remember, without being given any clues). Questionnaires can also be used to rank brands against competitors across various product attributes.
- **In-depth interviews**. This technique involves asking people to talk about the brand and about the advertising in an open-ended way, with some guidance from the researcher. It is a technique which requires great skill from the researcher in not 'leading' the respondent, but it can yield a great deal of information, and has the advantage that the respondent may identify issues which the researcher was not aware were important.
- **Focus groups**. This is a similar technique to the in-depth interview, except that the respondents are brought together as a group and invited to comment. This has the major advantage that the group members often spark off new discussion routes and can explore their ideas: since they often need to justify what they are saying to the group, the method compels them to think about what they are saying rather than simply telling the researcher what they think he or she wants to know. The danger with focus groups is that one or two members might sway the thinking of the others. Results are generally

quick to obtain, and a large proportion of commercial market research is now conducted using focus groups since they appear to have better predictive value than questionnaire surveys. They are notoriously difficult to analyse, however.

- **Sales patterns**. Although sales levels *per se* are generally a poor way to assess promotional success or failure, the pattern of sales can be indicative, provided it is used in conjunction with other methods. For example, repeat purchases can indicate greater loyalty, and surges in sales can indicate the success of sales promotions. Personal selling is almost always assessed in terms of sales volume, but seasonal factors can also be taken into account. Nielsen retail measurement services provide continuous tracking of product sales to consumers, based on information gathered at the retail point-of-sale. They can provide detailed information on sales, market share, distribution, pricing, promotional activity and merchandising. They can also try to measure consumer behaviour by monitoring more than 250,000 households throughout the world.
- **Pre-testing**. Advertising can be pre-tested by showing the advertisement to a typical customer and assessing his or her responses. Focus groups are especially useful for pre-tests, but of course the test assumes that people will actually pay attention to the advertisement in the first place – it is much more difficult to test whether an advertisement is eye-catching or not. This can be checked using a portfolio test, in which a series of advertisements is shown and the respondent is asked which ones he or she can remember.
- **Physiological measures**. This is a set of laboratory techniques in which individuals' responses are measured using such technology as eye cameras (which record the route an individual's eye takes when reading an advert), pupil dilation response (which measures the degree to which the person's pupils dilate when they see an advert – this is supposedly an indication of interest), and galvanic skin response, by which the electrical resistance of the skin is measured (also considered to indicate interest).

CHAPTER ROUNDUP

- Promotion is about communicating the other elements of the marketing mix to potential and/or existing customers.
- Promotion encourages customers to act.
- Promotion develops a two-way communication system and helps build relationships.
- New and existing media both have an impact on other elements of the marketing mix.

FURTHER READING

Since the marketing mix is such a large part of practical marketing, the reading tends also to be comprehensive. For more detail on the mix elements:

Baker, M. J. *The Marketing Manual*, Butterworth Heinemann. Chapter 7.

Blythe, J. (2009) *Essentials of Marketing.* 4th Edition. Harlow, Prentice Hall. Chapters 1, 6, 7, 8 and 9.

Blythe, J. (2008) *Principles and Practice of Marketing.* 2nd Edition. Andover, Lengage. Chapters 1 and 12–22.

Brassington, F. and Pettitt, S. (2006). *Principles of Marketing.* 4th Edition. Harlow, Prentice Hall. Chapters 7–19.

Kotler, P. *et al* (2008) *Principles of Marketing.* 5th Edition. FT Prentice Hall.Chapters 13–22.

Jobber, D. (2009) *Principles and Practice of Marketing.* 6th Edition. Maidenhead, McGraw-Hill Chapters 8–17.

Section 3 of Frank Jefkins and Daniel Yadin book *Advertising*, Prentice Hall gives good overview of the types of advertising.

Looking at B2B communications part 2 of Norman Hart's book *Business to Business Marketing Communication*, Kogan Page, gives good outline of the basic B2B methods.

Chapters 1 and 2 of P.R. Smith's book *Marketing Communications; An Integrated Approach*, Kogan Page gives a good insight into the marketing communications mix and plan.

http://www.berr.gov.uk/index.html: The official website of the Department for Business Enterprise and Regulatory Reform. It contains a large number of articles and statistics on innovation, as well as advice for innovative businesses.

http://www.myoffers.co.uk: This website directs users to many sales promotions, providing a useful set of examples.

http://www.advertisingarchives.co.uk: This site contains advertisements going back over a hundred years.

http://brand.blogs.com/mantra/2005/02/lovehate_brand_.html: This is a chat room for people to post their messages of love or hate about brands. It offers some interesting insights into what goes wrong with brand messages.

http://www.strangenewproducts.com

National broadsheet newspaper

Marketing magazine

Product-based magazine in your organisation's area of specialism

REFERENCES

BBH Global (2012) http://www.bartleboglehegarty.com/#!/global [Accessed on 22 June 2012].

Booms, B.H. and Bitner, M.J. Marketing strategies and organisation structures for service firms. J.H. Donnelly, W.R. George. (ed.). In: *Marketing of Services.* 1982, Chicago: American Marketing Association 47–52.

BMWAG (2012) http://www.mini.co.uk [Accessed on 22 June 2012].

BT (2012) BTLife Blog http://www.btlife.bt.com/btcustomers/bt-family-watch-the-story-so-far/ [Accessed 27 June 2012].

Hegarty, J. (2011) *Hegarty on Advertising; Turning intelligence into magic*. London Thames & Hudson Ltd.

Levitt, T. (1986). *The Marketing Imagination*. New York, Free Press.

Sweney, M. (2011) BT Family breaks up after 6 years. Guardian, http://www.guardian.co.uk/media/2011/dec/23/bt-family-breaks-up [Accessed on 22 June 2012].

The Nielsen Campaign (2012) http://www.nielsen.com/uk/en/measurement/retail-measurement.html [Accessed on 22 June 2012].

QUICK QUIZ

1. Define a promotion, in less than 20 words.
2. What are the elements of the promotional mix?
3. Give one word that is fundamental to promotional mix.
4. List four differing media that could be used.
5. List two types of media that would be best to use if you were looking to communicate with High Court Judges about a new book that could help them in court.
6. List three measurements which can be used to assess the success or failure of achieving the objectives of a promotional campaign.

ACTIVITY DEBRIEFS

Activity 8.1

This will depend largely on the last shopping experience you had. Good, bad or indifferent the process you went through will be influenced by the marketing communications you may have seen before or during this purchase. Did you need extra information or was it already provided by a magazine advert, web banner or research you had undertaken before the purchase? If the sales person asked you questions they were looking for information to ensure the product would satisfy your needs and this was part of personal selling. However, if you did not need that interaction some other communication must have given you the required information.

The level of interaction will be driven by you as the customer, however research suggests that sales in retail outlets are increased if the customers are engaged with, even if this is a simple 'good morning'.

Activity 8.2

Scotiabank

1 How did Scotiabank translate its vision statement into an advertising campaign? The vision statement was about treating people as individuals and finding solutions which would help make them wealthy – a very customer-orientated vision. The bank used this to develop a campaign showing people in typical 'problem' situations, then showing how the bank could help solve the problem.

2 What sales promotion techniques did Scotiabank use? The bank used the cash-back mortgage, the business and personal banking facility, and a hand-holding approach to online banking. These sales promotions encouraged loyalty, but they also encouraged people towards dependency on the bank for sorting out all sorts of financial problems.

3 How did the three principles translate into an integrated communications campaign? By using the problem–solution format, Scotiabank was able to show typical, relevant problems and show the solution (thus meeting the focus on the truth of people's lives principle). The bank showed how it could help people to generate wealth for themselves (the getting ahead principle) and by understanding how people were usually treated by other banks they were able to see things from the customer's perspective.

4 What difficulties might there have been in offering a single, integrated message to such a wide range of potential customers? The main problem would be ensuring that people felt that the message was relevant to them. Seeing people in typical problem situations would certainly have helped to convey the message: most of the situations would be fairly stereotypical of people's involvement with banks.

Activity 8.3

Viral marketing

1 Advertising is heavily regulated: it must, by and large, be truthful. No such regulations exist on contacts between friends, so why is viral marketing more credible than advertising? Credibility is about the source, not about the regulations surrounding it. People are more likely to trust someone they know, especially if the person has no obvious vested interest, rather than a stranger with an obvious interest in making the sale. Interpersonal communications will always be more credible than impersonal ones because the individuals concerned can read each others' facial expressions and body language more easily.

2 How might the power of word of mouth be transferred to advertising? Some advertising models word of mouth by showing friends advising each other: this is a common ploy in household products advertising. Another approach is to encourage people to tell a friend by offering incentives, either to the adviser or to the friend or to both. In general, giving a reward to the friends works better than giving a reward to the existing customer.

3 What type of organisation might benefit most from viral marketing on the internet? Any organisation which is offering goods which are useful to computer owners and users, and any organisation aiming for a younger market would benefit from internet-based viral marketing. On a more subtle level, any organisation which has difficulty in identifying the members of its target market would gain from viral marketing, because people tend to become friends with people much like themselves and will therefore tend to send them items they find interesting.

4 What other advertising media might be useful in driving customers to the website? Almost any other medium can be used to drive customers to the website: firms often use billboard or press advertising to do so, and even TV can be used. Recently, firms have been using e-mail viruses to drive potential customers to websites, but this is widely regarded as unethical. Probably print is most suitable because the URL can be printed – broadcast media such as TV and radio are impermanent, and it is unlikely that someone watching a TV ad would be quick enough or alert enough to write down a web address.

Activity 8.4

Full Stop

1 What are the main communication factors which would prevent the NSPCC reaching its goal? One major problem the NSPCC has is that child abuse is a distressing topic: many people are likely to shy away from overly-emotional portrayals of abuse victims, and thus the impact of the advertising will be lost. On the other hand, the issue has to be confronted in a realistic way. A further factor is the difficulty of conveying complex information about how to recognise and report child abuse, when the advertisements are only a few seconds long.

2 How might the NSPCC be more proactive in contacting potential abusers? The NSPCC could run a hotline for parents who feel unable to cope and could also liaise closely with the police and other agencies to work with parents who are or who might become abusers. Although currently much of this work is carried out by local authority Social Services departments, the NSPCC could also contribute.

3 What other communications media might the NSPCC use? Most media are already used by the charity, including TV, radio, direct mail, press, outdoor media and internet-based media. The charity should look at viral campaigns, thus approaching a younger audience who are comfortable with 'word of mouse' communications.

4 What are the main problems for the NSPCC in producing an integrated campaign? The NSPCC has a major problem in that it is trying to communicate to a wide range of audiences, each of which needs a different message and each of which will interpret messages intended for others. For example, a message intended to help abusive parents control themselves better may be construed as sympathetic to the abuser by some other observers. Also, the charity uses a wide range of media, each of which will offer a different type of media experience for the audience.

5 How might the NSPCC improve the integration of its campaign? Although it is difficult to integrate the campaign fully, some progress might be made by ensuring that the charity's main aim is always prominent. In this case, the NSPCC needs to ensure that its Full Stop strapline is used in all the communications, and to retain a common theme in the advertising. Integration would be easier if fewer media were used, but this would undoubtedly reduce the coverage the campaign receives.

Activity 8.5

The answer depends on your own research. However, consider the following: you will find that classified advertising in newspapers is higher than display advertising. People generally buy newspapers for the news stories, but they also find it interesting to see what activities are happening in their local area, as well as the products they could buy listed in the classified adverts.

QUICK QUIZ ANSWERS

1 Tell potential customers what you do, where they get it and how much it costs.

2 Advertising sales promotion and personal selling, should include one or two of ambient advertising, websites, word of mouth & mouse and product placement.

3 Synergy.

4 Television, cinema, billboards, press, web advertising and radio.

5 Web advertising on appropriate sites and the press, especially specialist legal magazines.

6 Questionnaires, interviews, focus groups, sales patterns, pre-testing and physiological measures.

CHAPTER 9

The marketing mix – people, process and physical evidence

Introduction

We have now looked at the 4Ps of the traditional marketing mix, however increasingly today in developed economies we see that most products contain an element service. Supermarkets, banks, education and garages, to name a few, all sell intangible products we generally call services. In the case of supermarkets, for example, they sell products but also provide customer service; the pleasure and the experience of shopping. These are the intangible aspects of buying your weekly shop from a supermarket.

So in this chapter we will look briefly at the elements of service marketing mix: people, process and physical evidence. How do we market something when we can't show it to the customer, or, in some cases, when we can't give them something tangible for their money?

We will look at how we make the staff fulfill the needs of their customers, how we make the process of achieving the sale a pleasurable one, and what it is we will give the customer to show their friends what they have purchased.

After working through this section, and carrying out the associated reading, you should be able to:

- Explain the contribution of people, process and physical evidence to the marketing mix.

Topic list

Syllabus reference

3.11	Explain the importance of a co-ordinated services marketing mix, its characteristics and implications for the marketing of service products: ▪ Co-ordinated approach to people, physical evidence and process ▪ Characteristics/implications: inseparability, intangibility, variability, perishability and non-ownership

1 The remaining 3Ps – people, physical evidence, process

Products and services are seen as differing in many aspects, but in reality it is difficult to see where the line is drawn, so it is important that we include 7Ps in our marketing mix, so we need to consider:

- **People** – the staff who have direct interaction with customers
- **Physical evidence** –the tangible outcome of the service
- **Process** – the activities that occur to provide the service offered.

Virtually all products have some physical aspects and some service aspects. It would be a mistake to divide products into services and physical products, as if there were some definite dividing line between them. Having said that, some products have a much greater service element than others, and for convenience in writing we refer to these as service products. Service products have the following characteristics:

- **Inseparability of production from consumption**. In most cases, services are consumed at the time they are produced: one enjoys the meal while sitting in the restaurant, for example. There will be residual benefits in many cases: a haircut lasts for quite a long time after leaving the hairdressing salon, and a foreign trip continues after the airline has provided the transportation service.
- **Intangibility**. Services cannot be touched: the benefits are mainly in the mind and the emotions. Some aspects are tangible, of course, which is the physical evidence aspect of the marketing mix. Some services are less tangible than others, of course: an insurance policy is a great deal less tangible than a restaurant meal.
- **Variability**. Services are usually variable in that there may be differences from day to day, or from customer to customer. Sometimes the chef has a bad day (or a particularly inspired one), and of course a good hairdresser has to take account of the client's physical features and specific tastes. This means that each customer will come out of the salon with a different hairstyle from other clients.
- **Perishability**. Services cannot be stockpiled. Once an aircraft takes off, any unsold seats will remain empty and cannot be used the following day. Likewise, a hairdresser's time cannot be sold later – if a client misses an appointment, the stylist can usually only sit down and wait for the next customer. This is a major problem for service industries, which is why many of them offer discounts or other incentives to fill quiet periods. Restaurants sometimes offer discounts to early-evening customers, and bars often run 'happy hours' when drinks are cheaper.
- **Non-ownership**. Because services are intangible and perishable, the customer does not own them. In other words, there is no second-hand value for a service. There are one or two exceptions to this general rule: it is possible to sell an endowment insurance policy, for instance.

2 People

> **Key term**
>
> **People**: can be those individuals who work for an organisation that provides a product to a customer.

In markets where the service element predominates, there will be a greater emphasis on the final 3Ps of the marketing mix: people, process and physical evidence. People are usually taken to mean the **'front line' staff** who deal directly with customers: the waitresses, truck drivers, receptionists, lawyers, accountants, hairstylists and so forth who deliver the service. Some commentators also include other people who may be present when the service is provided, that is, other customers. This can be an important factor – if we consider a restaurant, a bar or even a retail store, other

customers affect the atmosphere and consequently our enjoyment of the service. An extreme case would be a nightclub, where the other customers are actually the product: most clubbers are not there for the music or the quality of the drinks, they go in order to meet other people.

THE REAL WORLD

IKEA's co-workers

IKEA is a gigantic operation. The stores cover several acres, and each store employs 60 or more staff (called co-workers). The stores carry thousands of different products, and the whole experience can be so confusing for people who are shopping there for the first time that IKEA provides pencils, paper, tape measures and maps so that people can find their way around the vast stores and can make notes on what they want to purchase.

Inevitably some people become confused, disorientated, frustrated and error-prone in such an environment. Sometimes they will pick up the three-drawer model when they meant to pick up the four-drawer one, or they will get lost and wander in circles. Staff at IKEA are extremely well trained: they are cross-trained in sales and stock operations so that they can usually solve any customer problem, but more importantly they are trained to spot customers who are struggling or frustrated.

Co-workers are empowered to take a wide range of corrective actions. Apart from solving the immediate problem (being out of stock of an item, or helping the customer to find something) they can, when the situation requires it, offer customers a free meal in the IKEA on-site Swedish restaurant, or free delivery of an item, or cash coupons or even money off the purchase price of the product.

Over 200 million people visit IKEA stores in any one year – testimony to the effectiveness of the company's customer care policies.

▸ **Key term**

Service: the totality of features and characteristics offered to the customer when meeting their needs.

As the case of IKEA shows, the people element in service provision can create competitive advantage. Empowering the workers to resolve problems instantly helps to create a positive working environment, but it also provides the customers with exemplary service – which is, of course, what service products are all about.

▸ **Exam tip**

Some students have become confused over defining the people element. For most purposes, remember that the 'people' in the service marketing mix are the people working for the service provider, not the consumers.

Also, do not forget that the services mix includes all 7Ps – do not just write about the last three or you will definitely lose marks! Finally, if you are writing about a retailer, 'product' in services markets means the benefits the retailer adds, not the products they sell. These benefits include things like location, convenience, quick service, free delivery, advice on products, servicing back-up, guaranteed fresh produce and so forth.

3 Physical evidence

▸ **Key term**

Physical evidence: the physical attributes of an intangible product.

Physical evidence is the **tangible aspect of service provision**. The classic examples are the documents one receives from an insurance company as evidence of having a policy, the décor and ambience of restaurants and retail stores, and the tickets for airlines and railways. In many cases, physical evidence is used by consumers to help make a judgement about the likely quality of the service – a lawyer with a smart waiting room and luxurious offices gives an impression of success, which in turn inspires confidence in the client that the lawyer will be successful in fighting the case. Likewise, banks and insurance companies often have prestigious offices because this gives an impression of financial probity and solidity – important factors for financial services companies.

THE REAL WORLD

JD Wetherspoon

In 1979, law student Tim Martin decided he wanted to own a pub. Unlike most students with the same ambition, Martin actually went ahead and bought the pub he usually drank in. From the beginning, Martin decided that Wetherspoon was going to be different from the other pubs around.

For one thing, Wetherspoon has no music. There is no juke box, no live bands and no piped music anywhere in any Wetherspoon pub. Second, Wetherspoon has a wider range of beers than do most pubs – and it is the beer that makes the profits. Wetherspoon operate by keeping the price of the beer relatively low, but offering a quiet atmosphere, no-smoking areas and all-day food.

Each pub has its own name, but operates under the overall Wetherspoon brand: the pub name and the company name appear prominently on each of the 800 Wetherspoon pubs in Britain. The company was floated on the London Stock Exchange in 1992 and continues to expand throughout the United Kingdom. In recent years, the company has also diversified into J.D. Wetherspoon Lodges and Lloyd's nightclubs. Each of these operations has the same philosophy as the central J.D. Wetherspoon brand.

Maintaining a pleasant, safe atmosphere is central to Wetherspoon's policies. The company has removed all financial incentives for customers to 'trade up' to larger or more alcoholic drinks: for example, most pubs sell a double measure of spirits for less than the cost of two separate singles, but Wetherspoon has removed this because it sees it as an incentive for customers to buy more alcohol than they otherwise might. Strange behaviour – most companies seek to encourage people to buy more of their products. The company also sells its soft drinks at much lower prices than most other pubs or restaurants.

John Hutson, managing director of Wetherspoon, says, 'We believe that a combination of food served all day, reasonably priced soft drinks, an absence of financial incentives to 'trade up' to larger quantities of alcohol, combined with good facilities and a heavy emphasis on staff training are the right direction for the pub industry to take. No company which serves alcohol can be immune from bad behaviour from time to time, but these policies should help to reduce its effects and, as a company, we will, as in the past, continue to consider sensible policies for our business and the community in this complex area.'

In another somewhat surprising development, Tim Martin called on the government to ban smoking in all pubs. Citing the Californian experience, where all smoking in public places was banned in the 1990s, he said that a significant number of people were avoiding pubs because of the smoky atmosphere. 'I believe that a total ban would be the best way forward, and not result, for example, in a situation where customers can smoke in pubs in Newcastle, but not in nearby Gateshead, because neighbouring councils have different agendas,' he said. 'However, it would be commercial suicide for a pub company to prohibit smoking in the absence of a nationwide ban by the government. Going it alone, in my opinion, is not a viable option in the pub world.' The government clearly took him seriously – smoking was finally banned in pubs throughout the United Kingdom in 2007. Some pubs have found that business dropped off, but many others have reported increases in business as non-smokers return.

The United Kingdom is a pub culture, like Ireland: much of Britain's social life revolves around drinking, and the corner pub is often the cornerstone of the community. What J.D. Wetherspoon has done is recapture the old atmosphere of the pub – a place for conversation, perhaps some food, and a comfortable and safe environment.

ACTIVITY 9.1

Consider the JD Wetherspoon example.

1 What is the role of physical evidence in Martin's thinking?
2 Why would Wetherspoon seek to have smoking banned in all pubs?
3 Why ban music in the pubs?
4 Why might Wetherspoon seek to limit people's drinking?

ACTIVITY 9.2

Next time you visit a service organisation – a restaurant, store, bar, etc – try listing the different things the management has done to create physical evidence. How have these elements combined to create a brand image?

4 Process

Key term

Process: looks at a series of activities the customer undertakes with the organisation to achieve satisfaction and may include elements such as negotiations, procedures and organisational policies.

Process is the **series of events that takes place in order for the service to be delivered effectively**. Even when the physical aspects of the service product are similar, the process can differentiate the products markedly: consider the difference between a hamburger from McDonald's and a hamburger from Hard Rock Café. Process can also change the dynamics of the service operation, **reducing costs** and **increasing efficiency**.

THE REAL WORLD

EasyJet

EasyJet, the low-cost, no-frills airline, has been the subject of many case studies and is widely used as an example of how an innovative approach to marketing can produce tremendous competitive advantage. This does not mean that things have always gone smoothly for the airline – in fact, at one point it looked as if the company was going to become a victim of its own success!

The demand for cheap flights, and the availability of new routes, was growing faster than the airline's ability to buy or lease aircraft. EasyJet could not afford to relax on opening up new routes, because a failure to seize opportunities in that regard would have left the routes open for competitors, of which many had grown up since the early days when Ryanair and EasyJet were the only two budget airlines in Europe. Also, passenger numbers were growing so fast that EasyJet's prices were rising – unless one booked very early indeed, the aircraft would be filling fast and the computer system would raise the air fare, thus destroying the company's main selling point.

The choices were simple: either the company would have to raise fares across the board and use the money to fund new aircraft (thus destroying the firm's only competitive advantage), or it would have to find ways to make the existing aircraft work harder. EasyJet chose the latter course.

Aircraft suffer from some limitations. They fly at the speed they fly: although it is possible to speed up a little, the cost in fuel outweighs the savings made. They have a fixed number of seats: unlike buses or trains, passengers cannot stand in the aisles. They cannot tow trailers, or have extra carriages put on, or in any way expand their capacity. Many airports nowadays do not operate on a 24-hour basis, because of environmental and noise considerations, so short-haul aircraft are effectively grounded overnight. The only slack in the system that EasyJet could identify was the turnround time on the ground: the less time spent on cleaning and servicing the aircraft ready for its next batch of passengers, the more time it could spend in the air.

EasyJet called in the consultants, but rather than hire time-and-motion consultants, the airline brought in a group which specialises in developing innovative corporate cultures. For the next three months the consultants interviewed all the people involved in turning round the aircraft – the baggage handlers, the caterers, refuelling companies, airport staff, EasyJet front-line staff, ground engineers, pilots, cabin crew and even the cleaning contractors. The consultants then were in a position to set up the right conditions for people who actually do the job to pool their ideas.

One of the early discoveries by the consultants was that people carrying out the various tasks did not understand how their processes fitted with other people's activities, because they had little or no idea of what the other teams actually did. Worse, they did not understand how each job was reliant on every other job. The consultants arranged for cross-disciplinary groups to meet and explain each others' jobs. The result of this was some creative ideas for cutting ground time. For example, ground engineers normally wait until all the passengers have disembarked before coming on board to discuss servicing needs with the pilots: this inevitably causes delays as it can take 10 minutes or more for passengers to collect their hand baggage and leave the plane. Discussions within the focus groups led to the idea of supplying ground engineers with headsets so that they can talk to the pilots from the tarmac while the passengers disembark, getting most questions out of the way before needing to board the aircraft. Another innovation is for the cabin crew to begin cleaning the cabin before the aircraft arrives – the cabin crew collect unwanted magazines and newspapers and any obvious rubbish while the aircraft is in its final approach and the seat belt sign is on.

Ideas were disseminated by videoing the sessions and allowing staff to see what the groups discussed. Ideas continue to flow from the staff, because they have developed an innovative culture. After all, who can understand the job better than those who do it all day, every day?

The net result of the exercise is that average turnround times are down from 50 to 33 minutes, and in one notable case an aircraft was turned round in only 7 minutes. This may not seem a lot, but if an aircraft makes an average of four return flights a day, over an hour per day will be saved in downtime. Over a working year, this equates to more than 60 return flights from Luton to Nice – which is equivalent to over a million pounds per aircraft in extra sales revenue.

CHAPTER ROUNDUP

- The additional 3Ps which make up the 7Ps are:

  People – the staff who have direct interaction with customers.

  Physical evidence – the tangible outcome of the service.

  Process – the activities that occur to provide the service offered.
- As with the 4Ps, the 7Ps must work together.
- When one element is changed we must be mindful of how this will affect the six other parts of our mix.

FURTHER READING

Since the marketing mix is such a large part of practical marketing, the reading tends also to be comprehensive. For more detail on the mix elements:

Baker, M. J. *The Marketing Manual.* Butterworth Heinemann. Chapter 7.

Blythe, J. (2009) *Essentials of Marketing.* 4th Edition. Harlow, Prentice Hall. Chapters 1, 6, 7, 8 and 9.

Blythe, J. (2008) *Principles and Practice of Marketing.* 2nd Edition. Andover, Lengage. Chapters 1 and 12–22.

Brassington, F. and Pettitt, S. (2006). *Principles of Marketing.* 4th Edition. Harlow, Prentice Hall. Chapters 7–19

Kotler, P. *et al* (2008) *Principles of Marketing.* 5th Edition. FT Prentice Hall. Chapters 13–22.

Jobber, D. (2009) *Principles and Practice of Marketing.* 6th Edition. Maidenhead, McGraw-Hill. Chapters 8–17.

http://www.berr.gov.uk/index.html: The official website of the Department for Business Enterprise and Regulatory Reform. It contains a large number of articles and statistics on innovation, as well as advice for innovative businesses.

http://www.myoffers.co.uk: This website directs users to many sales promotions, providing a useful set of examples.

http://www.advertisingarchives.co.uk: This site contains advertisements going back over a hundred years.

http://brand.blogs.com/mantra/2005/02/lovehate_brand_.html: This is a chat room for people to post their messages of love or hate about brands. It offers some interesting insights into what goes wrong with brand messages.

http://www.strangenewproducts.com

National broadsheet newspaper

Marketing magazine

Product-based magazine in your organisation's area of specialism

REFERENCES

Booms, B.H. and Bitner, M.J. Marketing strategies and organisation structures for service firms. J.H. Donnelly, W.R. George. (ed.). In: *Marketing of Services.* 1982, Chicago: American Marketing Association 47–52.

Levitt T. (1986) *The Marketing Imagination*. New York, Free Press.

QUICK QUIZ

1. Describe the people in a high class restaurant.
2. Describe the physical evidence provided when you have your car serviced.
3. Describe the process you would to go through to obtain home insurance.
4. List some examples of good and bad customer service you have received recently.

ACTIVITY DEBRIEFS

Activity 9.1

JD Wetherspoon

1. What is the role of physical evidence in Martin's thinking? Physical evidence is exemplified in Wetherspoon's by the unique environment. There is no loud music, no TV and no noisy pub games, so customers have a relaxing and quiet atmosphere in which to enjoy their evening out.

2. Why would Wetherspoon seek to have smoking banned in all pubs? Banning smoking in pubs has been advantageous to Wetherspoon because of their belief that many people avoid pubs because of the smoky atmosphere. Smokers are now a minority of the UK population, and smoking is becoming socially unacceptable: Wetherspoon's brand image (comfort, safety and clean surroundings) does not fit well with allowing smoking. Although many pubs appear to have lost business due to the ban, Wetherspoon remains relatively buoyant.

3. Why ban music in the pubs? Wetherspoon's emphasis on the physical evidence aspect of the service mix means that they are aiming for customers who seek out a quiet environment. Music detracts from this.

4. Why might Wetherspoon's seek to limit people's drinking? An important element in the people factor in the marketing mix is the other customers. Customers who become drunk might also become noisy, or even abusive and violent. This would harm the Wetherspoon image: it is not worth damaging the brand simply for the short-term gain of selling a little more alcohol.

Activity 9.2

For example consider Subway and McDonald's seating, colour scheme, lighting, restaurant layout. Both offering takeaway food but both have differing approaches to the process; different line and queuing process, the colour of the seats and overall feel is different (McDonald's are bigger in many cases) and finally the staff are trained in differing areas to support you through the purchase process.

QUICK QUIZ ANSWERS

1. The front of house staff, waiters and bar staff, but chef will influence the physical evidence and the owner the décor and so on.
2. Your car returned clean, tidy and working well; service book stamped dated and a clear bill showing what you have paid them to do.
3. It may be through website or comparison sites, easy to input the information, quick response and a price that is clear on the screen and payment by many differing methods.
4. Will all be different and personal to you and your perception of good service.

CHAPTER 10

The marketing mix – evaluation

Introduction

In this final chapter we are mainly concerned with the measurement of the success, or otherwise, of our marketing activities. There may be a myriad of different key performance indictors (KPIs), targets, goals, aspirations or objectives against which performance can be measured as we move through time. Alternatively, it could be a decision about monitoring how the market responds to our marketing actions, in order to give the organisation real-time feedback.

Importantly, the organisation wants to know whether the customers' needs have been satisfied effectively and efficiently both from the organisation's point of view and that of the customer.

After working through this section, and carrying out the associated reading, you should be able to:

- Describe the different methods for measuring marketing outcomes.
- Show how a co-ordinated marketing mix contributes to customer satisfaction and competitive advantage

Topic list

Syllabus reference

3.12	Explain the different methods used for measuring the success of marketing activities: ▪ Budget measurement ▪ Objectives attained ▪ Sales/revenue, profit/loss ▪ Efficiency/effectiveness ▪ Zero defects/returns ▪ Customer service complaints ▪ Increased awareness and changing attitudes ▪ Repeat purchase and loyalty

1 Methods of measurement

> **Key term**
>
> **Measurement**: without some type of measure you will be unable to see if you have achieved your objectives, you may fail or fly right past what you intended to achieve.

Measuring success in marketing is not easy. Because much of what marketers do is concerned with establishing specific attitudes in consumers' minds, or with creating an image for a product, the difficulties inherent in assessing intangibles often result in no accurate assessment being undertaken.

Factors involved in measurement are as follows:

> **Key term**
>
> **Budget**: is a statement which sets out resources required to achieve an objective, and can therefore be used as a measurement and control tool.

> **Key term**
>
> **Control**: is part of measurement within your objectives. It requires you to take action to adjust performance.

- **Budget measurement.** This is the degree to which marketing expenditures remain within the budget estimates. It is usually only relevant if the budget is based on sales turnover, but many firms do measure against budget, at least as part of the assessment of marketing success.
- **Objectives obtained.** Naturally, this relies on setting realistic objectives in the first place (see Unit 2). In some cases, objectives are easily measured: in other cases, for example, when trying to measure the success of a communications campaign, outcomes are difficult to measure. Communications activities can only be measured by communications outcomes – measuring by marketing outcomes such as increased sales is problematic since sales might have increased (or decreased) for any one of a great many reasons. If the objectives have been correctly set, using SMART (specific, measurable, achievable, realistic and time-bound) as a checklist, the objective will be measurable.
- **Sales revenue, or profit and loss measurements.** The difficulty here is that many factors other than marketing activities can affect sales revenue, and even more is this the case with profit and loss. For example, a major economic downturn can wipe out sales, and at the same time a sudden fall in raw material prices or a currency fluctuation can make dramatic changes in profit and loss. These can easily mask any effects caused by marketing activities.
- **Efficiency and effectiveness.** Effectiveness is the degree to which something has worked and efficiency is the degree to which something has been achieved for a minimum of effort and expenditure. Each of these will involve other measurements (notably effectiveness) but they are useful as a way of understanding the impact of different marketing activities.
- **Level of defects or returns.** This appears at first sight to be an engineering issue, but in fact marketers need to be assured that goods going out to customers are fit for purpose. This is especially true in the case of services. Companies may aim for a zero-defect policy or, in other cases, expect a certain amount of complaining as being inherent to the business. If levels of complaints or returns are *rising*, the company may well want to do something about it.

- **Customer service complaints**. Two issues need to be addressed here: first, the level of complaints itself, as being indicative of customer dissatisfaction, or a mismatch between what the company provides and what the customers want; and second, the extent to which complaints are dealt with to the customer's satisfaction. Complaints which are satisfactorily dealt with tend to increase customer loyalty, which is why some firms actively encourage complaining.
- **Increased brand awareness**. This is usually measured by formal market research and is one measure of success in promotion. It does not necessarily translate into sales revenue outcomes, however – being aware of a brand is not the same as intending to buy it. Obviously increased awareness of the brand will probably increase the number of people who will be interested in buying, but in some cases people are aware of a brand in a negative way.
- **Changing attitudes**. Like brand awareness, this can be measured through good market research. Making changes in people's attitudes is one of the key functions of promotion activities, although in general attitudes tend to be stable and most promotion probably only acts as a reminder or 'nudges' people towards a purchase.
- **Repeat purchase and loyalty**. Some companies can measure this easily: many large retailers operate loyalty schemes, and many online retailers can track purchases. For other firms, especially those who are not close to the final consumers of their products, measuring repeat purchase and loyalty involves market research exercises.
- Often today you will also see organisations develop a whole set of 'Key Performance Indicators' (KPIs) to measure the success of their marketing effort. This can be as simple as making progress toward strategic goals or often success is simply the achievement of an operational goal (for example, lower sick days within a care provider). Accordingly, choosing the right KPI is reliant upon having a good understanding of what is important to the organisation. A very common method for choosing KPIs is to apply other management frameworks such as balanced score card. Alternative indicators can be highlighted as KPIs. These can be summarised in the following sub-categories:
  - Quantitative indicators that can be presented as a number
  - Practical indicators that interface with existing company processes
  - Directional indicators specifying whether or not an aim is likely to be reached
  - Actionable indicators are sufficiently in an organisation's control to effect change
  - Financial indicators used in performance measurement

KPIs, in practical terms, offer another way of measuring the intangible and tangible outcomes of marketing activities.

THE REAL WORLD

Meningitis Research Foundation

The Meningitis Research Foundation case study considers the evaluation of marketing activities and the understanding of how an organisation measures success or failure in its marketing activities.

These types of marketing campaign focus on providing information to the public about disease and they look to raise awareness of the disease among a number of different groups or segments, eg the public, health professionals and those responsible for health policy. Therefore a number of goals that could be achieved by a campaign could include:

- Assessing the needs of the public for information, education, guidance and support
- Developing the profile of the disease, so that it remains high in the minds of those who are responsible for health policy and resource allocation
- Marketing can also increase and/or maintain donations to the charity

Recently the Meningitis Research Foundation ran an awareness campaign – 'Race Against Time' – to promote the awareness of the symptoms of meningitis. This campaign was launched across the UK with various events in different cities, from a balloon launch in a school to a mini Olympics in a sports stadium. All events distributed literature covering the main symptoms of meningitis. The same literature was also delivered to all doctors surgeries in the UK. Simultaneously, a press release was issued nationally focusing on the continued need for awareness of meningitis. Foundation staff also took part in TV and radio interviews.

Another recent fundraising campaign was the 'Slimathon'. In this promotion, members of the public were encouraged to register to take part in a sponsored slim. This enabled the Foundation to look at a number of different outcomes – individuals' contact details for future communications, fundraising and, once again, opportunities to raise awareness of meningitis. This campaign was launched just after Christmas and corresponded with the New Year when many individuals are contemplating losing weight or making the customary New Year's resolutions.

Another element of marketing from a charity point of view is the support they get from celebrities. Meningitis Research Foundation has a number of celebrities who act as patrons including Ewan McGregor, Phil Collins, James Dyson and soccer legend Pat Jennings.

The marketing mix for not-for-profit organisations can be slightly different than that of a profit-making businesses. The emphasis can become directed at promoting the Foundation itself and its attempt to maximise fundraising so that it can continue to achieve its charitable objectives. The success of marketing activities can be difficult to quantify. However, the Foundation has, in the past, estimated its success by looking at the number of responses it receives. These can be through interviews, letters direct to the Foundation, focus groups, professional meetings, press clippings, calls to the helpline and through health professionals requesting resources, as well as their patients.

(Biz/ed, 2005)

ACTIVITY 10.1

Consider the Meningitis Research Foundation example:

1. How might Meningitis Research Foundation be able to assess the effectiveness of its campaign?
2. What type of marketing outcome would be reliably researched by Meningitis Research Foundation?
3. What problems could you identify in the research process?
4. Will there be any bias in the research?

Exam tip

You will be expected to be aware of the methods used for measurement and the ways in which they can be used, so you should be aware of the drawbacks and limitations of each. You should also consider if some are inappropriate with a marketing-orientated company.

Many students make the error of assuming that advertising can be measured by increased sales, for example, whereas advertising can only be measured by communications outcomes such as increased brand awareness or changed attitudes.

2 Putting it all together

You will need to be able to assemble all the elements of the marketing mix in order to make recommendations. Although the mix is dealt with as seven discrete factors, marketers (in practice) have to use all seven in the correct proportions and at the correct time to be successful. The co-ordinating mechanism is the brand personality, but the starting point for everything is the needs of the target customers.

In order to compete effectively, you will need to:

- Design a mix which is compatible and co-ordinated effectively.
- Think about your target market, their needs and expectations and also (of course) what the firm wants from them in return.
- Think about possible competitive responses. Competitors do not sit idly by and let you take their customers away – they will do something and it might be something serious.
- Think of the impact on the other elements of the mix if you start adjusting an element.

ACTIVITY 10.2

Take a product you know well and consider how the different elements of the marketing mix may have been utilised. For example, consider where and how it is advertised, and what sort of pricing options or deals are available.

Table 10.1 For example – purchase of a cold drink

	Product	Price	Place	Promotion	People	Process	Physical evidence
Product	Cold can						
Price		Good value					
Place			Vending machine				
Promotion				Large, colourful box			
People					No one was involved		
Process						Money in change given	
Physical evidence							The can of drink was cold

THE REAL WORLD

Bringing it altogether – The Brazilian market

This case looks to identify all the elements of the marketing mix and highlights how a marketer needs to plan their approach in new and expanding markets.

Organisations wanting to launch successful products in the Brazilian market need to connect with a vast population of 195 million which has become the 6th largest economy in the world. With a speed of growth that European markets can only dream of, the economy grew by 7.5% in 2010 and has a vast and growing middle class that has money to spend on products. It is not just the scale of the prospect that requires careful consideration, it is also the nature of the opportunity. Many of the 91 million customers in Brazil are online and on the move. This provides a huge opportunity to develop and use cost-effective digital media systems to communicate and build relationships with these customers.

One successful organisation in the Brazilian market is the drinks giant Diageo, which is trying to keep pace with a customer base that moved from zero technology to smart phones without any of the transitional technologies we have seen in between. With the government now looking to provide free WiFi, Brazilians have become, in a very short space of time, the third highest users of the internet on the globe. To illustrate the point Brazil has over 200 social networks, so this networking activity needs to be harnessed to communicate effectively. Add to this the love that Brazil has for YouTube and you can see why organisations such as Burger King and Visa use budget video campaigns to launch their new products, and how Nissan achieved viral success with their *Pôneis Malditos* campaign in 2011. Nissan claimed that new sales almost doubled on the basis of this campaign. Even more transitional media are seeing the benefits of using the digital platform. For example, Harper's Bazaar looks to offer the rising middle class the opportunity to browse and purchase fashion and home furnishing via a new website, rather than the more transitional magazine approach. This is being followed by H&M, Brewdog Beer, Gap and many more who are already trialing digital formats in Europe before they enter this market. However, it is also important to point out that Brazilians like their brands to have a Brazilian flavour and to be relevant to their lives.

That said, there have been failures. Products that launch without adequate distribution and product availability have not been successful, which is why organisations such as Volkswagen and Santander are waiting to use the World Cup in 2014 before they develop their Brazilian offering; making their product appear local with sponsorship of the World Cup and ensuring the infrastructure is in place. This is also true of Apple and Burberry who are looking at 2014 as their launch window as they develop their local manufacturing base. This follows the successful launch of Bentley Motors, who based themselves in Sao Paulo and had a business model operated by Brazilians from day one.

Unilever has seen that just trying to import your standard product does not work. The company has had to tailor its ice creams to suit other tastes by introducing new local flavours such as passion fruit and guava. There are also local and regional variations which must be considered before developing a marketing approach for the whole country. For example, vodka in one region may be totally different to that in another. This may be tied to local events such as carnivals or local music, but even this might be a totally different experience in different parts of the country.

There are difficulties that arise from not locating in Brazil itself. The Brazilian government is quite protective of its home based industries and therefore import taxation can be high. There are also investment, manufacturing and employment laws, all of which need to be taken into account when looking at the marketing mix for the future. Smaller organisations have more difficulties in these areas as they do not have the resources to support long-term relationship building prior to income generation.

Finally, language can present a barrier in negotiations and needs to be considered. It is an important element in the planning process to ensure you have the skills and resources to achieve organisational goals. Link this to a conservative media owned in large part by one organisation and the fact that there is no outdoor media and you can therefore start to see the importance of having a strong, well constructed marketing mix.

(Snood, 2012)

ACTIVITY 10.3

Consider the case study on the new Brazilian market.

1. What elements of the marketing mix can you identify?
2. What are the important elements that have a unique requirement for the Brazilian market?
3. What is important about the promotional aspects of the marketing mix?
4. Why is the Brazilian market so enthusiastic for 'western' products?

3 Summary

The **marketing mix** is a useful concept in that it brings together all the **tactical tools** that marketers have at their disposal and explains how each one affects the overall marketing effort. It should be used as a recipe: each ingredient, added at the right time and in the right quantity, contributes to the final result. It is important to remember that the elements all affect each other, and the total finished marketing plan will reflect all the elements.

It is also worth remembering that every firm supplies some services along with its physical products. These service elements (people, process and physical evidence) are often the only differentiators a firm has. One should also bear in mind that not everything fits neatly within the marketing mix 'silos' – like most models, it is for guidance and convenience of thought, it is not a prescriptive blueprint for action.

CHAPTER ROUNDUP

- Methods of measurement can be numerous, including outcomes against our plan, sales volume, market share and organisational goals achieved.
- Developing a method that best suits the organisation and shows how well it is doing towards its objectives is fundamental.
- Measurement methods must look to measure at least the ability of the organisational plans, strategies and tactics to achieve customer satisfaction.

FURTHER READING

Since the marketing mix is such a large part of practical marketing, the reading tends also to be comprehensive. For more detail on the mix elements:

Blythe, J. (2008) *Principles and Practice of Marketing.* 2nd Edition. Andover, Lengage. Chapters 1 and 12–22.

Blythe, J. (2009) *Essentials of Marketing.* 4th Edition. Harlow, Prentice Hall. Chapters 1, 6, 7, 8 and 9.

Booms, B.H. and Bitner, M.J. Marketing strategies and organisation structures for service firms. J.H. Donnelly, W.R. George. (ed.). In: *Marketing of Services.* 1982, (Chicago:American Marketing Association 47–52.

Brassington, F. and Pettitt, S. (2006). *Principles of Marketing.* 4th Edition. Harlow, Prentice Hall. Chapters 7–19.

Jobber, D. (2009) *Principles and Practice of Marketing.* 6th Edition. Maidenhead, McGraw-Hill Chapters 8–17.

Kotler, P. *et al* (2008) *Principles of Marketing.* 5th Edition. FT Prentice Hall.Chapters 13–22.

Levitt, T. (1986) *The Marketing Imagination*. New York, Free Press.

http://www.berr.gov.uk/index.html: The official website of the Department for Business Enterprise and RegulatoryReform. It contains a large number of articles and statistics on innovation, as well as advice for innovative businesses.

http://www.myoffers.co.uk: This website directs users to many sales promotions, providing a useful set of examples.

http://www.advertisingarchives.co.uk: This site contains advertisements going back over a hundred years.

http://brand.blogs.com/mantra/2005/02/lovehate_brand_.html: This is a chat room for people to post their messages of love or hate about brands. It offers some interesting insights into what goes wrong with brand messages.

http://www.strangenewproducts.com: It is a website for weird and wonderful new products. The products themselves are genuine: some of them are definitely useful, others are useful but no one would buy them, and some are just plain crazy.

National broadsheet newspaper

Marketing magazine

Product-based magazine in your organisation's area of specialism

REFERENCES

Biz/ed (2005) *Meningitis Research Foundation Case Study Home Page*. http://www.bized.co.uk/compfact/mrf/mrfindex.htm?page=15 [Accessed May 2012].

Snood, L. (2012) *Breaking into Brazil*. http://www.marketingweek.co.uk/breaking-into-brazil/3033886.article [Accessed May 2012].

QUICK QUIZ

1 What does PLC stand for?

A Product-loving consumer.
B Product life cycle.
C Product launch controller.

2 Which of the following is true?

A Screening comes before idea generation, but after concept testing.
B Concept testing comes after market testing, but before commercialisation.
C Screening comes after idea generation and before concept testing.

3 Which of the following is true?

A People can include other customers.
B Product, for a retailer, means the products on the shelves.
C Price is the only element of the mix which does not affect the other elements.

4 A new product which changes people's lives radically is called:

A Continuous innovation.
B Discontinuous innovation.
C Dynamically continuous innovation.

5 Which of the following is true?

A Early adopters buy after innovators, but before early majority.
B Early majority buy before late majority, but after laggards.
C Late majority buy after laggards, but before early majority.

6 Which of the following lists the elements of the traditional promotional mix?

A Price, advertising, PR and personal selling.
B Personal selling, advertising, PR and sales promotion.
C Selling, advertising, sales promotion and personal communication.

7 Pitching the price low to start with, in order to gain market share is called:

A Penetration pricing.
B Skimming.
C Demand pricing.

8 Pitching the price high to start with, then reducing it as competitors enter the market is called:

A Skimming.
B Penetration pricing.

C Competitive pricing.

9 A firm which sells books on the internet is an example of:

A A wholesaler.
B An agent.
C A retailer.

10 The practice of moving goods through the distribution chain from raw materials to end user is called:

A Physical distribution.
B Logistics.
C Marketing.

ACTIVITY DEBRIEFS

Activity 10.1

1 How might Meningitis Research Foundation be able to assess the effectiveness of its campaign? The Foundation will hope to look at the responses it gets back. It could look at fundraising as another measurement and it would be hoped it had historic information to help compare and contrast success rates from other campaigns. It may also be difficult for the Foundation to identify which campaign achieved the result.

2 What type of marketing outcome would be reliably researched by Meningitis Research Foundation? Increased public awareness could be measured – of course this would need to be researched before and after the campaign. The increased level of fundraised money would also be a particular measurement. The Foundation was also looking at increasing awareness within particular target groups – health professionals for example – so it could use surveys or focus groups to see if this has been achieved.

3 What problems could you identify in the research process? Time, cost and self-selection of individuals are just some of the issues that need to be taken into account during the evaluation process. It is likely that due to the emotive subject matter individuals will have very strong opinions, express particular views or may have ulterior motives about joining a focus group or answering a questionnaire.

4 Will there be any bias in the research? Dependent on the different types of measurements used the research could be affected by participants' degree of computer literacy if online questionnaires were used, for example. The honesty of individuals when answering questions about health matters is something that should be taken into account when looking at a subject area such as meningitis. Once again, the possibility that an individual may be self-selecting if they have had personal experience of the illness is one to consider.

Activity 10.2

What you should see is an effective and co-ordinated marketing mix which all links together, for example:

Product – Lucozade – Sport Lite, a brand

Price – competitive with Coke and Pepsi, but higher per litre as energy fitness based

Place – available in all shops, garages, vending machines, gyms and accessible for impulse purchase or on the way to sports activity

Promotion – high impact sports related re-hydration after and during exercise, increased performance. Not a drink but 'body fuel'

People – friendly with a smile in the gym or corner shop

Process – ease of access to the benefits of re-hydration, linked to place and bottle design

Physical evidence – easy to use bottle top, hand size and grip shaped.

Activity 10.3

1. What elements of the marketing mix can you identify? All the elements are present: 'Product' – Vodka and so much more, 'Price' – high because of brands, high needs for new products and protectionist governments, 'Place' – available in the right places, produced in Brazil and 'Promotion' – developing the aspirational Brazil, not forgetting of course the development of 'Process', 'People' and 'Physical evidence', which can be observed.

2. What are the important elements that have a unique requirement for the Brazilian market? Cost-effective large scale digital communication is what Brazil offers, with a vast use of social networks and the internet. Promotion is very important, as is getting the right image, brand and language. However, the transitional and conservative media need different approaches. They like their products to be produced in Brazil, so a view of how organisations achieve this is also very important.

3. What is important about the promotional aspects of the marketing mix? Language and an understanding of the conservative nature of the media. Developing a relationship with the new Brazil so that organisations have an understanding of the new growing and affluent Brazilian customer base. Brazilians want to be communicated to in the correct language. Working with local people and suppliers to ensure the message is right.

4. Why is the Brazilian market so enthusiastic for 'western' products? Brazil sees the opportunity to purchase successful global brands as another facet in its development from a 'third world' country into a major economic force. It is a huge growing market that existing organisations see as a replacement to the failing transitional markets of Europe and the USA.

QUICK QUIZ ANSWERS

1 B is the correct answer. The others are invented.

2 C is correct. The order is: idea generation, screening, concept testing, business analysis, product development, market testing and commercialisation.

3 A is true. For a retailer, product is the service element the retailer adds, not the products on the shelves, and price affects all the other elements of the mix.

4 B is correct. Continuous innovation is merely a minor adjustment, and dynamically continuous innovation is still recognisable as its predecessor, whereas discontinuous innovation is truly new to the world.

5 A is correct. The order is: innovators, early adopters, early majority, late majority and laggards.

6 B is correct. Price is part of marketing mix, and personal communication is usually regarded as being part of PR.

7 A is correct. Skimming means pricing high to start with, and demand pricing is about setting the price at a point which controls demand.

8 A is correct. Penetration pricing means pitching the price low to gain market share, and competitive pricing means pricing according to what competitors are charging.

9 C is correct. Any firm which sells to final consumers is a retailer.

10 B is correct. Logistics is the science of supply – it includes physical distribution and is included in marketing.

Index

Index

Notes

The Chartered
Institute of Marketing

BPP
LEARNING MEDIA
Notes

Notes
The Chartered
Institute of Marketing

Notes
The Chartered
Institute of Marketing

Notes
The Chartered Institute of Marketing

Notes
CIM
The Chartered
Institute of Marketing

Review form

Please help us to ensure that the CIM learning materials we produce remain as accurate and user-friendly as possible. We cannot promise to answer every submission we receive, but we do promise that it will be read and taken into account when we update this Study Text.

Name: ______________________ **Address:** ______________________

____

____

1. How have you used this Text?
(Tick one box only)

☐ Self study (book only)

☐ On a course: college ______________

☐ Other ______________

2. During the past six months do you recall seeing/receiving any of the following?
(Tick as many boxes as are relevant)

☐ Our advertisement in *The Marketer*

☐ Our brochure with a letter through the post

☐ Our website www.bpp.com

3. Why did you decide to purchase this Text?
(Tick one box only)

☐ Have used companion Assessment workbook

☐ Have used BPP Texts in the past

☐ Recommendation by friend/colleague

☐ Recommendation by a lecturer at college

☐ Saw advertising in journals

☐ Saw information on BPP website

☐ Other ______________

4. Which (if any) aspects of our advertising do you find useful?
(Tick as many boxes as are relevant)

☐ Prices and publication dates of new editions

☐ Information on product content

☐ Facility to order books off-the-page

☐ None of the above

5. Have you used the companion Assessment Workbook? Yes ☐ No ☐

6. Have you used the companion Passcards? Yes ☐ No ☐

7. Your ratings, comments and suggestions would be appreciated on the following areas.

	Very useful	*Useful*	*Not useful*
Introductory section (How to use this text, study checklist, etc)	☐	☐	☐
Chapter introductions	☐	☐	☐
Syllabus learning outcomes	☐	☐	☐
Activities	☐	☐	☐
The Real World examples	☐	☐	☐
Quick quizzes	☐	☐	☐
Quality of explanations			
Index	☐	☐	☐
Structure and presentation	☐	☐	☐

	Excellent	*Good*	*Adequate*	*Poor*
Overall opinion of this Text	☐	☐	☐	☐

8. Do you intend to continue using BPP CIM products? ☐ Yes ☐ No

On the reverse of this page is space for you to write your comments about our Study Text. We welcome your feedback.

Please return to: CIM Publishing Manager, BPP Learning Media, FREEPOST, London, W12 8BR.

TELL US WHAT YOU THINK

Please note any further comments and suggestions/errors below. For example, was the text accurate, readable, concise, user-friendly and comprehensive?